Social Media in Emergent Brazil

T0136714

WHY WE POST

PUBLISHED AND FORTHCOMING TITLES:

Social Media in
Southeast Turkey
Elisabetta Costa

Social Media in
Southeast Italy
Razvan Nicolescu

Social Media in
Northern Chile
Nell Haynes

Social Media
in Trinidad
Jolynna Sinanan

Social Media in
Rural China
Tom McDonald

Social Media in
Emergent Brazil
Juliano Spyer

Social Media in an
English Village
Daniel Miller

Social Media in
South India
Shriram Venkatraman

Visualising Facebook
Daniel Miller
and Jolynna Sinanan

Social Media in
Industrial China
Xinyuan Wang

How the World
Changed Social Media
Daniel Miller et al

Download free: www.ucl.ac.uk/ucl-press

Why
We
Post

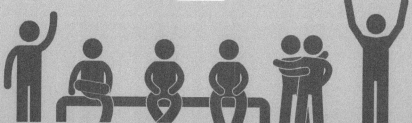

Social Media in Emergent Brazil

How the Internet Affects Social Change

Juliano Spyer

First published in 2017 by
UCL Press
University College London
Gower Street
London WC1E 6BT

Available to download free: www.ucl.ac.uk/ucl-press

A CIP catalogue record for this book is available
from The British Library.

ISBN: 978–1–78735–167–7 (Hbk.)
ISBN: 978–1–78735–166–0 (Pbk.)
ISBN: 978–1–78735–165–3 (PDF)
ISBN: 978–1–78735–168–4 (epub)
ISBN: 978–1–78735–169–1 (mobi)
ISBN: 978–1–78735–170–7 (html)
DOI: https://doi.org/10.14324/111.9781787351653

To my parents Ana and Marcos, for pointing the way, and to Thais, for sharing the adventures.

Introduction to the series Why We Post

This book is one of a series of 11 titles. Nine are monographs devoted to specific field sites (including this one) in Brazil, Chile, China, England, India, Italy, Trinidad and Turkey – they have been published in 2016–17. The series also includes a comparative book about all our findings, *How the World Changed Social Media*, published to accompany this title, and a book which contrasts the visuals that people post on Facebook in the English field site with those on our Trinidadian field site, *Visualising Facebook*.

When we tell people that we have written nine monographs about social media around the world, all using the same chapter headings (apart from Chapter 5), they are concerned about potential repetition. However, if you decide to read several of these books (and we very much hope you do), you will see that this device has been helpful in showing the precise opposite. Each book is as individual and distinct as if it were on an entirely different topic.

This is perhaps our single most important finding. Most studies of the internet and social media are based on research methods that assume we can generalise across different groups. We look at tweets in one place and write about 'Twitter'. We conduct tests about social media and friendship in one population, and then write on this topic as if friendship means the same thing for all populations. By presenting nine books with the same chapter headings, you can judge for yourselves what kinds of generalisations are, or are not, possible.

Our intention is not to evaluate social media, either positively or negatively. Instead the purpose is educational, providing detailed evidence of what social media has become in each place and the local consequences, including local evaluations.

Each book is based on 15 months of research, during which time the anthropologists lived, worked and interacted with people in the local language. Yet they differ from the dominant tradition of writing social science books. Firstly they do not engage with the academic literatures on social media. It would be highly repetitive to have the same discussions in all nine books. Instead discussions of these literatures are to be found in our comparative book, *How the World Changed Social Media*. Secondly these monographs are not comparative, which again is the primary function of this other volume. Thirdly, given the immense interest in social media from the general public, we have tried to write in an accessible and open style. This means we have adopted a mode more common in historical writing of keeping all citations and the discussion of all wider academic issues to endnotes.

We hope you enjoy the results and that you will also read our comparative book – and perhaps some of the other monographs – in addition to this one.

Acknowledgements

This work has been done in continuous co-operation with several friends from the settlement where the evidence used in this book was obtained. They were active collaborators with whom I openly discussed my ideas about, and understanding of, technology, family, social life, prejudices, personal history and affection. Unfortunately I cannot mention any of their names here to protect their privacy.

My wife and I owe an enormous debt of gratitude to Professor Daniel Miller, my mentor and supervisor on this project. He has offered generous amounts of feedback, support and patience with my shortcomings and delays. Above all, he has been an exemplar of a scholar: one that loves the discipline and loves doing research. We are also thankful to Daniel's wife, Rickie Burman, for offering encouragement in past years and for welcoming us many times into their home.

This project involved a team of researchers who worked together for several months before leaving for field work, then kept in regular contact by reading and commenting on each other's monthly reports, and finally collaborated further to produce an online course, a comparative volume and their own individual monographs. Thank you to Dr Elisabetta Costa, Dr Jolynna Sinanan, Dr Nell Haynes, Dr Razvan Nicolescu, Dr Tom McDonald, Dr Shriram Venkatraman and Dr Xinyuan Wang.

Dr Alex Pillen, my second supervisor, has been part of this academic adventure only since I arrived back from the field, but she has indicated and then helped me to navigate a body of literature in the discipline essential to analysing central aspects of my ethnography. More importantly, her availability to read and comment on my chapters, and her enthusiasm for the potential of the research, transmitted much needed support during the writing process.

Dr Rosana Pinheiro-Machado offered 20 very rich pages of commentary after reading an initial draft of this monograph. She has also given me informally, during the opportunities we had to meet, insightful guidance regarding my work, as well as about anthropology in Brazil and in general.

I am also indebted to Ciara Green, Dr Diana Lima, Francisco Oliveira from Instituto Imbassaí, Gabriela Franceschini, Isabela Casellato, Dr João Matta from ESPM, Joilson Souza from IBGE, Laura Haapio-Kirk, Marcelo Maghidman and Dr Marta Jardim. They supported this research in different but substantial ways.

Several friends and colleagues offered comments and support that contributed with the completion of this work: André Avorio, Andrea Reis, Aoife Bennet, Asuka Sawa, Bea Aragon, Dr Carlos Toledo, Cosimo Lupo, Dinorah Paiva, Dr David Jeevendrampillai, Edmilson Filho, Fábio Souza, James Matarazzo, Dr Joseph Bristley, Dr Koldo Bizkarguenaga, Louise de Faria, Dr Maria Luiza Gatto, Laura Poutney, Luciana Costa, Dr Martin Fotta, Manoel Fernandes, Dr Matan Shapiro, Dr Matilda Marshall, Dr Pwyll ap Stifin, Rafael Pereira, Dr Samentha Goethals, Dr Scott Thacker, Dr Shireen Walton, Susanna Inzoli, Toca Feliciano, Dr Tomoko Hayakawa, Vaguinaldo Marinheiro, Vanessa Ribeiro, Dr Yenn Lee and Dr William Matthews. I would also like to thank the friendship and support of the following families: Almeida Prado, Garzarelli, O'Byrne, Pisano and Westman.

I am grateful for the convenors of the seminar series for PhD students at UCL's Department of Anthropology, the academic staff of the digital anthropology programme at UCL and the organisers of the Oxford Digital Ethnography Group (OxDEG) for the opportunities to present parts of this work, receive feedback and interact with other researchers.

Professors João de Pina-Cabral and Luiz Fernando Dias Duarte kindly shared digital versions of their work published in Brazil that otherwise I could not have read.

A generous grant from the European Research Council (grant 2011-AdG-295486 Socnet) enabled the 'Why We Post' project, and consequently this book, to happen.

A big thank you also goes to the administrative teams at UCL Anthropology, the European Research Council at UCL and Oxford's Saint Benet's Hall for the continuous support during this research. I thank particularly Chris Hagisavva, Chris Russell, Keiko Homewood, Martin O'Connor and Paul Carter-Bowman from UCL, Pascale Searle from the ERC and Steve Rumford from Saint Benet's Hall.

During the last six years of constant travelling, Thais and I have received loads of support from our families, especially Ana Maria, Marcos and Florencia, Walter and Flávia, Astério and Zete, Iracema, Thiago and Charles, and our adopted English family Caroline and Daniel.

Thais, my love, none of this would have been possible without your presence, your sunshine, the joy and excitement you bring to life and the inspiration it is to see you participating and giving your best to those around us. It is encouraging and it is sheltering. Thank you.

Hopefully this book will repay part of my debt. Needless to say, all errors and shortcomings are my responsibility.

Contents

List of figures

Antonio Balduíno had always had great scorn for those who worked. He would have preferred to kill himself one night in the harbour than to work [...]. But now the Negro viewed workers with a new respect. They could quit being slaves.

Jubiabá, Jorge Amado

1
The field site: emergent Brazil

This book about emergent Brazil is intended to address one fundamental question: is social media a force to reduce the inequality that remains such a potent legacy of a 300-year-old history of slave-based colonialism?[1] The answer we might have anticipated is that this new infrastructure of communication is on the same side as other forces of social transformation such as the increasing presence of the state, the economic stability provided by formal employment, the growing influence of Protestantism (and its promotion of literacy and individualism) and the overall expansion of transportation and communication infrastructures. However, the ethnography presented in this book provides evidence that points to a different answer: that social media may be popular also because it allows locals to retain the type of dense social relations that migration and new modalities of work are diluting. According to this argument, social media allows some locals better to survive the changes modernisation is causing. It renews the possibilities for attacking the growth of individualism and provides new means for the cultivation of collective and traditional networks of support. This alternative hypothesis explains the enthusiasm locals show for using social media to spy on each other and to spread rumours. As such it comes to similar conclusions to those found in other books in this series, such as Costa[2] and Miller *et al*[3] – namely, that social media is often used to bolster forms of conservatism.

The following pages provide a summary of the findings of each of the chapters leading to the overall conclusion of the book. This is followed by a short discussion of Brazil in relation to its colonial legacy, of the field site chosen for this research and of the methodologies applied during field work. Basically the book divides into two parts. The first three chapters explore the way in which low-income Brazilians use and understand social media. It also relates these ethnographic observations to our knowledge of the historic and socioeconomic background of this population. Each of these chapters presents 'landscapes' or broad views: of the settlement itself (Chapter 1), of how locals communicate in and outside social media (Chapter 2) and of the different types of visual content they exchange (Chapter 3).

The second part of the book then focuses on specific aspects of these people's lives in order to address the consequences of their use of social media. The questions with which these chapters engage include: Is social media affecting traditional family relationships, in which women tend to be subordinate to men and younger people are expected to obey older relatives (Chapter 4)? Is social media a new channel for students in these poor neighbourhoods to connect with people beyond their socio-economic circles, enabling them to access new knowledge and information resources (Chapter 5)? And finally, in a place where the presence of the state is still weak, are locals using social media politically to make themselves less vulnerable within society (Chapter 6)?

Social media in their own terms

The field site where I lived – I call it Balduíno – is undergoing a rapid process of urbanisation and development as, in the context of neoliberal economic expansion, it is located within a region that recently became one of Brazil's important tourist destinations. Growing opportunities of work attracted thousands of low-income families, whose presence transformed old rural settlements into dormitory neighbourhoods now hidden in the outskirts of its gentrified areas.[4] This book analyses the impact social media has on the lives of these families as, within the last decade, the internet has become an important aspect of their lives.[5] Migrant families can now use social media to cultivate bonds within the locality and manage family relations in a different context – one in which the extended family is not as present and parents work for at least part of the day, leaving children alone at the settlement. It also offers alternative ways for them to remain in touch with relatives living elsewhere.

One initial finding about how locals use social media might seem at first quite peculiar. Affluent Brazilians might consider the 'normal' use of Facebook to be a situation in which platforms would align intimate content with people's closest relationships, while the more public materials would be shared with broader audiences. In line with this, middle- and upper-class users these days limit the posting of content considered personal to 'friends', individually accepted to be part of their online networks. Often these more educated Brazilians employ different social media platforms to reach different people[6] (for example, LinkedIn to relate to work contacts or Twitter to interact with other specific audiences). Yet things in Balduíno are different.

First, locals do not use various social media platforms according to specific types of relationships. Instead of having particular domains to meet different types of contacts, they appreciate the way that a social media platform such as Facebook brings them together quite indiscriminately with everyone else who uses the same platforms. Additionally they do not use privacy settings to limit access to the content they upload or share. What Balduíno locals put on Facebook is certainly seen by their online 'friends', but it is also publicly[7] available to anyone with an internet connection.

Based on this evidence, my initial conclusion was that locals revealed their intimate worlds indiscriminately online because they did not appreciate the potential dangers this practice might expose them to. After all, I thought, they have only a few years' experience in accessing the internet. Most also have little education, so it would be unlikely that they follow debates on 'serious' media outlets about the apparent challenges social media is bringing to society. The problem with this early interpretation is that it was based on partial access to the content that people shared on social media; I subsequently also realised that my views about privacy did not correspond to the reality of my informants. What I considered intimate photos – such as those shown in Chapter 3 – are in fact frequently posted in their timelines, but actually represent something similar to the fancy dress or suits people put on to go to a party or to church on Sundays. This content shared on Facebook timelines is not intimate: it shows culturally prescribed actions, with the intention of displaying one's moral values and achievements.

After six months building relationships in Balduíno I was gradually let into the more trusted exchanges that take place in private-facing social media such as Facebook chat and WhatsApp. This proved a shocking discovery, both because of the surprising types of content they share (images of violence and of bizarre nature; politically incorrect humour; gossip, as discussed in Chapter 3) and also because I could then see that the notions of 'public' and 'private' I had in mind did not help to portray their ways of using social media.

At this point, the notion of polymedia proved valuable in analysing the disparity of types of content that people exchanged on the different social media platforms. Polymedia proposes that, because we now have a great variety of possibilities of communicating online, users attribute functions to each platform that reflect shared moral views.

To draw an analogy with the landscape around Balduíno, Facebook timelines are often similar to the community's central areas – places of higher visibility where everyone is constantly assessing everyone else's behaviour. As people move to more peripheral locations, however, the landscape and vegetation provide places to meet in which, similarly to online chat solutions, people could act and speak to each other more freely; here they were no longer under scrutiny.

I felt at this point that I needed to use different terms to 'private' and 'public', so this book instead refers to 'lights on' and 'lights off'[8]. 'Lights on' indicates genres of information that are made visible in order to display to the community one's moral values and achievements. 'Lights off' is where conversations of collective interest often take place, such as cases of violence that locals want to discuss intensely, but never on Facebook timelines or in analogous public spaces to avoid becoming the target of revenge.

Another surprising aspect of how locals in Balduíno communicate is their development of 'speech encryption' techniques. These allow them to modify their speech to limit the understanding of some sensitive conversations, even when these take place surrounded by people. This phenomenon, also discussed on Chapters 2 and 3, is not at all related to computer technologies. It rather involves a technique of omission, by which people leave out sufficient context from conversations to permit only those with intimate knowledge of the subject under discussion to understand what is being said. Linguistic anthropology has studied this practice among populations of similar background to my informants and uses the jargon of 'indirection' to refer to it.[9] This discovery was enlightening: it shows that what makes social media both relevant for the people of Balduíno and expresses their delight in life online is entirely different from that for cosmopolitan educated urbanites in Brazil.

Affluent users usually see the internet in terms of shortening distances: the world has become 'a global village' so we can now establish and cultivate relationships with likeminded individuals independently of place and time.[10] But the central issue for people living in these low-income settlements in Brazil is not excessive distance but excessive proximity. People live in spaces of dense sociality, in part because they are often surrounded by relatives and trusted peers, but also because houses are built literally on top of each other. So for people who live under constant exposure to others' surveillance, social media represents a new frontier: it enables them both to speak secretly with others nearby and also offers, as Chapter 4 shows, new opportunities for spying on people's lives. From this perspective we can see how social media not only reflects but also develops practices, such as speech encryption, which have already emerged as a response to these circumstances.

Why do they love social media?

The previous section has shown that these low-income Brazilians, far from failing to understand their consequences of internet exposure, actually showed quite an immediate and spontaneous appreciation for the possibilities of social media. This in turn explains why they have been broadly responsible for their own digital inclusion. To better appreciate this phenomenon, we move from the general background presented in Chapters 1 to 3 to apply a theoretical toolkit (polymedia, 'lights on' / 'lights off' and indirection) to focus on specific themes. This toolkit allows us to examine cases around the communication of intimacy, education and work, as well as institutionally mediated relationships. Based on the analysis of the common ways in which locals in Balduíno are using social media, the conclusion points to three main reasons why these Brazilians are so positively disposed towards online sociality.

The most obvious reason for low-income Brazilians to embrace social media is that it is economically advantageous. The discussion on mobile phones and the internet (Chapter 2) shows how locals are constantly updating themselves on the intricacies of the different data plan schemes currently available on the market. In addition, having often limited amounts of data to exchange per month, they set up their mobiles to upload or download files only when the phone is connected to a Wi-Fi network. Locals are equally keen to discover the Wi-Fi passwords of the places they work or of their schools, and to share this information with peers. They also know of locations that have free Wi-Fi. At their homes it is common to find broadband plans to which one person subscribes, but which is in fact paid collectively with the other families living in the vicinity. Consequently having access to social media does not just make communication with distant relatives cheaper and more interesting; it also helps those who are communicating with family members and neighbours (by voice or text) to spend less than they would with mobile phone calls.

Using social media is also clearly associated with other practices of consumption that project socioeconomic distinction. The growth in popularity of social media in Brazil that took place in the mid-2000s coincides with a period of shared prosperity in the country, which effectively reduced society's great inequality gap. This is when the (inaccurate) term 'new middle class' eventually came to symbolise this widely shared realisation that the low-income population could become avid consumers. Low-income families perceive the purchase of a computer as a suggestion that its owners are benefiting from formal employment and/or have access to bank credit. These first computers to arrive in family homes, bought through the payment of countless instalments, are often placed in the living room, allowing their symbolic prestige to be appreciated by passers-by.

Social media is one step beyond other products in terms of encapsulating prestige, however, as the very use of social media implies the acquisition of a certain level of literacy. Chapter 5 reveals evidence of how, in contrast to the repeated claims from their teachers, students in Balduíno improved their reading and writing skills because they were afraid of shaming themselves with grammar and spelling mistakes online, when they are 'in front of everybody'. As the final sections in Chapters 4 and 5 explain, evangelical Christians in particular see, at various levels, social media as an important tool for distinguishing them from the non-evangelical. Finally, the use of social media displays not just financial progress, but also intellectual achievement – a key factor in distinguishing between the poor and the affluent in Brazil.

This is not to say that social media is remedying the very serious problems concerning public education in the country. Though social media is perceived locally as a source of information and knowledge, Chapter 5 shows that this seldom encourages locals to study in ways that would advance their careers. The change brought by social media is in terms of self-esteem: people previously ashamed of their low levels of literacy and peasant background now see they can learn how to use this highly sophisticated machine. In a similar way to embracing evangelical Christianity, adopting social media can represent an act of redemption, through which people feel they are no longer as cut off from the rest of society.

However, it is misleading to look at social media's popularity only as a consequence of its practical advantages and of the economic improvement experienced by low-income Brazilians. As Chapters 4 to 6 describe, the government is more present than ever in Balduíno, but locals still feel (and indeed are) marginalised and insecure. Local schools are very problematic places: many families distrust teachers and resent the associated lack of motivation among those working in these communities. Instead of being perceived as places to improve one's career options, schools are treated more like day-care centres in which young people are looked after while their parents work. Similar deficiencies exist in terms of public health and police services, while locals are suspicious of government politics.

Meanwhile, the lives of these locals have been changing rapidly in the past 50 years. Broadly speaking, until the 1950s work structures resembled the feudal system of medieval Europe, with peasants cropping the land of 'masters' in exchange for part of the production. The transition to modernity, which took place over centuries in Europe, is happening here within a generation. Local adults talk about a time in which money was rarely seen. In 30 years locals in Balduíno have gone from not having piped water and electricity to being connected to the world through cable television and broadband. They went from just one Catholic chapel to the presence of over 20 different Protestant denominations within the settlement. Similar transformations took place in relation to transportation and urbanisation. Although people welcome many of these changes, they require them also to make great efforts to change their ways of living (for example, mothers leaving children to work outside the home) and to face considerable new challenges, including the growth of violence related to crime (Chapter 6).

What the ethnography shows over and over again is that people still feel insecure, marginalised and dependent upon extended families and support networks to improve their living conditions.[11] So we see that while the symbolism of social media relates to economic achievement, the practices – how it is actually used – relate rather to strengthening the possibilities for cultivating such established networks and extended family relations. Social media allows people to be present in the settlement while being physically absent. By gossiping, sharing problems, jokes and religious commentaries, they demonstrate their mutual interest and availability to each other. It is the circulation of such gossip and rumours that delineates the limits of those belonging to Balduíno. This is a conclusion that contradicts common assumptions coming from the social sciences, namely that social media extends only individual-based networks.[12] To the majority of low-income Brazilians living where this ethnography was produced – a very parochial and typical low-income site – social media strengthens the traditions and the relationships connecting them with the place where they live.

This all leads to one further conclusion that contradicts the assumption of affluent, educated Brazilians. They would see the development of social media as a modernising and progressive force, in contrast to evangelical Christianity which they would see as representing backwardness and conservatism. However, the ethnography presented in this volume indicates that it is evangelical Christianity that encourages the values associated with modern life and growing affluence, such as promoting nuclear family structure or investment in education. Compared to this, the role of social media is much more ambiguous. When associated with morals nurtured together with Protestantism, it reflects people's efforts to acquire cosmopolitan tastes. But for the remaining part of the population, social media is largely embraced for the help it gives local people in preserving traditional forms of sociality and community – concepts that they still very much need in order to adapt to the wide, abrupt changes brought by recent modernisation.

Social media in emergent Brazil

Between 2003 and 2011 nearly 40 million Brazilians moved above the poverty line.[13] These people have helped to form a social group of 60 million that belong to a 'new working class'[14] (also described as 'classe C'[15]). Evolving in the context of neoliberal economic policies, this population represents close to one third of Brazilians today, and their tastes, morals, religious values and world views have an increasing impact upon the country's economy and politics. For the first time many of these Brazilians are experiencing the advantages and protection of formal employment and have access to bank credit. Consequently they have started to have the opportunity to acquire things such as cars and private health insurance, to afford air travel and to be able to send their children to university.

A noteworthy aspect of this recent phenomenon is the love that this population shows for social media.[16] For example, young people from poorer backgrounds have been largely responsible for their own technological inclusion, initially by making internet cafés successful businesses in their neighbourhoods, areas often deprived of government assistance.[17] In recent years, by embracing less-expensive Android smartphones, these people are finally able to stay (privately and continuously) connected to the internet.[18]

This drastic socioeconomic change is often credited to the ability of recent governments to curb hyperinflation, universalise literacy and instigate internal growth, at the same time reducing inequality by injecting resources into the most vulnerable strata through welfare programmes such as *Bolsa Família* (Family Allowance).[19] Yet specialists tend to undervalue the contribution that these Brazilians have made to rid themselves of poverty.[20] Affluent educated commentators will normally claim that the internet is a modernising force that expands one's possibilities through making available broader horizons of learning. Evangelical Christianity, many will also argue, does the opposite, fostering narrow-mindedness and intolerance.[21] In this view, because of these Christians' Bible-centred values, they favour creationism over evolutionism, condemn gay rights, oppose abortion, abuse members of non-Christian faiths and reject divorce. However, the ethnographic evidence gathered here indicates that to low-income Brazilians, it is evangelical Christianity – including historic Protestants and Pentecostals – that makes people want to acquire formal education. Evangelical churches provide literacy courses to their adult members, and reading the Bible can progress to reading other books. The influence of this meritocratic Protestant ideology also has effects outside churches – especially among young social media enthusiasts, who now believe that they have more opportunities to prosper than their parents ever did.[22]

Social media reflects the ambiguities of this transition. In the initial months of field work, when I was introducing myself as an anthropologist studying social media, locals in Balduíno consistently reacted in one of two ways. Some responded that I had come to the right place because (as they put it only half-jokingly) using social media there was 'an addiction' (*um vício*) and it was spreading even among those who could barely read and write – which is true. However, others found it very strange that having come to such a large country as Brazil, and being able to choose a prosperous southern city, I had ended up in a small, poor and barely known settlement in the north,[23] where most are lucky to get a high school diploma and then find work as a driver, cleaner or security guard.

In short, some locals were saying that Balduíno was the perfect place to study social media; others thought that it was the least relevant, especially as I was conducting research related to technology. I explain below the reasons for choosing a small place instead of a city neighbourhood. For now it is enough to say that both in cities and smaller localities Brazil's under-educated poor are coming to terms with the rapid changes and fragmentation of social ties resulting from mass migration from rural hinterlands to cities. In this field site, formerly a rural setting but not yet fully urban, social media expresses both the hopes of some locals who are embracing new dreams and ambitions, and the fears of others who find themselves more diminished as the world expands around them.[24]

The title of this book indicates this is a study about social media in 'emergent' Brazil.[25] I refer to an 'emergent' working class to emphasise a process of change – from a general condition of stagnation to the possibility of experiencing socioeconomic fluidity. This is the consequence not only of an increase in purchasing power, but also of the acquisition of education, of limited quality as yet but at least now available. Recent data presented in later chapters shows a sharp decrease in illiteracy as peasant families relocate to urban settings, have better access to governmental infrastructure and are now exposed to Protestant values. While parents in Balduíno tend to have had up to four years of education, their children now have easy access to 12 years in public schools. A few are earning university degrees in areas such as psychology, physiotherapy, odontology and law, and consequently emerging from the condition of unskilled worker to become skilled professionals. Furthermore, the term 'emergent' is linked to how visibility becomes an important element in these low-income settlements and neighbourhoods.[26] It is not enough to be prosperous; people in such areas need to express and display their personal and family achievements.

Evangelical Christians are keen on making themselves and their religious experience visible (and audible) to others. They do this through the very formal dresses and suits with ties that they wear to attend services, through the importance of constantly displaying their faith, through the high volume of the speakers used in these churches and also through repeatedly exposing the blessings they claim to receive from God.[27] Outside of churches, both evangelical and non-evangelical families are under pressure to demonstrate to their neighbours that they too are able to acquire branded items and other symbols of prosperity. In this book, therefore, 'emergence' refers to this effort of wanting to become visible. Social media is important as both a window and a mirror: it provides a way for people both to see the world and also to portray themselves to the world.

One of the advantages of studying social media anthropologically is the ability actually to visualise social ties and the ways in which they are perceived. These online networks often include a list of 'friends'[28] and technical solutions so that each user can group or label different types of contacts. Social media also makes relationships visible because of the different types of exchanges that these connections produce, or do not produce. Online social relations materialise and record people's interactions. In this context, the more obvious path to study social mobility on social media is to examine the communication between people of difference socioeconomic classes. Interestingly, however, the change taking place at Balduíno has had little expression in inter-class ties. There a domestic servant or a builder is not becoming closer to his or her affluent boss because of Facebook or WhatsApp. However, intra-class associations are changing as the popularity of social media continues to increase,[29] and the exchanges it fosters commonly reflect tensions between groups such as young and old, Protestant and non-Protestant and men and women.

It is significant that the moment social media became a topic of national debate in Brazil was also the period in which large numbers of low-income Brazilians began to have the means to be online. Orkut, a social networking site owned by Google, was launched in 2004; it became the meeting ground for Brazilian internet users in 2006 and was abandoned relatively quickly around 2009 through a massive migration to Facebook (which has remained as the most important social media platform for Brazilians to this day).[30]

I am pointing this out because the shift from Orkut to Facebook in Brazil happened at least partially because of similar class issues to those that boyd[31] framed in relation to the United States as a phenomenon of 'white flight'; only that there the movement was from MySpace to Facebook. As this spontaneous migration took place among Brazilians, the expression 'orkutisation'[32] began to circulate. It is a neologism applied by affluent users to denounce the 'invasion' of an online space by undereducated 'low taste' people, for instance by the view expressed on social media that Facebook's purchase of Instagram would 'orkutise' Instagram.[33] The term generally conveys acts of 'symbolic violence' aiming to ridicule, shame, insult and hopefully drive away users of low-income background who may seek to use platforms viewed as more exclusive and sophisticated, such as Twitter and Instagram.

In short, this is a study of social media – but of social media in relation to a particular social group that has recently experienced a level of socioeconomic empowerment. This interesting group apparently uses social media intensely because of the consequences of social change and the possibilities of upward mobility in the communities where they live.

Choosing a location

Our research group chose to move away from traditional units, such as villages and towns, and look to the new kinds of 'in-between' settlements where people increasingly live today. Often we categorise our living space as either urban and rural, yet this understanding does not include in between places like exclusive gated communities located in suburbs nor 'isolated urban areas' such as Balduíno. This settlement is physically separated from the county's centre, and yet most of its inhabitants are not associated with rural activities such as cropping or fishing. Furthermore, the relatively small size of these places in comparison to cities also helped us to compare communication happening on and offline.

Socioeconomic inequality, which is key to this study, is an important topic of debate among economists, historians and social scientists researching Latin America.[34] Brazil currently ranks as the fourth most unequal country in the Americas, and is far larger than its neighbours that rank as more unequal; it is also, according to the GINI index,[35] the 13th most unequal country in the world, largely as a consequence of colonialism. In the nineteenth century Brazil had seven people of African ancestry for every white person, and racial segregation explains how today blacks and mixed race Brazilians earn on average 58 per cent as much as whites. In the United States, by contrast, the earning gap is 76 per cent.[36]

This study took place in Bahia, a state located in the Northeast region of the country and the centre of the first 200 years of Portuguese colonial presence in South America. Today the region has the highest inequality rate in Brazil.[37] Nearly one-third of all Brazilians live there; 72 per cent are non-white, 80 per cent belong to the lower economic strata (classes C, D and E)[38] and 88 per cent still depend on the (often poorly rated) national health care system (SUS).[39] It is the only region in Brazil in which the middle class is not predominant and, despite massive migrations to the southern cities in the twentieth century, 27 per cent of its population still live in rural areas – half of which are among the poorest in the country.[40]

Income, education and race further attest to the colonial socioeconomic roots of the Northeast's segregated society. Those at the top of the social ladder are predominantly white (49 per cent) and have spent on average 11.2 years at school. In the middle 70 per cent are black or of mixed race, and spent an average of 6.1 years at school. Those with the lowest incomes are 78 per cent non-white and attended school for an average of only 4.6 years.[41] Yet this is also the region that has showed most signs of socioeconomic improvement during the period of quick economic growth in the 2000s. Perhaps the greatest sign of change appears in the severe decline in the illiteracy rates: while a staggering one-third of the population over 50 years old cannot read or write, this is now true of only 2.1 per cent of teens between the ages of 15 and 17.[42] The size of middle-income groups grew from 28 per cent of the population in 2002 to 45 per cent a decade later. Out of the total population of

56 million, 18.6 million are part of this emergent working-class stratum known as 'classe C'.[43]

The field site

I have called the settlement where this research took place Balduíno.[44] It is only about 100 km to the north of the city of Salvador, now the capital of the state of Bahia, and legally forms part of the county of Camaçari. The following historic and demographic information is useful in understanding the scale of changes that have taken place in the past few decades in the coastal region where Balduíno is located.[45]

Historical context

Brazil is the largest country of Latin America, with a territory larger than the contiguous United States. It occupies 49 per cent of the eastern coastal side of South America, from the equatorial Amazonian forest to the subtropical borders with Argentina and Uruguay in the south. Like all its neighbours, Brazil is a relatively new sovereign state; it became a monarchy autonomous from Portugal in 1822 and a republic in 1889. Its formation is rooted in a process of colonisation conducted mainly by the Portuguese state, which arrived on its coast in 1500 and established a settlement – today the city of Salvador – five decades later.[46] Similarly to the case in the Spanish colonies in the Americas, the presence of the Portuguese in the New World brought the Catholic Church, and Brazil still has the largest Catholic population in the world. In contrast to Spain, which economically had a more urban colonial presence and a focus on mining precious metals, Portugal produced wealth in Brazil mainly through slave-based plantations.[47] Together with many of the English colonies in the New World, the plantations exported initially sugar and cotton to Europe. And given the size of the land and the importance of agriculture to the Portuguese colonial enterprise, Brazil was the main destination of the slave trade from Africa to the Americas.[48]

Some of the key elements in the formation of Brazilian society are thus Catholicism and slavery, in the context of a rural-based economy and with long-lasting effects. Information from the 1950 census for Camaçari,[49] a neighbouring county to Salvador, reflects its proximity to Brazil's colonial roots. This official data indicates that among a population of about 13,500 there were nine people classified as brown (*pardo*) or black to each white person. The same source shows that the county was predominantly Catholic, having one mother church, one church and six chapels in its territory, but the census also mentions the existence at that time of one Assembly of God, a Pentecostal church. (It does not mention representatives of Afro-Brazilian religions such as the *candomblé*, popular mainly outside of wealthier white social circles). As with the whole of Brazil at that time, Camaçari was predominantly rural: only 31.2 per cent of people lived in urban areas and one-quarter of the country's active population (those aged ten and above) worked with agriculture, livestock and/or forestry. The main industries produced charcoal, cassava flour, bricks and bread. Horticulture and fishing are also mentioned as relevant, mainly in its coastal 'villas', each with populations of up to 900 people (Fig. 1.1).

Balduíno was one of these 'villas' in the coastal area of Camaçari county. Such micro-urban hubs, all of them near river mouths, have probably existed since colonial times when they were local ports for boats to load farming goods, possibly sugar, from Brazil's early economic activity. (Not far from Balduíno are the remains of a Portuguese castle built from 1549.) But by the 1950s large-scale farming in the region was

Fig. 1.1   The Coconut Coast, an area in transition from a rural and isolated region to an international tourist destination

reaching the end of its cycle after centuries of decline.[50] Landowners mostly used the coast to produce coconuts, a crop that is cheap to maintain and that kept the land productive. And as farms were abandoned or broken up to be given as inheritances, merchants established themselves in these villas. Here they acted as commercial intermediaries, taking the local coconut crop to markets at cities and then bringing to the region products such as coffee, sugar, cachaça (a substance distilled from the sap of sugar cane) and cloth.[51]

The reduced economic significance of these businesses is reflected in the forms of transport that the merchants used. No roads linked Balduíno to nearby cities, so goods were either transported on the back of horses and mules or carried along the coast by small sailing boats (*saveiros*). Today it takes roughly one hour, depending on traffic conditions, to go from Balduíno to Camaçari city, but until the 1950s merchants walked with their cargo on 9-hour journeys, starting at 7 am and ending at 4 pm.[52] They usually slept in Camaçari that night to attend the market the next morning, then headed back to Balduíno in the afternoon. Sailing journeys to Salvador and back could take weeks as progress depended on favourable winds.[53]

The people

In addition to landowners and merchants, the society of settlements such as Balduíno in the first half of the twentieth century had another component. These were people of mainly African but also of mixed (European and Amerindian) descent who lived as fishers and croppers of cassava and other vegetables in family plots surrounding the centre of the settlements.[54] Even today locals can be spotted fishing in the river using straw baskets; these are placed in rocky, sloping sections of the river, a technique descending from native Brazilian practices.[55] Besides cropping and fishing, this population worked for farmers in temporary manual jobs (such as gathering and peeling coconuts); they also exchanged with merchants and scavenged products such as *piaçava* (fibre and coconut), and the seeds of the *babaçu* and *ouricuri* plants.[56] The lives of these workers were closely connected through kin and fictive kin relationships, with women managing the house and raising children, and men (when present) working outside of Balduíno.

This book focuses on this section of the population. Today it is a group that includes families of similar backgrounds (under-educated manual workers of African or mixed descent) who, attracted by work opportunities associated with tourism, have been migrating from Salvador and the hinterland of Bahia state. They are distinguished by the subordinate position[57] they hold in relation to the local elites. The implication is that this population is not just outside the settlement's central areas for socioeconomic reasons, but also because the vegetation, trails and mud homes provide a screen to obscure them from the affluent society. As Chapter 2 shows in detail, camouflaging takes place in various practices of this population, including their forms of communication. As Chapter 3 argues, such practices represent on one hand the acceptance of being subordinate ('lights on'), but on the other an increased possibility of action ('lights off'). A simple example is found in religion, as mentioned above – in the opposition between the various concealed *candomblé* yards in the surroundings of the settlement and the hyper-visible Catholic chapel at its centre.

The logic of this camouflage resonates today with the settlement's location: close to, but kept separate from, the more recent arrival of a gentrified strip by the ocean.[58] Such settlements are generally perceived by the affluent as a necessary evil to be otherwise avoided. The owners of summer homes and businesses employ the cheap labour force of cleaners, cooks, gardeners, security guards, waiters, drivers and builders, but are increasingly restricting the presence of these locals outside of working situations; they seek, for example, to avoid this low-income population on 'their' beaches.[59] Locals often contest their subordinate situation, in which others seek to render them invisible, by passively resisting the arrogant will of bosses, by ridiculing them behind their backs and by stealing food and other products from their employers.

According to the 2010 national census, there were 11,244 people living in Balduíno, including its surrounding rural vicinities and the gentrified strip by the coast. While in the settlement three to four people live in each house, across the road there is one person for every three to four houses (as these tend to be second homes used only on weekends, vacations and holidays). However, the official figure for population is probably inaccurate, with 15,000 being a more realistic estimate. This is the figure used by one of the local political bosses to calculate the number of voters in the area during the 2012 mayoral election. This number accounts for the constant flow of temporary workers and the already established population living in the five main squatting areas (the earliest dating from the mid-1980s and the most recent from 2012) that surround the centre of the settlement (Fig. 1.2).

Fig. 1.2 A view of the more urbanised squatting area in Balduíno

A migrant family from Salvador

Like every other older child or teenager in Balduíno, 11-year-old Lara almost cannot take her eyes off or stop using her smartphone. Being so young, she is still not bothered that her relatively inexpensive Nokia mobile has problems connecting to the internet. She is more interested in its large and visible casing, with a modern-looking screen and keyboard. Lara uses her phone mainly as other children do, to play simple action games, take photos and listen to music (Fig. 1.3). When she is at home or with her female peers during school breaks, she uses it to play highly sexualised songs of *Pagodão* or *Pagofunk* music genres, popular among many under 20 years old. The phone's external speakers allow Lara and her friends to practice sensual and acrobatic dance routines together, their moves following the action the lyrics describe. (The locally most popular tune in 2013 had as its chorus: 'the pussy has the power' (*o poder está na tcheca*)). More recently, however, Lara has stopped participating in these; she has been attending a Pentecostal church and is now part of its children's dance group.

Lara's parents met as neighbours in a *favela* in Salvador. Nadia, aged 44, has been working in the past few years as a cook at a restaurant

Fig. 1.3 A child using her smartphone

across the road. She cannot read or write, and before moving to Balduíno she worked mainly as a domestic servant. Her two previous partners have died, of health-related issues, and today all her five children (four from previous relationships) still live with her. The oldest is 27 and Lara is now the youngest: her brother died of a heart problem at the age of three. Jonas, Lara's father, used to be an amateur singer in a music group. Being barely literate, he retired at 43 due to a back injury suffered while working as a deliverer of boxes of beer and fizzy drinks in Salvador. Jonas is an alcoholic and spends most or all of his money on cheap spirits. (As he does not work, I saw him regularly in the settlement, usually 'merry' and walking the streets trying to borrow money from anybody he knew and singing beautifully at the top of his voice.) Nadia explained to me once that *candomblé* could cure his alcoholism if he really wanted to quit. Despite this problem, however, she says he is worth keeping: he does not beat her, is a good father to Lara and has never sexually abused her other daughters.

Lara's family arrived in Balduíno almost 12 years ago after Jonas was offered a job as a housekeeper. Since then they have managed to acquire a small plot, 5 m by 8 m, and to build a humble brick home at an older squatting area. Now, however, they are squatting again. The family has kept their house, but moved much of their furniture to three

Fig. 1.4 The newest squatting area

little shacks, built on a plot that they hope will eventually become the site where Nadia's children will build their homes.

This family is not unusual in Balduíno. There are locals living in better conditions, particularly those who inherited plots of land, work in public services or have consolidated their employment at a tourism-related business; such people have steady incomes and access to work and government benefits. But there are also families living in worse situation than Lara's. These are generally people who have arrived recently, with no local network of support. Many of them live in newer squatting areas (Fig. 1.4), where crack cocaine is increasingly replacing cheap cachaça as the drug of choice and sexually transmitted diseases, including AIDS, are silently spreading.

Tourism, migration and urbanisation

The most recurrent themes of conversation in Balduíno are all related to migration. Locals whose families have lived there for several generations blame newcomers for 'taking over their settlement and contaminating it' with problems from the cities: pollution, greed, stress and crime. This argument connects with another favourite theme, the decline of family values. These views constantly arise as locals complain that young people today are lazy and materialistic (Fig. 1.5); they have lost respect for the elders, and their behaviour is viewed as immoral, especially regarding young women's 'promiscuity' and lack of concern for marriage, is viewed as immoral.[60] Such tensions are occasionally associated with the use of social media. According to this moral framework generally held by adults, the internet is one of the elements that represent modernity; as such it is embraced by young people as an 'addiction', along with the consumption of expensive branded items, general lack of morals and the use of drugs. So discussions about migration are less about blaming a specific category of people (as most have arrived in the past few decades) than about intergenerational conflicts of taste, values, conduct and world views associated with urban lifestyles.

The theme of migration further connects Balduíno with a phenomenon of crucial importance taking place across Brazil as a whole. After the Second World War a prolonged drought affected the hinterland of the Northeast region, encouraging a pattern of migration in which poor rural families moved towards urban centres. This phenomenon is the main cause that shifted the balance of population distribution in the country from being predominantly rural in the 1950s (70 per cent) to predominantly urban (80 per cent) by the turn of the twentieth century.[61] Balduíno is not a city, yet the migrant families who arrive have the same socioeconomic background and origin as those travelling to cities. Nor is

Fig. 1.5 An older adult making hats to sell to tourists

it predominantly rural, as it is now perceived as part of the metropolitan area of Salvador. Given the national importance of this phenomenon of urbanisation in rural areas, the national census bureau (IBGE) has had to come up with a new designation – 'isolated urban area' (*area urbana isolada*) – to classify this type of transitional settlement.[62] Such places are detached from cities, but most of their inhabitants do not work in productive activities related to the rural domain.

Various factors at different levels act to intensify the rhythms of change in the 'Coconut Coast', a coastal area 193 km in length where Balduíno is located (Fig. 1.6). The early construction of an unpaved road (in the 1950s) connected Balduíno to Camaçari city. Wealthy car owners began to purchase plots there and to build country houses, seeking to escape the city and spend weekends away with family and friends. In the 1960s Arambepe, a beach locality also in Camaçari County, was a site on the international counterculture map: known as a free-love natural sanctuary for young hippies, it was visited by artists such as Janis Joplin and Mick Jagger.[63] The flow of people to the Coconut Coast increased because, due to the area's geography, Salvador cannot expand to its southern coast.

The opening of the Coconut Road (officially called BA-99) in the 1970s consolidated the process of development towards the north. In the

Fig. 1.6   A map of Brazil indicating the location of the Coconut Coast, in the northern coastal area of Bahia

1980s the city's population growth and the escalation of crime encouraged well-off families to move to gated communities in the fringes of Salvador, from where they commuted daily to the city.[64] The gradual expansion of infrastructure facilities eventually brought water, electricity and telephones to most of the northern coast's localities, finally prompting the launch of projects to develop large-scale tourist resorts in the 1990s and 2000s. These resorts today are tourist versions of gated communities;[65] holiday makers prefer the safety and convenience of staying at these resorts by the coast and only make occasional day trips, using private drivers, to Salvador.

The settlement

This development brought highly urban characteristics to a traditionally rural environment at the Coconut Coast. Near the ocean are often swampy plains of varying width covered by vegetation and cut by streams that eventually form lagoons, some over 1 km in length.[66] This land next to the ocean is now almost exclusively occupied by people with greater economic muscle and more educational qualifications; they arrive from urban centres (Fig. 1.7). The Coconut Road separates this strip from the continental coastal elevations rising to up to 150 m above the sea level, covered with typical sandbank vegetation that intertwines with the Atlantic forest under regeneration. These elevated areas, now separated from the sea, are often where settlements such as Balduíno are located. There the characteristics of the population and the use of land is different. Instead of planned housing and business infrastructure, low-income migrants are often moving in to houses located in squatting camps.

Satellite images from the area reveal very different patterns of occupation on either side of the road. On the strip near the sea, streets form more or less square blocks that contain plots of regular sizes. If they are not hotels, they are predominantly residential areas of gated houses (some inside gated communities) with gardens, inside parking areas and, at times, swimming pools. Owners use private cars to move around. Residents are local business executives, independent professionals, business owners or retired couples who travel regularly to Salvador to meet friends and family or to go out. Across the road in settlements such as Balduíno, urbanisation follows a rhizome-like pattern (Fig. 1.8). Instead of sequences of regular street blocks, a main street begins by the road and branches out into a series of smaller, unpaved streets. Nearer the main street is often a commercial area of pharmacies,

Fig. 1.7   The Coconut Road separates the tourist areas from the working-class settlements in the region

markets, service providers and shops in general – usually not present in the gentrified parts. At these places homes are raised next to one another, and owners constantly expand their properties by building up to two storeys above ground level.[67] At these settlements exposed bricks on walls are almost ubiquitous because constant efforts to expand one's home depend on saved money that is only occasionally available. The inhabitants predominantly use public transport (buses and vans) to go to the city, while they walk or take the informal but popular moto-taxi services (a single motorcycle used as a taxi) to move about inside or near the settlement.

The rhythms of the two sides of the road are often interlinked: as the wealthier area gets busier during weekends and holidays, the population of the settlement is at work in restaurants, hotels and other tourist-related businesses. During Mondays and Tuesdays many of these employees have their days off, and the settlements are livelier with cars, motorcycles, buses and people coming and going, gathering at bars or cafeterias (*lanchonetes*). However, as the large hotels are now open throughout the year, processions of private buses enter and leave the settlements three times a day every day, transporting the staff to and from their places of work.

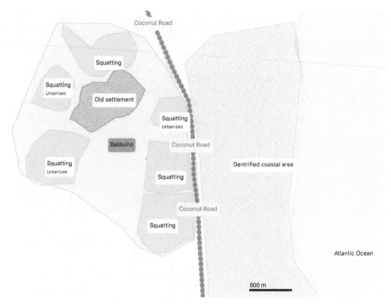

Fig. 1.8 Diagram of a typical settlement in the region, separated by the Coconut Road from the gentrified coastal strip and retaining the old 'villa' and the recent areas of squatting

A young peasant woman migrates to Balduíno

Aged 29, Vanessa works as a cleaner at a smart bed and breakfast establishment catering to European and North American tourists who prefer small, off-road places to crowded chain hotel resorts.[68] She is single and lives by herself in one-bedroom accommodation in Balduíno. Two years ago she joined an evangelical Christian church and recently many new things have been happening in her life. For the first time Vanessa has a place for herself; she can own things like a laptop, a washing machine and an Android smartphone. The access to digital communication and social media in particular represents to her becoming part of the modern world of consumption and technology – a world that about ten years ago she could only experience through the glamourised lives of soap opera characters.

Vanessa's story is not very different from those of her neighbours in the settlement. Many grew up as peasants in farms or small family plots, working first at home from the age of four or five (washing, cleaning and carrying for younger siblings) and then cropping from nine years upwards. Schools in rural areas are often distant and in general structurally poor. As Vanessa reached her teens in the early 2000s, she left the farm to move to a neighbouring small city and become a domestic servant.[69] As is often required in this type of job, she slept at the homes of the families who hired her. (Even today Brazilian middle-class homes often include tiny rooms by the laundry area, designed to be occupied by these female servants.) She worked from morning until night washing, cleaning and cooking, as well as looking after the family's small children. After some years, however, the long hours of work, the lack of privacy, the complaints made when she left the house after work to see friends, the difficulties posited when she considered going back to school at night and various instances of mistreatment she endured eventually piled up;Vanessa began to dream of alternative possibilities of life and work.[70]

The ticket to a new life arrived from a relative, who described a place near Salvador where there were abundant opportunities of work. 'There, you are only unemployed if you want to be,' the relative told her. This sounded promising, so in 2010 Vanessa quit her job and took a bus to Salvador, travelling from there to the state's north coastal area. She started living with her relative in Balduíno and working as a baby-sitter, but gradually moved towards formal employment.[71]

Fig. 1.9 An example of a hotel in which local people work

The transition Vanessa is experiencing has advantages, but it does not free her from feeling abused and exploited. She now enjoys access to government benefits, for example being entitled to jobseekers' allowance. Her employer also provides private health insurance that is often better and more efficient than public health services. She recognises all of these conveniences and has thus remained in the same job for the past four years (Fig. 1.9). However, like others in Balduíno, she will refer sometimes to her working conditions as a form of 'modern-day slavery'. She now has money to rent a home, pay for a gym membership, buy things and to contribute a 'tithe' every month (a financial offering) to the church she attends.[72] She is continuously in contact with friends and family living near and far. Yet there are still incidents that make her aware of her historical condition of social vulnerability. Having her bag occasionally searched as she leaves work – 'just like a criminal', she says angrily – brings forth the feeling of humiliation she had working as a domestic servant. Like others working at the same hotel, she defies the authority of owners in various ways, such as eating food that should be only consumed by guests. She explains, 'I am not a lesser person than anybody; why should I eat a lesser type of food?'

Christianity[73]

Roman Catholicism arrived during the early years of the Iberian colonial presence in the Americas through religious missionaries such as Jesuits. It was the official religion of Brazil until the late nineteenth century. According to the census, however, the popularity of Catholicism has fallen, from representing 91.8 per cent of the population in the 1970s to 64.6 per cent in 2010. Over the same period the number of Protestants has increased from 5.2 per cent to representing today nearly one-quarter of all Brazilians.[74] The numbers projected by the 2010 census indicate that in 30 years Protestants and Catholics will have communities of the same size in Brazil.[75]

My informal estimate is that between 30 and 40 per cent of people living in Balduíno are Protestants.[76] Yet such statistics only really come to life by walking around the settlement. In this relatively small locality I counted 24 different church organisations in operation.[77] These include established groups such as the Assembly of God, one of the oldest Pentecostal churches in the country and the first to arrive in Balduíno in the 1960s, and various others of different sizes, including Baptists, Methodists, Jehovah Witnesses and Seventh Day Adventists, plus a number of neo-Pentecostal churches, the most important of which is the Universal Church of the Kingdom of God.[78]

The religious shift from Catholicism to Protestantism follows the pattern of poor Brazilians relocating from rural areas in the Northeast to the peripheries of cities as mentioned above.[79] Protestant Pentecostal conregations consist predominantly of urban, young, female and non-white individuals, who spend less time at school and earn less money than the average population.[80] In Balduíno churches help both migrants and the younger generation of locals as they navigate the often challenging and unhappy experiences of moving away from family-based support networks; the need to adapt to living in cities, to urban forms of violence and to different types of work and employment all contributes to the stress.[81] In such contexts the adoption of Protestantism enhances the possibilities of forging new social relations and renewing values.[82] Conscious of the size and scope of the influence Protestants have gained in Brazil in recent decades, a friend who works as an executive market researcher informally describes such religious organisations as the country's 'non-official welfare state': they provide the most vulnerable with material support as well as immaterial benefits such as care and attention.

Locally, the most successful of these organisations are the Assembly of God, whose local leadership manages around 20 small branches operating in and near Balduíno, and a neo-Pentecostal (originally Baptist) church; the latter follows an aggressive apostolic strategy called Vision G12 that started in South Korea. Both of these more popular churches have up to or around 400 attendees during each of their main weekly services.

In Balduíno, having higher than average purchase power, evangelical Christians are buying computers to keep their children at home; they also pay for them to have extra-curricular activities as they fear the influence of non-Christian values, particularly regarding exposure to sex and drug consumption. But the consequences of the growing presence of evangelical Christianity are not restricted to those who choose to embrace these new forms of religion. Independently of their faith or religious views, young people in general perceive gospel as one of the genres of music they listen to regularly – and it is equally true that young Protestants also follow non-religious pop artists.[83] So it is not strange to locals that young men include gospel hits in the music tracks they listen to while drinking alcohol during a barbecue party.[84] And while in the past everyone in the settlement participated in *candomblé* 'parties' (which involve ritualistic dance and music, spiritual incorporation, sacrifice of animals, and free food for attendees), today many non-evangelicals have stopped going or letting their children participate in these events. This has taken place following the continuous attacks of evangelical Christians, who systematically denounce Afro-Brazilian faiths as being inspired by the devil.[85]

Moral and class distinctions

In spite of the variety of evangelical Christian organisations that exist today in Brazil,[86] this Protestant population often identify themselves (and are called by others) as 'believers' ('*crentes*') or 'evangelicals' ('*evangélicos*'). These terms, and also 'evangelical Christian', refer broadly to a population which includes historic Protestants, Pentecostals and neo-Pentecostals. But although originally these groups had very different identities and ways of understanding and practising Christianity,[87] their differences are not as clear in present-day Balduíno. While the 'Theology of Prosperity'[88] is traditionally associated with neo-Pentecostalism, the elite church in the settlement is the Pentecostal Assembly of God (Fig. 1.10), whose members portray themselves as both strict and prosperous.[89] (As a junior Assembly minister explained, it is all right to ask God for a car as long as the purpose of having the car is to help the church.) During the week's main services, shiny new cars and motorcycles crowd the entrance of this church, nearly blocking the traffic in the settlement's main street.[90]

Members of other organisations, such as Seventh Day Adventists, are not as strident about appearance and conspicuous consumption, but are equally concerned to display their religious devotion as well as achieving prosperity (Fig. 1.11). So while non-evangelicals are often informal workers or public servants, evangelicals invest in education and build their prosperity, both through dedication to formal employment or through energetically running small businesses.

For these reasons, the clearest symbolic frontier among locals in the settlement – particularly when it comes to adults – is between non-evangelicals and evangelicals. Non-evangelicals' perception of evangelicals does not distinguish between what they see as moral and material arrogance: the 'celestial' pride Pentecostals display through strictness and devotion merges with the neo-Pentecostals' appetite for financial 'worldly' success. Catholics, non-church goers[91] and disciples of Afro-Brazilian religions similarly tend to portray evangelicals as hypocrites who enjoy lecturing others about the Bible but are greedy and selfish beneath. More specifically, what many dislike about evangelicals is their claim

Fig. 1.10 A small branch of the Assembly of God in Balduíno

Fig. 1.11 Evangelical Christians wearing their best suits and dresses for service

of superiority: they think too much of themselves ('*se acham*') and behave as if they are better than everyone else. For them, evangelicals pretend to follow Jesus's teachings about loving other people, but in fact they love only themselves and those close to them.

This polarisation of opinion also happens in other domains. Though evangelical Christianity is a national and international phenomenon, evangelicals are often portrayed by the more affluent media outlets, as well as in academia, as close-minded fanatics.[92] The negative perception relates to how these Christians adopt very conservative behaviour. Because of their Bible-centred values, they favour creationism over evolutionism, condemn gay rights, oppose abortion, abuse members of non-Christian faiths and reject divorce. Consequently, outside narrow academic circles which may include social scientists studying low-income groups, evangelical Christianity is treated generally as manipulation from 'merchants of faith'.[93]

Few recognise, however, the ways in which evangelical organisations contribute to society. Some churches provide literacy courses to their adult participants (who are often ashamed of not being able to follow the readings during service), and reading the Bible can evolve to reading other books. Churches may also facilitate the contact of church members with specialised services, including doctors and lawyers. And by 'recycling the souls' of drug addicts and criminals through faith in God's healing powers and the promotion of new lifestyles, they provide a much better service to society than the Brazilian state could hope to offer today.[94] Finally, evangelical Christianity may be seen as a positive influence as it curbs domestic violence and alcoholism, promotes intimacy among couples and supports young people's ambitions to study and evolve professionally.

A local adult and his 'rebellious' choice to be a fisherman

At 44 years old, Jorge has a solid, muscular body and warm laughter. When he is home (always wearing his swimming trunks), we often see him surrounded by friends, beer bottles and peals of laughter while fish is cooked on the grill. A father of three grown-up children, he is a '*filho da terra*' ('son of the land'), meaning that his family has been in Balduíno for some generations. Like other fishermen of that region, he carries a reputation of being a lady's man. A fan of Bob Marley, Jorge also stands out for steadfastly refusing to sell his catch to hotels or to affluent visitors in general. His fish is only for locals like him, and he charges less to families who he knows have lower incomes. Although he is illiterate, Jorge is among the very few locals from Balduíno invited to dinners and parties at upscale homes across the road, although his partner is usually reluctant to attend them, as these occasions make her feel poor and ignorant in relation to these 'barons' (affluent people). The invitations arrive because of Jorge's charisma, and the fact that he also takes tourists and their boats on fishing trips for sport or pleasure.

Like many adults in Balduíno, Jorge grew up attending *candomblé* parties. For some years as an adult he participated regularly in the activities of a local *candomblé* yard, but today he distances himself from this experience. Often boisterous and loud, Jorge adopts a serious expression when talking about *candomblé*; displaying both respect and fear, he says that this has not been a positive experience for him and his family and that today he is satisfied with his own beliefs. The only time of the year he attends church is during the yearly Catholic festival that pays homage to St Francis, the local patron of fishermen. This occasion begins with a long singing procession to the sea and ends with many hours of drinking, dancing and celebrating (Fig. 1.12).

In common with most children in Balduíno, Jorge grew up being severely beaten by his mother. One of the reasons she punished him was for his insistence in identifying himself as a '*pescador*' (fisherman), a label

Fig. 1.12 A Catholic procession

that his mother dreaded.[95] To her, this meant a primitive and backward type of person she associated with Afro-Brazilians; she did not believe that a fisherman would prosper in life, and instead wanted Jorge to say that he was a '*pedreiro*' (builder) – for her an exciting and promising career. Being a builder implied making money (something fishing did not really provide before tourism developed in the region) and offered the possibility of prosperity and becoming someone of relevance.

Jorge's mobile phones are constantly at hand as they are the main form of interactive telecommunication in the settlement. But he has mixed feelings about the internet – which, for him, translates broadly to 'advanced technology'. As a fisherman, he recognises how much easier and safer his work has become, involving as it does numerous days and nights spent far out at sea. Electronic equipment such as GPS, underwater sonars and the ability to check the weather forecast at any time online – something which his 20-year-old, technologically savvy son does for him – has improved the conditions considerably. At the same time, Jorge says that social media is 'emptying his home'; other family members (all literate) are there in body but not in mind. His partner and children chat continuously with others through Facebook and WhatsApp (Fig. 1.13). Because Jorge cannot read and write, he says he feels left behind by his family in his own house.

Fig. 1.13   Literate adult woman connected to social media

Methods

This ethnography results from a process of long-term immersion[96] in the daily lives of the people living in Balduíno between 2013 and 2014. I used classic anthropological methods as proposed by Malinowski,[97] which translate in short into cultivating trusting relationships with the aim of incorporating the world views of the people that I studied. Consequently I considered social media not to be the exclusive focus of this book, but rather as something that mediates relationships existing in a context.

A result of this methodological choice was to cultivate bonds with people of different ages, not just with those who have abilities or experience in online sociality. Some of my informants were 'heavy users' while others needed the children's help to use social media; others, such as the elderly, only spoke about it because it was a popular topic. Similarly, WhatsApp and Facebook were a recurrent subject of conversations I had in the field site. However, I also talked about, and asked questions about, other topics independently of their association with social media (such as religion, celebrations, work, health and family) because they were relevant to my informants.

A similar study could have emerged from field work carried out in a city's low-income neighbourhood or in a *favela*. As I have explained at the beginning of this chapter, however, Balduíno was an equally good choice: given its relatively small size, I could follow people around more easily as they went to market, to school or attended church services. Although the settlement is increasingly exposed to urban forms of violence, it is still a relatively safe place to live.

I left to do field work knowing that my destination was the northern coastal area of Bahia, but I had not yet decided the exact settlement in which to live. I first stayed for three weeks at the home of a friend who lives by the coast, an architect and environmental activist who decided to move from New York to that region of Bahia in the early 2000s. Balduíno is the settlement located across the road from where her house is. After a few exploratory visits it seemed convenient for the aims of my research in terms of its size and the socioeconomic profile of its population; there was also the advantage that my friend could show me the area and make initial introductions to people she employs, as well as taking me to shops that she visits as a customer. These initial contacts helped me find a temporary home in the settlement and gave me the opportunity to meet many other locals.

Choices to study social media use

During field work I 'friended', and was 'friended', by a total of about 250 people on Facebook. These were people I first met face to face and only then sent a friendship request. My proximity to them varied – I interacted with some regularly, I spoke occasionally with others and I simply followed most through the content they posted on public-facing Facebook timelines. Then, in early 2014, as WhatsApp became a useful communication tool to a significant portion of the settlement, I also began to use it extensively as a research tool. Most of the content that appears in the 'lights off' section of Chapter 3 came to me after I explained to closer informants that I would like to see what locals circulate using direct exchanges – including the content that, in their view, would not be pleasing to my taste as a professional, educated person. I left the settlement having routine interactions on WhatsApp with about 100 people. Also, thanks to WhatsApp and social media in general, I carried on observing and interacting with locals after field work ended, contacting them on a few occasions to clarify or ask for further information about certain topics.

In relation to different modalities of field work on and about social media, I appreciate the relevance of anthropological research conducted exclusively online, such as Boellstorff[98] and Wesch.[99] My masters dissertation on YouTube's 'beauty gurus'[100] was based on participant-observation of people who maintained social relations among themselves exclusively through YouTube while living in different parts of the world. However, a similar methodological choice for this research would lead to different and probably equivocal results. I entered local, private-facing networks of exchange only after months living in the settlement. Indeed I gained a clearer understanding of this practice, as Chapters 2 and 3 describe, only through the help of trusted informants, and after learning about the various forms of face-to-face communication and the different physical locations where they take place.

As I hope the ethnography will prove, it was crucial to be in the settlement in order to contrast the information circulating and locals' self-presentation online and offline, and to examine social media based on traditional values and forms of face-to-face communication. As I explain in Chapters 2 and 6, much of the conversation taking place on locals' social media relates to events happening in the locality. Some of the content that appears on Facebook timelines consists of fragments of dialogue happening inside social circles; they make sense only when combined with other bits of information obtained by being there, participating in and witnessing local events.

Ethical issues

This research follows one general rule in relation to ethics: not to expose or endanger the people that contributed to it. The items below are common procedures that are now more necessary considering the particularities of online practices, including, for example, the fact that locals as a rule do not use content filters to restrict access to the information posted on public-facing social media. I took the following precautions during field work and afterwards:

- I created a profile on Facebook independent of my personal account to conduct this research. On this research profile I stated clearly my role as a researcher and the institution that I was associated with; I also explained my research interests. I adjusted the privacy settings of this account in such a way that the profiles of my contacts would be hidden.
- Informants who participated in interviews authorised the use of their content by signing a consent form presented to them after the interview finished. In the cases of interviews with people under 18 years old, the consent was also signed by their parent or legal guardian.
- All the information that I used to produce this book has been thoroughly anonymised. This means that I have attributed new names to people and changed other information, such as age and gender, that could potentially lead to those involved being identified. I also changed the names of places, including that of the settlement itself.
- All images used have also been digitally altered to hide the identities of informants.

2
The social media landscape: hiding in the light

The social media landscape in Balduíno is very simple: people use Facebook and WhatsApp. Before Facebook there was Orkut, a now deceased Google project; like Facebook, it provided a platform that enabled users to post content openly to contacts. Before WhatsApp there was MSN Messenger, a private chat service offered by Microsoft, enabling interaction between individuals or within small groups. Facebook and WhatsApp have technical and design advantages over these predecessors, but it is significant that the core characteristics of Facebook and WhatsApp resemble those of Orkut and Messenger.

As Chapter 1 has shown, participation on social media by 'emergent' Brazilians took off during the mid-2000s, in parallel with a broader phenomenon of economic mobility. At least initially this happened under ongoing attacks from more experienced and affluent users, who wanted to resist the 'orkutisation' of social media in the country. While these wealthier and more experienced users now access a variety of platforms to reach different groups, the low-income population concentrate their activity in the most popular services.

In Balduíno today Facebook and WhatsApp are effectively the reason why many locals choose to be online; many would also not make a distinction between Facebook and the internet. Facebook and WhatsApp are useful in themselves as ways to communicate with other individuals and groups; they also provide the intermediary between people and content circulating online. YouTube, for instance, is largely used for entertainment and learning, but it is through the social relations on Facebook that many of its videos circulate. News items about everyday politics, crime and sports also acquire visibility through Facebook pages that news outlets update and locals follow and share. Both Facebook and WhatsApp allow users easily to upload and interact with visual content, important to a population with limited literacy skills. WhatsApp is also useful for sharing files, including video clips, voice messages and music files, and as a free substitute to phone calls. The younger, more technically savvy users in Balduíno are familiar with services that have greater importance among the educated urban elites in Brazil (such as Twitter, Instagram and SnapChat), but these platforms receive relatively little attention in the settlement. Instagram is actually appreciated more as a way to follow celebrities such as the footballer Neymar, or to have the cosmopolitan experience of interacting with people in foreign countries, and though SnapChat has been increasingly attracting local users, there are still a few who devote regular attention to it. People in Balduíno do not lack the necessary equipment or the curiosity to find out about these other platforms; they simply choose to be where everyone else is – not just those of the same age, but also older parents and relatives.

This chapter – and also Chapter 3, which discusses visual postings – will consider how visibility, and increasingly invisibility, are key to understanding the shifting relationships between emergent groups and wealthier Brazilians. They are also important in appreciating how the low-income population perceive and use social media. The next section explores in detail what it is that I mean by visibility or invisibility regarding communication practices, but here is a brief introduction to this key subject.

To more affluent Brazilians it makes sense that a subject of collective interest should be discussed openly and publicly.[1] For them, if a certain event is collectively important it should be broadcast and spoken about openly so everyone can see it and participate in the discussion. However, in Balduíno the reaction tends to be the opposite: many of the situations that make people talk on the streets do not appear on public-facing social media. Often these events make locals discuss public matters[2] anonymously, with hints about such conversations appearing only occasionally and indirectly on 'visible' Facebook timelines. On the other hand, topics which wealthier Brazilians often consider personal or intimate are the main type of content that locals in Balduíno share regularly, without content filters, on their Facebook timelines.

What follows is a presentation of background information about local perceptions of social media in Balduíno. I propose the argument that social 'invisibility' is an important aspect of the lives of people here. This introduction is crucial to unpack the common online practices which involve exposing personal intimacies on Facebook timelines while carefully concealing some information that circulates broadly in the settlement.

Invisibility as a strategy

When I talk about invisibility in relation to the ethnography in Balduíno, I am actually referring to two correlated processes. The first describes why some people are rendered invisible in society even if this is not what they desire.[3] The second element takes place when those treated in this way use such invisibility as a cloak to hide the actions they may take against those who have the power to make them socially 'disappear'.[4]

The particularity of racial segregation in Brazil – in contrast to places such as the United States or South Africa – is its institutional invisibility, as until very recently race was not dealt publicly through the law. As Schwarcz explains, ours is 'a silent racism [...] that hides behind an apparent universality and equality of the law.'[5] The constitution incorporated with the proclamation of the Republic in 1889 had no clause or explicit reference to any form of racial differentiation.[6] If, before abolition in the late nineteenth century, slaves were considered as property (i.e. non-citizens), this invisibility remained even after abolition, with race becoming almost a taboo topic.[7] The legacy of slavery survives through a gradual hierarchy of prestige based on criteria such as formal education, place of birth, gender, family background and socioeconomic class[8], and this form of discrimination is still in practice today.[9] Social mobility and economic opportunities, then, are not associated directly with skin colour but with embracing certain moral codes,[10] mostly beyond the reach of the predominantly poor descendants of Africans and Amerindians.

Within this context, slaves and former slaves invented strategies of negotiation and resistance through bluff and deterrence,[11] using the invisibility imposed by society to their advantage. As within the country as a whole, low-income people in Balduíno share the view, resulting from the history of slavery, that those of lower status[12] do not have the same institutional protection as wealthier social strata;[13] they need to become less exposed to possible attacks and situations of confrontation, and yet still be capable of protecting themselves should such situations arise.[14]

Many folk tales from the days of slavery, such as the Anansi spider stories of the Caribbean and the Saci Pererê[15] in Brazil, are about the way in which lower social groups take revenge as 'trickster' figures – a scenario that anthropologists also find in many African folk traditions.[16] The 'ethos' at the centre of the novels of Jorge Amado, one of Brazil's most popular novelists, who lived in nearby Salvador, reflects the use of social media in this field site. He recounts many stories of how people assumed to be weak and invisible then achieve success at the expense of the powerful and self-important. In one of his best known works,[17] the protagonist Dona Flor has two husbands: one is a hardworking, decent 'living' man, and the other a drinking and partying '*malandro*'[18] (trickster) figure, visible only to his wife. So again and again it seems that the individual's subordinate condition becomes a strategy to use to gain a degree of power. Things are purposely hidden from sight, taken from context, not mentioned. Social media apparently attracts people for what is shared on public-facing Facebook timelines, which often reveal elements of distinction, intimacy and personal enjoyment. As Chapter 3 shows, these can be imported whisky bottles, a gym membership or specific types and brands of clothing. And yet as important as – or more important than – what takes place in public-facing exchanges is a local understanding of what circulates openly and what is exchanged directly through social media platforms.[19]

Invisibility in this case, then, has nothing to do with physics, digital technologies or science fiction. It is about doing or not doing things according to who is looking at that moment, and about acting in ways that are more or less visible to certain people.

Learning one's place in the world

Growing up in Balduíno, young people construct their identity in society through acts of daring (*ousadia*), undertaken among peers in hidden peripheral areas of the settlement, and the consequences o\f their discovery. The latter involve violent reprimands from their parents, often carried out in the family's backyards so that neighbours can hear and understand that the parent is fulfilling his or her duty towards their children.[20] Such a dynamic of social relations is schematic and flat. It is obviously one aspect of many more complex social and historical relations taking place in this particular location in Brazil,[21] and yet this description reflects the life experiences of the vast majority of Balduíno's low-income population. Most adults claim that they are grateful for having had loving parents, responsible and concerned enough to want to teach them 'the difference between right and wrong' as they were growing up. A parent who does not beat his or her child tends to be seen as cold and distant. Some of today's adults are also honest about the consequences of this particular experience: that because of these constant acts of daring followed by violent repression, they became more successful at hiding their actions from authority.[22] Thus learning the 'difference between right and wrong' in order to become 'honest and hardworking' (aesthetic understanding) constantly meant also learning to differentiate between what can take place visibly or openly and what has to take place secretly (pragmatic understanding).

An individual's possibilities of action vary depending on his or her visibility. While rigid social norms condemn stealing, for example, such norms can be reinterpreted when the person is not being watched: appropriation then becomes tolerated. Not surprisingly, the practice is widely reported by business owners and managers of tourism-related activities.[23] Quietly acquiring things such as food, cutlery and bed linen, they claim, are acts not limited to a few 'rotten apples' out of many low-income employees. On the contrary, such petty pilfering is actually so widespread that theft-related expenses are at times considered part of the costs of running a business in the regioin. However, it is important to note that this habit of 'liberating' things when others are not looking is not only related to inter-class tensions; locals report similar practices occurring, and recurring, inside the settlement. Residents of Balduíno who leave fishing nets or lobster traps untended for too long at the river or at the beach often go back to find their catches have been stolen. Finally, the invisibility of taking things is similarly expressed in forms of indirect confrontation. Bosses are often the subject of a form of silent confrontation, leading them to claim that the low-income, under-educated population as a whole rejects opportunities to evolve professionally. The perspective of employers is that instead of showing a good attitude and working hard, their workers in large part prefer to boycott and ridicule their superiors.

So if this section started with the exposure of young people to a moral visible sphere where they are punished, we can see how other deep traditions have evolved in which adults create an alternative morality, belonging to a hidden, peripheral sphere. The 'lights off' underworlds relate to popular accounts of trickster figures and tales of how apparently powerless, poverty-stricken individuals actually succeed by remaining out of sight of the elites whom they then overcome.[24] Such a perspective is essential to understanding how new social media platforms are seen as ways to continue, expand or reject the possibilities offered by existing in a segregated society. Cosmopolitan, affluent perceptions of social media may consider areas used for broadcasting as forums where public-facing conversation should happen. Following this rationale, posting on Facebook timelines should indicate an effort to reach more people. However, as the second part of this chapter shows, in many cases Facebook timelines are the ideal places to 'hide in the light'. In Balduíno the more visibly controlled social arena is turned into domains for private interactions to happen, while direct communication, usually thought to serve private or personal purposes, becomes the actual channel to discuss issues of collective interest.

Encryption and 'indirects'

The following section offers an analysis of invisibility as it has been defined so far in relation to communication. In the fields of linguistic anthropology and sociolinguistics researchers use the term 'indirection' to describe forms of 'oblique' or 'opaque speech' that 'convey something more or different from their literal meaning'[25]. In contrast to what is spoken directly and explicitly, indirection refers to forms of conversation in which 'meaning relies on the active participation of audience in making sense […] out of an utterance'[26] because what is said is separated from what is communicated.[27] This form of communication can refer, for instance, to the use of euphemism, metaphor and irony,[28] which rely strongly on shared context to be understood; such conversations are invisible, imperceptible or potentially misleading to those unaware of these contexts.[29] However, indirectness in Balduíno relates to a phenomenon previously studied among Afro-Caribbean people, who have historic ties to Brazil's Northeast region, and Indians who have migrated to Fiji.[30] Brenneis explains that these two experiences share 'conditions of immigration and of plantation life and labour', and evolved in the context of an egalitarian social sphere that is part of a larger stratified society.[31] This background relates to social life in Balduíno, where a more community-oriented and more egalitarian group of croppers and fishermen, mainly of African or mixed ancestry, cohabit a broader domain of class division and segregation. But although encrypted speech is an important part of the daily lives of people living in low-income settlements such as Balduíno, relatively few anthropologists have studied indirection as a means of examining social relations in Brazil.[32]

Speech encryption

Locals often observe about Balduíno that even today (despite the settlement's growth) 'every person knows everyone else'. This perception is not only associated with the condition of living in a small place; it also relates to a shared expectation that everyone is constantly observing, and being observed by, everyone else. It happens because of the densely interwoven sociality, the presence of kin and fictive kin living near each other, and the thin and porous separation between the 'inside' and 'outside' of many homes. People are more often together; they tend to have more family members around, and also develop ties through marriage, baptism of children, or by acquiring family-like connections through belonging to certain professions such as fishing or organisations such as churches.[33] In this context, conversations and noises coming from homes are constantly monitored by neighbours[34] – to a point, for example, that an evangelical teenager complained that he could not even yell at his brother at home because neighbours would spread rumours about him being a 'fake Christian'. However, it is wrong to imply that in these circumstances privacy is non-existent and that people do not care for and protect their intimacies. Actually, being able to speak reservedly is such a necessary element in daily life that locals have refined means to socially engineer private communication.

I call one of the common forms of 'indirection' in Balduíno 'speech encryption'. This is a way of forging privacy when there is no physical privacy[35] by disguising the subject discussed in conversations. In the settlement, the majority of locals, especially women,[36] are able to talk to each other in front of other people in ways that others cannot understand.[37] This linguistic technique is one of the outcomes of the recurrent experience presented earlier, in which parents (more frequently mothers) educate their children through violent beatings to display subordination in order to resist subordination. Before talking about it in relation to social media, however, it is important to note how the same practice previously existed in face-to-face interactions.

The first thing to notice about encryption is that it does not have a local name, suggesting that the objective of rendering something imperceptible starts with the practice of not being able to discuss it directly. 'Code' is not an accurate term for this practice as it suggests the existence of a defined secret language, which is not the case. In the instances of this form of invisible communication in Balduíno, no single set of coded words substitutes for others in a conversation. Instead locals apply a variety of formulas that can be combined to extract as much context from the conversation as possible, making what is being said meaningful only to specific people in a given circumstance.[38] This means that even an experienced 'speech cryptographer' will not notice a certain conversation taking place nearby if he or she is unaware of the context of the event or situation being discussed.[39]

Not only do the people of the region have no name for this technique, it is also not seen as a separate practice from communication. Speech encryption is part of speaking and interacting; it happens in many different instances of social life. Here is an example: during the hour before service starts in evangelical churches, believers kneel on the floor next to their seats to pray aloud individually, each one having often emotional and intimate conversations with God. But because others are present, when they have to refer to things considered humiliating or too intimate, they speak vaguely about 'a certain situation' that is happening to a 'friend' (not to them). Such habits represent ways to purposely 'invisibilise' speech so that only God knows what the person praying really means.

The more people spend time together and employ this form of communication, the more subtle and minimalistic are the resources they need to understand one another. Some report that they can understand close relatives simply by watching their faces. In cases of people with less intimacy, there are some frequent alternatives used to encrypt a conversation: attributing nicknames to refer to certain people, applying local slang words, speeding up pronunciation, changing the tone of voice, stripping out contextual data (places or times) and shifting the person being talked about.[40] The last example, frequently used, means that a person will seem to talk about her interlocutor while actually meaning someone else who is nearby. At a party, one could say to a friend with an ironic tone of voice: 'My God, what have you done to your hair tonight? And you think you are looking soooooo good...' The friend would look around discreetly as she understands the message is about another person. Karina, a university student from Balduíno, provided another example. She was at a lecture and a classmate had taken her baby into the class. It was very noisy and at a certain point, one of Karina's friends sitting nearby turned to Karina with a disapproving face and complained: 'Karina, come on, this is enough!', as if protesting about something she was doing. Karina understood that her friend was just expressing her frustration at being unable to concentrate on the lecture because of the baby's noise.

Encrypting conversations is just as important inside the home as it is outside. This is partly because neighbours can follow conversations in the common case of houses built with thin walls in close proximity. Yet it is also because of the power balances within the house, and the necessity women often feel to discuss things beyond the knowledge and supervision of husbands, fathers and other male relatives.

Another use of encryption is in work-related environments.[41] Michelle, a 46-year-old resident of Balduíno, mentions how some years ago she used to talk to the cook and babysitter who, like her, worked for an English 'missus'. Michelle said she felt mistreated as she learned that their boss would speak English with her husband or with guests only in certain occasions, when they wanted to say things about the employees of the house. She realised this was happening by noting the names of employees being pronounced, and she considered it a cheat as well as a display of arrogance. She then brought this subject up with her peers when her bosses were away and proposed that they should adopt a similar strategy.

One example she gave was the following: if the 'missus' was behaving badly with them because, for example, there was a dinner for guests later on, the cook would say to Michelle: 'Woman, didn't you take your cramp pills this morning? You are being a pain today!' And she would reply: 'Yes, I apologise, I went to the pharmacy but they were out of stock.' This practice allowed the staff to ridicule their bosses. Occasionally they would communicate among each other so that their employers noticed – but could not understand – that the staff were talking behind their backs. Finally, using encryption they could also coordinate actions, enabling them to anticipate – and so have good excuses to reject – requests to work extra hours.

Mobiles, internet and conversation encryption

One way of considering the local impact of mobile communication is by observing the importance it has beyond its practical utility[42] and assessing the complexity of information and knowledge that locals acquire and share as a way of taking as much advantage of mobile phones as possible.[43] Almost every person in Balduíno is able to describe clearly the (often complex) advantages of different mobile plans; it is also common for people to use two or more mobile lines to be able to speak to more people paying less money.[44] Mobiles are also essential to mothers already working or interested in moving into the labour market while continuing to look after their children.[45] However, it is only recently that social scientists have started to pay proportional attention to the importance of this technology, a situation applying both globally and to specific research conducted in Brazil.[46]

The increasing popularity of the internet has only made mobiles more necessary and present in Balduíno. To understand how they are used, however, it is important to remember that the term 'personal computer' does not completely fit the context of how computers were initially used in these settlements. Before they became more affordable to the 'emergent' population in the late 2000s and early 2010s, locals had to go to internet cafés to access the web, allowing other clients to spot one's interactions. Today computers at Balduíno tend to be shared at home and to have the status of expensive furniture, so the PC is not kept in one person's room. It often is placed in the living room, where it can be used collectively by the whole family and also admired by visitors because of its price and symbolic value as an indicator of modernity and prosperity. As a result it was the Android smartphone, rather than the PC, which became the first strictly personal computer-like equipment people experienced using in Balduíno. For the first time they could access the internet through something which belonged only to them, and that would not be accessed by anyone else.

Mobiles consequently became the decisive factor for locals to take on accessing the internet more regularly. Until the second part of 2013 only some teenagers and young adults had what we could technically call smartphones in Balduíno, but this equipment was mostly not used to access the internet. The most common model then was a Nokia phone with a non-touch screen above a physical keyboard. This eye-catching equipment – its relatively large body often increased in size by a brightly coloured case – served primarily to display a certain sense of modernity; it also enabled the user to listen to music, to take and show photos and to exchange files via Bluetooth. Since the main reason for locals to access the internet is social media, which before the arrival of WhatsApp happened mostly on Facebook, and the Facebook app for the Nokia system performed poorly, very few people saw reasons to use mobile phones to go online. WhatsApp, being a native mobile application, resolved precisely these problems. It is easy to navigate on smaller mobile screens and allows the user easily to send and receive messages, and to know if and when the recipient has seen each message. Given these affordances, after the initial months of 2014 it became difficult to find a teenager or young adult in Balduíno who did not have an Android phone.

The growing popularity of mobile internet access had practical outcomes in relation, for instance, to work and to resolve domestic matters. However, its importance also relates to allowing people to stay in touch with other members of their social circles[47] and to having increased the scope locals have of creating channels for encrypted interactions. Because they have phones, two people can choose when and where is the most convenient for them to talk, in ways that avoid them being seen together. To protect mobiles further from spying, young people will lock them with highly complex and long codes; they also disguise names using graphic alternatives so that those around them will not know who is calling, as the name of callers appears on the monitor. In the image shown here (Fig. 2.1), the informant's actual girlfriend's name 'Thailane' is written using only letters followed by an emoticon of a heart (S2). However, he was flirting at the same time with another girl (Thamiris), whose name he disguises with symbols (Th@m!r!s) followed by a disguised heart sign ($2). WhatsApp only advanced this possibility further, by expanding the means of file exchange and easy group communication for a relatively lower cost than voice conversation.

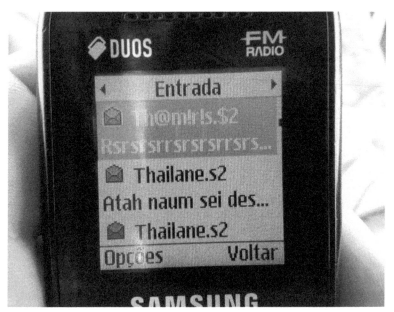
Fig. 2.1 A phone screen showing the encrypted name of a contact

Speech encryption and social media

This section began by showing how privacy is engineered in a context where 'everyone knows and is constantly monitoring everyone else'. Media anthropologist Patricia Lange addressed a similar issue while studying the various degrees of 'public-ness' of YouTube videos. She presents cases in which 'participants may share private experiences … in a "public way" [but] At the same time, they use mechanisms to limit physical access to the videos or to limit understanding of their contents'.[48] In other words, the video becomes available publicly and can potentially be seen by any person, and yet other forms of filters, either technical or social, prevent this from happening. Speech encryption, which locals in Balduíno are so used to applying in everyday situations, represents an expression of the social and technical mechanisms Lange refers to, as they limit the understanding of conversations taking place in public spaces.

The word 'mechanism' may suggest the filtering of content happens because of a technology made available through the social media platform (such as Facebook's content filters), but that is not the case. One of the mechanisms used for encryption on social media in Balduíno is literacy. As Chapter 5 discusses in detail, people of all ages in the settlement have limitations in terms of formal knowledge, starting with reading and writing, but young people in general are better educated than their parents, which makes social media more interesting and attractive for them. Literacy, and also computer literacy, makes social media an efficient hideaway place where young people can gather and interact openly, conscious that adults are not capable of following such interactions. So the real skill of people here is not to use private-facing social media such as WhatsApp to encrypt communication; it is in creating a sphere of the private within what would otherwise seem to be the entirely public arena of Facebook.[49]

Hiding under the light

Margarete was an attractive, 16-year-old high school student with good grades. She earned money as a babysitter and, in contrast to most teenagers in Balduíno, had only just begun to engage more seriously in romance. However, this was not good news for her mum, Tilia, a hardworking, under-educated person who depended on temporary cleaning jobs for her income. Tilia got pregnant as a teenager, and although she and Margarete's father are still together (something of a rarity for non-evangelical Christian couples), she blames the pregnancy for having limited her opportunities to prosper and evolve economically through schooling and work. Tilia thus reacted badly when she started hearing from people she knew that her older daughter had a secret boyfriend. She had high hopes for her daughter[50] and dreaded the thought of Margarete making the same mistakes as she did, and having to leave school to work because of needing to care for and raise children.

Tilia is on Facebook, and her first attempt to address this matter was to send a friendship invitation to Margarete with the obvious but unstated purpose of spying on her online life. When the daughter rejected this request, Tilia adopted a strategy with which she is more familiar. She spoke to a close friend who is also the mother of Raquel, one of Margarete's closest mates. The two mothers appeared unexpectedly one day when Raquel was online and demanded that she show Margarete's timeline and photos. Obedient to family hierarchies, Raquel had no alternative but to comply, but she did so knowing the limited understanding these older women have about Facebook. In fact, Raquel was well aware of Margarete's new relationship; she disapproved of it as well because she felt the boy was not committed to the relationship and would hurt her friend's feelings. At the same time, she did not agree with the mothers' attempt to spy on her friend's life.

What Tilia saw on her daughter's timeline was mainly selfies of Margarete alone, published together with several paragraphs of abstract reflections about the nature of relationships, the importance of friend-ships, faithfulness to God and similar material. As the texts were long and too complex for Tilia to read, she quickly asked Raquel to show Margarete's photo albums, but there was nothing incriminating in her daughter's galleries. Tilia expected to find proof of the relationship her daughter denied existed, but none of Margarete's photos showed her holding hands or even alone as a couple with the boy that – rumour had it – was going out with her daughter.

Margarete apparently never found out about this episode, and yet she had been prepared for it, anticipating her mother might seek to look at her profile through another person. Margarete helped to set up her mother's Facebook account; she was also the person in charge of turning on the computer and getting it ready for her mother to access Skype or other programs. As Raquel explained, Margarete was 'light-years' ahead of Tilia in terms of this kind of communication. As an analogy, Margarete's social media abilities resemble a modern FM/AM radio, while Tilia's are like an AM-only device; the former receives the same stations as the lat-ter, but it can also operate with a signal that the AM-only equipment does not capture. In other words, Margarete was too savvy to post anything that might look suspicious to her mother or her mother's friends.

This case demonstrates how speech encryption can be easily trans-ferred to public-facing social media. Text in general becomes an encryp-tion, firstly as a consequence of the literacy limitations of most adults. In addition Margarete disguised her messages using a generic philosophical wording: 'Don't ever ignore someone that loves you, worries about you and misses you. Because maybe one day you may wake up and find out you have missed the moon while counting the stars' or 'I grew up a lot. I learned, acknowledged [myself]. I met new people, but also let go of some people that did not add to my life. - ☹ feeling bothered'.[51] These posts, for example, indicated that she and her boyfriend were having a difficult time, apparently because she thought or had heard from others that he was flirt-ing with other girls. She then hinted they might break up. Her mother actu-ally looked at these messages, but could not really perceive this, although everything about the affair was there for anyone to see. However, inter-preters need to be better at reading and also to be immersed in the same context of relationships as Margarete was in order to associate the things to which she was abstractly referring with the actual events she experienced.

Often the internet is seen as an alternative form of communication, useful for keeping in touch when people are far away or cannot meet regularly. In this regard, Margarete's case is a useful illustration of an alternative application of social media. In Balduíno people often face the opposite problem: everyone is too close; they are regularly seeing and monitoring each other in the streets. Social media becomes desirable for offering ways to 'hide in the sun', a way of filtering out the excessive presence of others and so allowing individuals and small groups to interact more privately. To follow this kind of 'publicly private' conversation (as Lange describes it)[52] one needs to be more than merely connected on Facebook; people need to share everyday life experiences and to have a similarly higher level of literacy.

Margarete's case invites us to consider what really is different about the internet, and the effects these new possibilities of communication bring to places such as Balduíno. As her story indicates, social media is not often transforming the local ways of communicating; rather, the uses of social media relate to traditional forms of communication, as in this case with speech encryption. The novelty of being able to hide one's communication online only responds to the change the settlement is currently experiencing, now that people have greater mobility as they go out to work or travel regularly to Salvador or nearby settlements for various reasons.

Speech encryption on social media did not make Margarete different from her mother (see the discussion in Chapter 4). Her secret romance progressed and eventually her parents accepted the relationship, with the condition that the two would be together only during the day and under family supervision, standing outside of her home's porch ('lights on' dating). However, these restrictions did not prevent the couple from meeting secretly in the peripheral 'lights off' areas of the settlement. Fairly soon afterwards Margarete got pregnant and, like her mother and a number of other local women,[53] became responsible for raising her child. As a result she left school and had to depend on her partner and family for financial support.

Indirect messages

Though not as attractive and visible as the photos posted on Facebook showing prosperity, encryption practices similar to the example above represented a significant part of the written content posted on public-facing social media. Another popular genre appearing in locals' timelines is called 'indiretas'.[54]

There are interesting symmetries between encryption and these indirect messages, which as a practice means publicly posting a message referring critically to someone on Facebook without mentioning who that person may be.[55] Because of the secretive quality encryption has, its existence is less noticeable because the comments that use it appear to be meaningless or vague. In addition, encryption engenders privacy precisely to avoid confrontation between people while 'indirects' do the opposite: they expose situations of tension.[56] The indirect is also arguably the most popular and most talked about genre relating to the use of social media in Balduíno. Some people literally rolled their eyes as I asked them about it, reflecting a common feeling that indirects are both silly and take up too much of people's time online. Nevertheless, informants also acknowledged having used them on occasion.

In contrast to encryption, the name *indireta* is native and known by anyone independently of social media. Traditionally, locals mention the use of *indiretas* to defend the collective interest from actions carried out by people of greater power. For example, the police in Balduíno regularly close the settlement's main street to stop and verify the documents of people riding motorcycles, which in most cases are purchased and used informally. Because these 'inspections' are popularly understood as excuses for policemen to collect bribes, those whose bikes are apprehended will often remain on the street; as their number grows, some of them begin to talk out loud about the cowardice of a police force that 'takes the property of working men who have families to raise' while avoiding doing the work they are paid to do, namely 'going after drug lords'. This kind of confrontation is never directed at an individual,[57] however, and the person who voices the criticism is protected by being part of a group. As the indirect complaint is expressed, others in the same situation can confirm it by echoing these remarks, approving them or adding to them aloud, as a way of exposing group dissatisfaction and morally shaming the police. The policeman is placed in a tricky situation because responding directly to the attack is often read as a confirmation of responsibility for the act.

What seems new about indirects on social media is that the same mechanism often employed collectively to confront a perceived injustice is now more closely associated with individual disputes. Online, indirects often become a favourite weapon to use in responding to gossip. In Balduíno, while gossiping can be viewed as a form of levelling mechanism[58] to curb individualistic acts, indirects on social media respond to these accusations gossipers spread, and consequently reaffirm individual identity and individualistic choices. This form of confrontation is efficient; it allows the person to attack the reputation of a foe verbally without exposing themselves to direct retaliation.[59] To increase the efficiency of the practice, locals wait to publish their messages until the target of the attack is online together with others with sufficient knowledge of the context to make the information arrive at its intended destination. This may take place even when the two people most closely involved, the attacker and the attacked, are not online 'friends'.[60]

Luciene's indirects

In many regards, 24-year-old Luciene is a typical young woman living in Balduíno today. She has eight siblings from the various partners of her 54-year-old mother. Luciene and her twin sister only recently met their father, after some effort talking to close family and friends to track his location. The siblings, including Luciene, were raised by their mother or by their maternal grandmother. Following a common practice, some of them during late childhood were temporarily 'given' to better off families to work as home servants,[61] and, although these events tend to have traumatic consequences, Luciene's younger sister had a different experience. She grew up taking care of a wealthy elderly person in Salvador, was able to finish school and today owns a bakery in the city. But the other brothers and sisters stayed in the settlement, and are now low-wage workers or owners of small informal businesses.

Luciene got pregnant in her teens. She tried to live with her then partner, but things did not work out so she then started raising her daughter with the help of her own family. They live in a plot that, like so many others, is literally a maze, with passages and doors interconnecting the property from one side of the block to the other. Being an achiever, Luciene managed to finish high school; she reads and writes better than most other adults of her age, and is familiar with the basic functions of computers. Thanks to these skills she was given a low-ranking managerial position at an industrial laundry service in the area. Through this job she has a work phone with internet access, which enables her to upload photos to her Facebook profile any time of the day. Luciene's economic achievements and her interest in showing them, her religious beliefs as a recently converted evangelical Christian and her relationships are recurrent topics on the indirects that she posts almost every day.

Before she remarried, Luciene's indirects could often be about a person who was failing to meet her romantic expectations. She would post on her Facebook timeline messages such as 'When you like the person, he cares less, when you move on, he raises hell saying he loves you. What a joke.' Or: 'I tried. I tried everything. But new days will come.' After a break up, she posted an indictment of a female friend who became her ex-partner's new girlfriend: 'There is no such thing as a "former friend". There is a person that could not stand [my] personal light and now her mask falls.' There are also indirects referring to everyday events such as an apparent disagreement: 'To like me is optional, to respect me is mandatory.' More broadly, Luciene's indirects are about trust and betrayal. When the minister of a church refused to marry her because the groom was divorced, they did not invite the community of that church to the wedding. Later she posted: 'I don't care about what people feel or think about some of my attitudes. I have my own mind and you don't have to like it.'

Remember that these are not one-to-one conversations. They are posts uploaded on public-facing Facebook timelines. Luciene is adding to collective conversations with which others in her social circles are already acquainted. To a visitor unfamiliar with this genre of posting or with the events of Luciene's life, her indirects may look like a random fragment of a personal conversation mistakenly made public. This is because indirects also relate to the local condition of physical proximity, creating and enhancing possibilities of communication for people who are constantly seeing and interacting with each other. In these environments, a message like an indirect is not independent or complete in itself; it is only a part of conversations that are conducted simultaneously online and offline. Like encryptions, indirects purposely lack context; they are complementing a broader domain of interaction that encompasses the constant possibilities of seeing, hearing about or talking with others. So while generally meaningless to the more cosmopolitan practices of urban, educated Brazilians, a person living in such socially denser environments may not specifically understand Luciene's message, but he or she will probably recognise the genre and the intentions of these postings.

Social 'narrowcasting'

As the previous section argued, a more culturally nuanced understanding of social media in Balduíno emerges from thinking about the ways in which communication can be encrypted, or partially hidden, in a context subject to dense social and moral control. Like other teenagers, Margarete used social mechanisms related to local practices to engineer channels of private exchange, which enabled her to hide conversations from people constantly observing and controlling one another. This following section, then, deals with an opposite possibility, in which a debate about a matter of collective interest did not take place at open public situations but through private channels. So while Margarete's case illustrates ways of privately communicating in front of others (being 'publicly private'), this next topic is about forging a public arena using private channels (being 'privately public'). The idea bears similarities with the concept of a news programme in which transmission happens through "narrowcasting'[62] (information may travel through one-to-one or one-to-few 'nodes'). Adapted to the context of this settlement in Brazil, this solution is a result of locals' need to remain anonymous while still desiring to learn about and exchange information on sensitive events.

Again the previously cited study of YouTube videos[63] provides a useful framework in which to compare and analyse this form of communication in the settlement. According to Lange's research, while some people use public spaces to upload and share private material, others make videos to reach broader audiences – but they do so while concealing their own identities (name, surname) and personal information (physical location, phone number, etc.). So, for example, a Youtuber creates a fictional character and publishes videos in which he or she appears dressed as the character. The aim is for the character to achieve fame while its creator seeks to remain anonymous. The reasons for this choice, Lange explains, include wanting to avoid compromising professional credibility or having concerns about stalkers. With this anonymity, one also has a greater freedom to say and do things that may further the reach of the message, such as showing the interior of one's home on the video or talking about traumatic events that capture the attention of audiences.[64]

A similar situation takes place in Balduíno regarding the discussion of certain events. As Chapter 6 discusses in detail, it was only recently that a police unit (as well as other government services) opened in the settlement, and for various reasons these services are still not very reliable. Locals depend on their networks of solidarity for protection,[65] as well as for dealing with emergency situations, such as having to go to the hospital. Within this same context, discussions of collective interest often take place through face-to-face encounters, so that people can find out and share opinions about the event without leaving traces of doing so.[66] An event that people may talk about face to face or in small groups over several days or weeks is only rarely and discreetly mentioned on Facebook timelines. In other words, locals want to participate in these conversations and exchange information, but do not want to be associated with the topic, as they do not wish to become a target for revenge. The following case of a burglary helps to show how these networks of communication operate in practice.

In April 2014 three unknown men riding motorcycles arrived at a well-known hardware store in the settlement. They carried guns and demanded that the owner should give them all the day's sales money. This event generated a lot of discussion in the settlement for a number of reasons. Firstly the owner, Mr José, is a prominent evangelical Christian who has been living in Balduíno for over 40 years. Being well known is a condition that should protect him, as local thieves would avoid upsetting him in front of the community. The matter also generated wider tension, as these kinds of crimes at gunpoint in daylight are still rare in Balduíno. Significantly, independently of police involvement in the case, everyone in the settlement soon knew who the thieves were. The following day, neighbours of the three men came to the store to relate what they knew about the men and where they could be found. They had heard about the crime and associated the descriptions with motorcycle riders who moved in recently from the city, then living in shacks at one of the newer squatting areas. Although the settlement as a whole shared this information, the men's identity and location were not officially given to the police as locals did not want to be associated with an eventual arrest and become possible targets of revenge. (To avoid these acts of revenge, the police often kill criminals with more serious records on the way to the station and report the death as the consequence of a shoot out.) In this instance Mr José himself chose not to press charges, to avoid himself and his family becoming vulnerable to more attacks. Here we see that, in a similar way to the case of YouTube videos, the diffusion of the story (in this case, the details about the crime and its perpetrators) could circulate freely as long as locals hide their personal identities.[67]

The most obvious examples about how public debates happen privately, or through private interactions, tend to be related to violence, implying that people are fearful of speaking up to avoid acts of retaliation. However, items of collective interest do cover other subjects, including romantic infidelities (even more so when these involve 'sinful' evangelical Christians) and cases of illness. These interests show other reasons why collective conversations happen as part of private exchanges. These include a communal monitoring of morality and attacks on individualism.[68] When locals are in the central areas of the settlement and are being observed by others, therefore, they comply with moral rules that in other conditions they may not respect.

Open secrets

In this context, one of the two more talked-about stories of 2013 in Balduíno started on a quiet October morning after a 'sound car' (a car adapted with loudspeakers, normally used for local advertising) announced that Lyn, a 24-year-old mother of two, had died and that her family was inviting the community to her funeral the following day.

When locals use Facebook, they are often more concerned about what is not shown than in what is made explicit, and the same thing is true outside of social media. The broadcast of Lyn's passing generated uneasiness and curiosity especially because of the lack of information about the cause of death. She had not been killed or involved in an accident, so locals correctly deduced that she died of a health issue. The fact that the family had kept this information secret during the previous months and now avoided revealing the name of the disease prompted people to speculate, gossip and exchange and collect bits and pieces of information gathered informally from family members, work colleagues, neighbours and others who knew her. As in similar cases, though Lyn's death occupied the settlement's attention for many days, Facebook postings only mentioned her in terms of goodbye photos and religious messages in relation to her death.[69] The issue preoccupying the locals' attention did not appear on public-facing social media.

Having a very low level of literacy and no professional training, Lyn worked as a money collector on one of the many informal transportation vans used by locals to move to and from nearby settlements. This in itself made her more visible than average, as travellers constantly saw her opening and closing the vehicle's door to passengers and then collecting payment for their journeys. Every day these vans circulate dozens of times along certain defined routes. However, Lyn was also remembered in the settlement or another reason. She has been an attractive girl who had engaged in casual sexual experiences from an early age. Because of this she was by some labelled a 'piriguete', a derogatory reference to an (often young) female said to exchange sex for ostentatious fun – for example, at swimming pool parties or exclusive bars.[70] Men also describe *piriguetes* as whores who are paid indirectly for their favours, through the expenditure that is required before they agree to have sex.

Soon after the news of Lyn's passing began to circulate, locals associated her death with an event that had happened a few months earlier. She had suddenly fainted while at work in the van. This information circulated and Lyn, who had recently become a more active Facebook user thanks to a camera phone, discreetly referred to it in a short post that appears in her timeline, surrounded by many selfies, memes and photos of her children. In response to the gossip circulating about the reasons for her fainting, she wrote in a typical indirect style: 'People really like to know about other people's lives. When you want to know anything about me, come and ask me directly. Yes, I'm pregnant and no, it is not of your husband and not of your business. Go wash your dishes.' But by acknowledging the surprising event of being pregnant (leaving others to start to wonder: 'who might the father be?'), she managed to deflect the public curiosity about the fainting incident.

The most likely cause of Lyn's death was AIDS. Sexually transmitted diseases are spreading silently in the settlement, as a health agent explained to me, citing informally the confidential results of tests carried out locally.[71] Lyn was probably aware of her illness, as this same professional explained, because she had given birth ten months earlier and blood tests (for conditions including HIV) are compulsory in public hospitals. After having been informed of her condition, Lyn apparently went to a specialised hospital in Salvador to collect the government-subsidised drugs available for HIV patients. However, on seeing others from the settlement queuing to collect the same medicine, she gave up the treatment, (supposedly) to avoid being shamed and socially ostracised. Her infection with AIDS was probably the reason why she fainted at work. Yet, even with this debilitating condition, she managed to keep her secret until the end; it is not clear when her family found out about her illness.

Besides the mere curiosity about the real cause of her death, locals also discussed through face-to-face gossip networks which people Lyn had recently had sexual relationships with, speculating on who might also be contaminated with the disease.

Conclusion

Social media draws a lot of attention from Brazilians of low socioeconomic backgrounds. However, the reasons for this interest have been only poorly investigated. Part of the difficulty in accessing these people's online behaviour relates to how they are under-represented in sectors of society such as journalism, academia and market research. This historically subordinate stratum of society is more often talked about than allowed to speak directly, restricting its ability to reach public spheres beyond the local domain.[72] Online user statistics reveal how highly Brazilians are positioned on international rankings in terms of hours spent online.[73] The country has the second most active population on social media in the world, and the third largest population on Facebook.[74] Yet these data tend to be analysed and presented in terms of the understanding of social media held by the educated analysts.

Because of the strong class divisions in the country, a foreign correspondent with whom I spoke with during the early months of this research mentioned how strangely familiar to him, coming from Europe, was the Facebook communication of the Brazilians he had met, mostly educated, cosmopolitan and from the middle and upper class.[75] Their types of concerns and their diverse understandings about how the platform should be used seemed the same as the perceptions his Europeans friends had about things such as Facebook, Twitter and Instagram. There are similarities in what types of content are considered more or less private, what kinds of photos are made available to different groups in each person's networks and how contacts are structured based on the relationship, for example close friend, friend, acquaintance, family, etc. Using social media in Balduíno, however, is not like that at all. In the settlement there are different values, views and sensitivities which, if disregarded, compromise the perception of how the low-income population see and use social media. So the only way to understand this usage and its appeal is a long-term ethnographic engagement with that particular population.

As the next chapter shows through an analysis of images, people in Balduíno seem at first sight to use Facebook to expose their intimacies and to show off. Locals upload photos of their children, the inside of their homes and scenes from their work places, as well as of family celebrations. These posts often show them with motorcycles or cars, wearing fashionable clothing, holding expensive electronic products, consuming imported drinks, wearing work uniforms (to display their employed status), eating out, working out at the gym or simply holding money.[76] In addition, everything they post in public-facing social media can be accessed by anybody with an internet connection; although young people know about content filters,[77] they simply choose to ignore them. That is why in the beginning, as I spoke with informants, I constantly expressed my worries about thieves being able to see the expensive equipment they have at home or that paedophiles could target their children. But instead of addressing the issue of privacy[78] I was raising, they believed that I was insinuating – as neighbours often do through gossiping and rumours – that they could not be the legitimate owners of the products shown on their social media. Initially therefore, while I was worried that they might get robbed themselves for such inadvertent exposure, they thought that my suggestions echoed the rumours of 'jealous neighbours' questioning the origin of their belongings.

On these first encounters I was tempted to conclude that locals in the settlement lacked the education and knowledge to use social media properly. This explained why they used public-facing social media to show what I regarded as intimate material. Apparently they posted everything publicly because they did not know about other more sophisticated uses, and could not really appreciate the consequences of their actions. But this changed after six months in the field, when I finally gained access to their direct exchanges. At this point I could then see that the 'intimacy' appearing on Facebook timelines in Balduíno is very controlled and performed. They are not ignorant about privacy, because their truly sensitive issues circulate elsewhere.

The sections about speech encryption, indirects and hidden channels of public debate are examples of how much care and attention is given to limit access to information that the locals in Balduíno consider important. As I argue in the first section of this chapter, these traditional modes of behaving include ways of making communication invisible. Recognising this is the key to understanding the locals' use of Facebook, WhatsApp and other platforms.

Polymedia[79] is a helpful conceptual tool for this analysis, as it proposes that the understanding of specific platforms – be they Facebook, YouTube, Instagram or WhatsApp – should be considered not in isolation, but in relation to all the other media that are being used. But the case of Balduíno is trickier to interpret using polymedia for at least two reasons: firstly because it is tempting for the researcher just to dig into the abundant, ostentatious photographs and other easily accessible information found on Facebook timelines (as I did during the initial months in the field); and secondly because private communication is protected by social mechanisms and can only be reached through trusted relationships that take many months of the researcher's presence in the settlement to build. However, to move beyond misleading and often imprecise notions of 'public' and 'private', we need to observe how these two aspects of their social media contrast and complement each other. The alternative notions of 'lights on' and 'lights off', analysed further in Chapter 3 through the visual content shared on social media, emerge by comparing the positive display of one's own life, on the one hand, with the constant attacks and surveillance towards others that happens invisibly on the other. Locals in Balduíno display images showing prosperity, enjoyment and beauty. In less exposed channels they talk about other people's sex lives or crimes, and share porn, violence and politically incorrect humour.[80]

But while we might say that public-facing Facebook represents 'lights on' and that private-facing WhatsApp represents 'lights off', this chapter reveals a secondary level of complexity in how people apply social media in their daily lives. As the various cases presented show (and contrary to what may seem obvious), public-facing social media can be used as 'lights off' and private-facing media is the locality's true and effective field of collective debate. Above and beyond those possibilities we also saw the very popular indirect posting, which has ambiguous qualities of privacy and public-ness. Like dimmer switches that regulate the visibility in a room, indirects bring personal matters to be discussed outside of the protected area of private exchanges, but they do so in a protected manner.

Facebook and WhatsApp are successful in Balduíno because they allow people to relate to each other through these pre-existing norms and values. There were always private and public worlds that were fundamental both to the socialisation of young people and to the morality of adults. However, these do not correspond simply to conventional meanings of private and public. They also relate to a more complex world, which includes the ability to create 'invisibility' within what might otherwise have seemed the visible. We began by considering the way young people were brought up, within what at first seems a clearly distinct public area. The place where they were beaten and reprimanded in public view is in opposition to the private arena of the domestic world, and of the peripheral areas of the settlement. But in practice, and for this very reason, people cultivated a way of 'hiding in the light' – of using the public and the visible to create spheres of invisibility within.

3
Visual postings: lights on, lights off

Our use and understanding of images in anthropology has been changing.[1] It began with the anthropologist owning the camera and choosing what to record, evolved to cases of cameras being distributed so that informants could also contribute to what to show and finally reached the present situation, in which inexpensive camera phones are ubiquitously used in low-income settlements such as Balduíno. This is significant because now photographing and sharing this material are no longer part of an experiment that depends on the intermediation of the researcher. The images you will see in this chapter, apart from Fig. 3.8, were all initially chosen by locals and shown on their social media channels, responding to individual and social necessities and the interests of communicating and cultivating relationships. Yet given how widespread visual communication is on social media, it is surprising how little of this content appears in research about the internet.[2] The purpose of this chapter is therefore to move beyond talking about images and actually show some of the visual postings that people of Balduíno circulate online.

Photographs have been considered 'exchange objects'[3] ever since the early days of anthropology. Being the official photographer of various weddings and children's birthday parties in Balduíno provided valuable opportunities for me to participate in these social events. A school trip in which I accompanied a group of students spontaneously evolved into a long photo-shooting session as, during a break, children and teenagers queued up to try posing for portraits. For locals, photography was also one of the reasons to purchase smartphones – even before they began using mobiles to access the internet. From children to older adults, they use phones to carry and exchange files: music, video clips and photographs. Special kiosks in Balduíno charge customers to transfer these large databases to new phones, or to edit images and print them for different occasions. People commonly use their phones to show photos as part of online conversations, to illustrate the subjects being discussed.

It is not, however, the intention of this chapter to contribute to the vast body of work produced in the last few decades about visual anthropology, anthropology and photography and anthropology and film. Firstly, this is not a conventional piece that addresses issues of memory, representation, affect, presence and history, often dialoguing with seminal work such as Barthes,[4] Sontag[5] and Benjamin.[6] The content examined ahead does not include just photographs, but also different types of digitally produced images. Furthermore, while anthropologists have made relevant contributions to the debate about digital photography,[7] the focus here is not on the consequences of visual content on social media. Instead the analysis will prioritise the comparison of the genres that emerge from the postings and the interpretations that locals provide about this material.

Images and videos are particularly useful as a form of communication to a population with low literacy rates, but this must not be seen as the only reason for the intensive use of online visual material in Balduíno.[8] Locals have traditionally depended on oral communication to create and maintain relationships, but exchanging visual files is now becoming an important part of social relations.[9] Personal photos take the place of written descriptions in exchanges about residents' everyday lives and experiences. Sharing videos and memes simplifies the act of expressing opinion or commenting on events. Not being able to read or write no longer prevents a person from participating in 'small talk' with peers online; simply by sharing an image or video they can joke and show moral values in relation to themes such as politics and religion.[10] In addition, the ability to be online is in itself a state that carries prestige, especially to the less literate, and this is also a motivation to use visual content on social media. Since the computer is commonly associated with modernity and progress, the person who manages to use it is invested with these same attributes, and is consequently perceived as having better formal education.[11]

It was actually the exercise of contrasting the images exchanged on Facebook timelines and on direct chats (Fig. 3.1) that provided the initial insight to analyse social media in Balduíno through the concepts of 'lights on' and 'lights off'.[12] The logic of hiding or overly exposing information presented in Chapter 2 becomes more evident when we see the types of images that locals post and share. These visual metaphors help to distinguish the social relations and tensions happening in the settlement. Consequently the two main sections of the chapter separate the visual content exchanged openly from that sent directly to individuals or small groups.

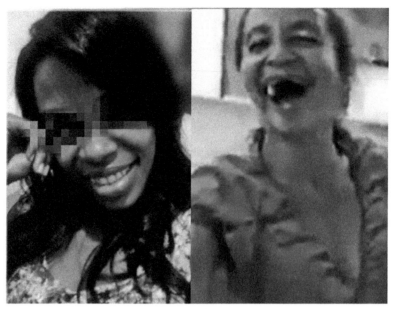

Fig. 3.1 'Lights on' shows the beautified self, while 'lights off' includes content related to sex, humour, violence and gossip

As Chapter 2 explains, 'lights on' refers to online spaces that are constantly being scrutinised and monitored collectively. Online posts of this kind are thus generally meant to be seen by neighbours they see on the streets.[13] Actually, the fact that an audience exists in a 'lights-on' situation affects the way in which Facebook is used. Not unlike living rooms with windows facing the streets, Facebook timelines become a way of displaying moral values. Hence 'lights on' postings work as a form of stage[14] on which socioeconomic improvement[15] is presented. Alternatively the 'lights off' online domain is an arena for gossip as well as for politically incorrect and yet highly popular content, mainly related to sex, violence and humour. Finally, between these two opposing domains is a shadowed space on social media which mixes elements of both: exposing hidden tensions, but doing so anonymously. The most common case is indirects (*indiretas*), which are so popular that there are Facebook pages dedicated to producing memes for this purpose.

The images presented in this chapter are the ones that appear more regularly on locals' social media. Most of these files come from public-facing Facebook postings from the same 30 informants. For the purpose of sample control, the collection of this material took place in a defined period during field work in the second half of 2013, aligning with the work of the 'Why We Post' team of researchers. The users I chose to be part of this case study represent the demographics of Balduíno in terms of age, education, religious preference and socioeconomic level. The most recent 20 posts that included a visual element on their Facebook timelines were then classified by keywords in order to identify recurring themes.[16] Next I applied an adapted version of the same methodology to collect and classify content that circulates through WhatsApp. The different themes present in each section emerged from identifying the most frequently recurrent visual content in circulation, both in the open and privately. The initial process of recording the sample of images enabled me to see beyond my preconceived ideas to include content that did not initially catch my attention.

As Torresan explains, synthesising MacDougall's analysis, '[Images] may not contain the whole story, they may not tell everything, but the specific index/icon quality of cinematographic images provides us with a form of understanding ethnographic realities that is sensorial, direct, and immediate, while also imaginative and suggestive of wider arguments'.[17] Therefore the expected outcome of this chapter is the 'recording of an engagement with a different culture'.[18] It evolved from the content shared on social media, my mediation and the ethnographic engagement of locals, who discussed with me the visual content and its circulation in the settlement.

'Lights off'

This is where sensitive interactions take place. It is there we learn what people are interested in, regardless of whether the subject is dangerous or morally or legally problematic. Simply by considering the time invested in this type of online 'face to face' direct contact, we can see that WhatsApp and Facebook chat are clearly more desired and useful domains of social relations than is public-facing social media. Young users may post on their Facebook timelines two or three times a day and follow what their contacts are doing there, but they will then remain connected for more hours exchanging direct messages.

'Lights-off' conversations include lots of text as it allows for more secretive and 'quiet' exchanges. If a person is typing, she or he can discuss any subject even if they are physically close to other people. The new possibility of making communication encrypted or invisible – discussed in Chapter 2 and again in Chapter 5 – helps to make reading and writing desirable practices. Together with long, almost endless chains of dialogue, however, the inhabitants of Balduíno also use social media directly to exchange files containing audio, images and short video clips. This activity then evokes topics of conversation, which produces more circulation of files.

One way of classifying the visual files shared in the 'lights-off' sphere is based on their source: material originally made in Balduíno is usually more sensitive as it relates to people and families known locally, so the circulation of this type of content is more controlled. One of the few cases related to violence that I saw circulating on (public-facing) Facebook timelines was a police sketch of a rapist at large in the region. However, he was an outsider, unknown in the settlement; as Chapter 6 explains, it is rare for local acts of crime to be shared openly. In general locally sensitive content generates more interest – for example, a photo of accident victims in the settlement – but the circulation will happen mostly through direct, one-to-one exchanges that are sent only to more trusted relatives and peers. They present the very problematic material with extra caution: these files are either played on the person's own mobile (to avoid sharing the file) or forwarded using Bluetooth,[19] so that those sharing the content cannot be detected. On the other hand, more visually disturbing content is less carefully handled, simply because it does not involve people from the settlement. These less sensitive exchanges demand less caution, so they take place through broadcast WhatsApp messages or inside WhatsApp groups.

In short, the main element that defines how a file is shared – with a greater or lesser degree of care – is less the type of the content, but rather its relation with people from Balduíno. A horrible video clip of a teenager being bullied, undressed and beaten is thus generally seen and forwarded more broadly, just like a porn file or a humorous image meme: the event happened elsewhere and the people shown are strangers. However, material of a less disturbing nature that relates to someone from Balduíno – such as the photo of a place where an accident happened – will receive special attention and be circulated inside more selected social ties.

The following case describes the context in which some photos of locals circulate in the settlement. One day I was talking to Roberto, a young evangelical Christian, about WhatsApp use, and also about the violence that often happens in or near the settlement. According to local accounts (I have no official figures) on more violent weeks two or more murdered bodies may be found in the settlement. Locals tend to react to the situation not with fear or stress, but usually by demonstrating curiosity about the deceased;[20] they will go out of their way and change regular routes to look at the body and gossip about what happened – and now, thanks to digital cameras on mobile phones, take photos and share the story, together with the visual aid. Roberto had just received from his brother a photo of a local killed earlier that week. He learned from his brother that the dead man was a bully who recently had come from Salvador and was living in a shack at a recent squatting area. According to shared rumours about the episode, this man was killed because 'he was causing trouble and his turmoil would eventually make the police come in'. The rumours circulating also mention that a woman pretended to want to have sex with him so that others could attack him naked, and consequently unarmed. Roberto added that he does not keep this type of file; after he has finished showing and discussing the case he erases it from his phone. In so doing he seeks to keep his distance from any possible consequences that the crime could produce. Outside trusted circles he will deny that he has seen or heard about the murder.

Though some of the material circulating through 'lights-off' channels is disturbing and often illegal, large amounts of it is not. Ranging from very disturbing content to that which is better termed 'politically incorrect', this material reveals the subjects currently attracting the attention of this population. The relevance of a certain file, or a certain type of file, is evident through how broadly shared it may become. For instance, the tension that WhatsApp is bringing to local families has been captured on various videos. These are made elsewhere in the country, but were intensively shared in Balduíno during the months in which WhatsApp was becoming popular. Many videos I received are of teenagers recording an adult parent or relative complaining about how social media has stolen young people's attention away from them.[21] Through clips and images shared on social media, Brazilians of lower socioeconomic background can participate in conversations connecting people living across the country. These group conversations happen through the exchange of files, which is also a special type of ethnographic evidence: one made by and for this population.[22]

What I do not show

The more common topics shared through 'lights off' conversations are sex, violence, bizarre things, humour, religion, dance and what I have labelled 'representations of the popular domain'. Politics is also important, but only during months leading up to elections. However, not all the content that I collected can be published in this book. Many clips have explicit sexual content or scenes of violence that are deeply disturbing, and it is sufficient to give a written overview of them.

Sex and pornography represented perhaps the most popular subject of files in circulation in the settlement, and this theme relates to the general interest locals have for cases of extramarital affairs – more about this in Chapter 4. Sex clips and images are not exclusively or even pre-dominantly shared by men, as one might expect. Many of the sex videos I received were actually sent by female informants; often the reason for sharing was not the personal enjoyment of watching the scenes, but of learning tricks that could be tried with a partner – such as how to per-form a certain sexual position or how to do erotic massages. One of the amateur files shows informatively the process in which a clitoris is cos-metically pierced. Other recordings are pornographic in nature but not intended to produce sexual excitement; instead they work as idioms rep-resenting certain ideas or views, and occasionally stimulating conversa-tions on certain topics. Among the most common types of video shared by adult females during some months were those featuring painful anal penetration or transsexuals with attractive feminine features and (sur-prisingly, in the narrative of the videos) large penises. These two recur-rent types of content hinged on the topic of machismo and of how men in the region create problems for women. Gender roles are changing as women become less dependent on men's money and protection, and this dialogue among female adults is reflected through these exchanges.

The content of 'lights off' channels also includes material bearing strong similarities to freak shows on travelling circuses from the past and present.[23] Bizarre things and humour are perhaps the two elements that combine to interconnect all the different types of files circulating among emergent WhatsApp users. The purely bizarre include videos of self-mutilation, sado-masochism, sex with animals and (very graphic) medical recordings of sur-geries (for instance haemorrhoids or penis enlargement). The content viewed as humorously bizarre depicts people defecating on the street, a female dwarf stripping and dancing naked, a deformed man with a large penis 'playing with himself' by a river and people with various forms of physical anomalies.

What I have shown here

Somewhat similar or thematically near to the videos labelled as 'bizarre things' are those I grouped as 'representations of the popular domain'. These files display people that embody visions about backwardness, particularly to teens and young people (Figs 3.2–3.3). In a way this cat-egory complements the selfies posted on public-facing social media – an antithesis to displaying one's own beauty and aspirations. Predominantly amateur videos made using smartphones, these show mostly older people displaying signs of physical degradation, especially a lack of frontal teeth, and often drunkenness. These subjects know they are being recorded

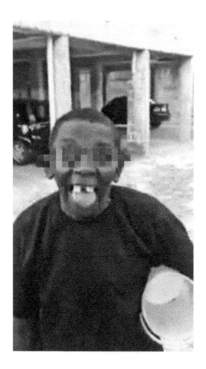

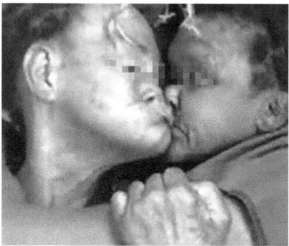

Figs 3.2–3.6 Screenshots from amateur video clips circulated in Balduíno among low-income viewers

Figs 3.2–3.6 Continued

and tend to participate in the video willingly, perhaps ignorant of how the recording is made for others to ridicule them. However, what is considered laughable is not only the display of elements perceived as ugly and decadent, but also a spontaneity, an openness about sexuality (for instance old people talking, singing about or performing sex), a sense of humour (even in relation to his or her own degradation) and a sense of enjoyment of life. Hence the popularity of these videos may also indicate how the people watching may be not just laughing at them but also with them. In so doing they are both negating but also identifying with these expressions of backwardness.

Dancing, sometimes involving children, could be viewed as a subcategory among the representations of the popular domain. However, I have separated them here due to the high quantity of videos on this topic (Figs 3.4–3.6).

Dancing may generally be seen as a way of expressing one's sensuality and sexuality, with the dances recorded here often being representations of sex acts. Even the dancers who are alone perform sexual movements. Again, this specific material produces an ambiguous perception. On the one hand there is the quality and exuberance of all dances; children and adults both exhibit physical co-ordination, energy, intensity and creativity. Nor is it uncommon for the recording of these videos to happen at home, with parents and relatives laughing appreciatively at the display and at the child's skill in emulating the adult world.

It is important to keep in mind how the images analysed so far are contrasted to the following material, which circulates openly on Facebook. While the primary focus of attention there is beauty and the accomplishment or future aspirations for the self, WhatsApp exchanges and Facebook chat conversations more often display 'ugliness' and the present-day reality of nearby or culturally similar others. 'Lights on' carries the benign and tame aspects of one's own aspiring middle-class life; through 'lights off' we see the types of experiences more commonly associated with the poverty of Latin America. 'Lights off' is not only sad and fearful – it can be, and often is, related to enjoyment and humour – but it is constantly somewhat dark in its essence.

'Lights on'

This batch of images bears some resemblance to how photography existed in the settlement before digital cameras and social media. The oldest types of photographic content that I saw inside people's houses were portraits of parents, grandparents and other family members, depicted in ways that have been analysed as visual records of roles and relationships.[24] These existing early images relate to 'lights on' in the sense of appearing to represent the highest moral conventions regarding respect for family and family hierarchies.[25] They are rare, however, given the absence until recently of businesses related to photography in the settlement, the general economic limitations of most families and the fact that these images often record special occasions such as formal marriages, which are still not common practices among many locals.[26]

As demands for formal employment increased in the area, ID-size photos became part of the process of official registration required by government bureaucracy in order to provide ID cards, employment registration documents and others. More recently, as money began to circulate more widely within low-income families and improved transport links facilitated visits to Salvador, some locals acquired pre-digital, inexpensive 'point and shoot' cameras. Their photos recorded mostly special occasions such as family trips or celebrations, as well as the family's children as they grew up. Most of this material is kept in picture albums or boxes stored in closets or drawers and looked after by adults. Especially in evangelical Christian families' homes, some of these photos are now being framed. They represent family bonds and also aspiration, expressed through clothing, background (referring to travelling), the forms of posing seen in magazines (for instance, a groom holding a bride in the air with the ocean in the background) and, more recently, selfie-like shots displaying affection among close relatives and friends. Today many of these framed photos that decorate people's homes were originally taken with camera phones and printed locally. This has become such an important aspect of people's lives that this relatively small, relatively poor settlement has a local business providing printing and framing services.

Such recordings of the modern and prosperous self often occur through continuously sharing large quantities of images taken in private settings.[27] These are meant to reach not those closely related, but often people outside of one's immediate social circles.[28]

Self-portraits, beauty and consumption

It is not the (great) quantity of images shown that makes the timelines of people in Balduíno particular in relation to those of Brazilians of different

Fig. 3.7 This type of exposed brick wall is among the most common visual elements in Balduíno, but it is avoided in photos as a sign of poverty and backwardness

socioeconomic backgrounds. What is interesting is the time invested in making these photos, and the particular elements in the picture that are either brought forth or erased.

Teenagers especially make great efforts to show neatness, for example, by constantly using spell checkers before posting content publicly and by avoiding capturing scenes associated with poverty. Misspelling words – a subject discussed in Chapter 5 – indicates that the person's family is 'backward' for not understanding the value of education or not having the means to send their children to school. Young people in particular can be very ashamed of having adult relatives who do not value education.[29] On social media this translates also into monitoring one's social media notifications[30] to erase any misspelled or misplaced comments left by older relatives. Similarly the view of unfinished brick walls (Fig. 3.7), arguably Balduíno's most recurrent visual background, is meticulously erased from photos – simply by consciously choosing not to take a photo showing this type of background. This particular image suggests that the family is struggling and unable to have a 'proper' house with finished plaster walls. Photos are thus purposely taken with neutral backgrounds such as inside painted walls.

Hair is often straightened and shows a fringe

In the following examples, displaying beauty means focusing on the hair (Figs 3.8–3.9). This is important for women in Balduíno as most

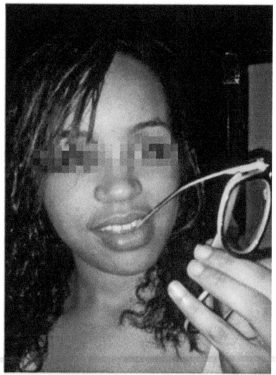

Figs 3.8–3.9   Selfies showing straightened hair

people there have African ancestry.[31] Given that the settlement was the colonial epicentre of the slave trade, straightening the hair[32] is generally perceived as corresponding to cleanness and progress. This is not just a matter of taste, as informants reported that the better-paying administrative jobs are not available to women who have 'Afro' hairstyles.

Selfies often display symbols of upward mobility such as clothing and accessories

Another key element to note is the use of this genre of photos to display one's prosperity through consumption.[33] In the cases of selfies taken by women, the clothing must be new and the subject should wear makeup, accessories and other items (Figs 3.10–3.11). These are highly posed and crafted photos. Many young people take these photos in front of the mirror, enabling them to display their smartphones in the image.

Figs 3.10–3.13 Selfies displaying a smartphone, a tablet computer and two scenes from a local gym

Figs 3.10–3.13   Continued

Many of these selfies are also taken at gyms (Figs 3.12–3.13) – both because the gym represents the type of consumption related to upward social mobility[34] and also because gyms have large-scale mirrors. These allow photos to be taken of the whole body, displaying together items such as tennis shoes, watches and smartphones.

The expectation of receiving complimentary comments and likes

Attracting attention through likes and comments is an important part of being online. These portraits are shared under the expectation of capturing attention, which is manifested through short comments saying how pretty the person looks (Figs 3.14–3.15).

These same types of selfies, which previously were displayed on the subject's Facebook timeline, are now also shared regularly in WhatsApp groups.

Figs 3.14–3.15 Selfies and the complimentary comments left by the friends of the person who posted the photo

Adults too use photography to show prosperity (Figs 3.16–3.17), which is also related to showing certain types of clothing. However, their portraits often reveal their inexperience with photographing and being photographed (though this tends to improve over time as they practice using social media). Instead of selfies, the photo is more often taken by another person while the subjects pose formally, as one would see in old family photos or images taken for ID cards. From my perspective the results are less aesthetically accomplished than those of the younger people in the settlement, but the preoccupation with finding neutral backgrounds is recurrent.

The opposite of cool

The social pressures to show neatness also appear clearly when this aspiration to beauty and perfection is denied. Take the story of Patrícia, a 13-year-old girl who lives with her parents and three sisters, aged 11 to 17. Each of the sisters has a distinct personality; Patrícia

Figs 3.16–3.17   Portraits showing adults

is the adventurous, outgoing teen who loves going out with friends and dreams of becoming a professional dancer to work with bands playing *Pagodão*[35] and other local music genres. She also has a mischevious streak, on one occasion taking a photo of her older sister Sara asleep on the sofa and posting it on Facebook. The photo was as uncool as a teenager in Balduíno could imagine: hair, makeup, type of clothing and angle for posing – everything was missing or wrong. Sara woke up later to find her Facebook profile filled with messages from friends, relatives and even people she did not know making fun of her. A few days later Sara saw a chance to get her revenge and took a similar photo of Patrícia. Instead of publishing it immediately, however, she decided first to torment her sister by showing her the photo. The prospect of appearing publicly in such a humiliating situation provoked a loud dispute between the sisters and their mother intervened, ordering Sara to erase the file.

Displaying enjoyment

If we follow also what adults post, we can see how this desire to look attractive and prosperous blends together. A topic that illustrates this well is the sharing of images that display enjoyment. Such photos suggest that one has the money to consume beyond mere survival. However, sharing photos displaying celebration also relates to a tension in the locality about the meaning of wealth. These images add to ongoing local disputes about what is more important in life: gaining money through work or preserving one's autonomy by resisting formal employment.

This tension is more explicit between migrants/evangelical Christians and natives/non-evangelical Christians. However, it also relates to opposing perspectives between young people who prefer formal employment and adults who resist formal work structures as something that enslaves the person. The perception is that prosperity can only be achieved in exchange for a discipline of work that has great impacts on family life and what is seen as personal freedom. More recent migrants arrive to fulfil the work demands of tourist resorts that are open around the year. Working there provides advantages, such as having a steady wage and becoming eligible for government unemployment benefits. However, it also imposes high costs on the effort of raising families, with children and other relatives being left behind during working hours and days. Hotel demands peak in the summer (during school holidays), and are also higher on weekends and holidays. Those working in this industry, especially women, have to get used to being away from their homes, and to cope with complaints and pressure from partners and older relatives, who often believe they should stick to traditional roles, caring for the home and children.[36] Displaying enjoyment is a recurrent way that locals use to address this issue on social media.

Swimming pools, sandy beaches and alcohol

In terms of showing enjoyment through prosperity, one of the most popular locations for taking photos is the swimming pool (Figs 3.18–3.19).

Figs 3.18–3.19 Photos showing people having fun at the swimming pool

There are no public or private pools in Balduíno (they are abundant in affluent properties across the road), so spending time at one displays one's social connections as much as it expresses an interest in achieving upward mobility. Visiting pools often results from friendships with housekeepers, or in some cases with bosses or former bosses who are the owners of these country houses. Although it is implicit that the person in the photo does not own the pool, the photos challenge the stereotypical image of the worker as submissive, unpretentious and poor.

Drinking alcohol (Figs 3.20–3.21) does not just show a desire to enjoy life, but also marks the person as not being an evangelical Christian, thus avoiding the negative connotations of this.[37]

The beach is associated with tourism and with the activities of tourists, so photos at the beach (Figs 3.22–3.23) also indicate an aspiration for upward social mobility.

Figs 3.20–3.21   Photos showing friends enjoying a drink together

Figs 3.22–3.23 Photos showing people enjoying themselves at a tourist site

Consuming food

Food indicates both enjoyment of life and prosperity. Meat is particularly symbolic of wealth, as non-jerked beef (i.e. beef that has not been dried and salted) was rarely consumed in this region in the past due to its high cost. Barbecuing, a practice associated with Brazil's more economically developed southern regions, is often accompanied by loud music – allowing both sound and smell to 'broadcast' the event through the neighbourhood. Barbecues actually represent one of the practices common to evangelical Christians and non-evangelicals, and both groups commonly post about them on social media. Notice how the

Fig. 3.24 Photographs of beef dishes at a barbecue

poses in the picture (Fig. 3.24) freeze the moment when everyone is engaging with the food.

Evangelical Christians and young people in general also display the consumption of fast food products, which tie them to the modern urban world (Fig. 3.25). The images show that he or she is able to afford to go to fast food restaurants and to order these products as paying customers. Similarly families post photos of children's birthday parties, particularly displaying very colourful sweets and commercial bottled refreshments (Fig. 3.26). These items also symbolise modernity and celebrate new possibilities of consumption, until recently not available to Balduíno residents.

Displaying bonds

The topic of enjoyment is also related to the enjoyment of being with people. Since Brazilians are generally perceived to be – and perceive themselves as being – intensely sociable,[38] it is not surprising that social occasions also emerge as a major theme to post about on Facebook (Fig. 3.27).

Figs 3.25 and 3.26 Photos showing fast food being eaten in a shopping mall and food at a child's birthday party

Fig. 3.27 A photo showing the bonds between family members

Peer relations

As Chapter 2 has demonstrated, local types of peer bonds are about risk taking, adventure and fun. The images below (Figs 3.28–3.29) suggest this kind of relationship being portrayed with reference to a 'ghetto' ethos, related to more evident sexuality, a hip-hop aesthetic and 'gangster' life-style. Branded clothing is key as it represents not just that the person is dressing up, but that he or she can afford to spend beyond survival to dress up. Locals explain that the point of wearing these fashionable items is to display one's association with criminality; the brands worn can only be purchased by somebody whose income is not merely the pay received by a (typically low-wage) manual worker.

Together with the ostentatious hip-hop style, Christianity is also displayed through fashion and practices. Through evangelical Christianity the idea of 'friendship' is being shown as a new genre of relationship, which appears in memes such as in Fig. 3.30. The image – of a male and female hugging – is contrary to traditional local assumptions about gender having to exist in separate domains. This position is backed by

Figs 3.28–3.29 Photos showing relationships between friends of around the same age

Fig. 3.30 A meme about male/female friendship. Translated, it reads: 'There are friendships that I sincerely want to keep with me for all my life'

Fig. 3.31 A photo showing the ties of friendship between a mixed-sex group of evangelical Christian teenagers

evangelical Christian values, which promote the building of companion-ship between husband and wife, and more broadly among the members of each church.

While non-evangelical groups avoid bringing males and females together in photos,[39] evangelical youth are less submissive to gender sep-arations (Fig. 3.31). They prefer to display, as a sign of modernity and 'civilised values', that men and women can have relationships that are not necessarily romantic or sexual.

Couples, romance and marriage

As we move from the informal display of people enjoying themselves to the more formal display of 'couples' per se, we also approach a very specific arena of ideal life, arising from religious rather than secular roots.

Not many couples share photos of themselves together, and those that do tend to be evangelical Christians. One of the ways in which they display their devotion to God is by portraying their fidelity within marriage. One may express this by uploading wedding pictures. These formal celebrations, for the costs they imply and for being a practice more associated with wealthier sectors of society, are also displaying aspirations and prosperity (Fig. 3.32). Young unmarried couples who show themselves online (Fig. 3.33) do so following a path promoted by Christian churches and also associated with modernity.

The presence of evangelical Christian churches influences the general perception about what families are and how family members are expected to behave. Fathers, who are traditionally less directly involved in raising children, appear and display themselves on social media. A man will demonstrate intimacy, as well as modernity, in the contact with his children and partner, emulating the structure of nuclear families (Fig. 3.34). Even non-evangelical couples feel the pressure to use these celebrations to present themselves as modern and prosperous. Such values are represented by the abundance of food in evidence, and also by the vibrant colours of the sweets and decoration.

Fig. 3.32 A photo celebrating the bonds of marriage

Fig. 3.33 A photo showing the ties of a romantic relationship

Fig. 3.34 A photo showing the bonds within a nuclear family

The way these new notions of friendship and partnership appear on social media also points to the value of using visual content that inform- ants themselves create and choose to display to examine changes in the norms of relationships in a society.

Displaying faith

Evangelical Christians display their faith through a rigorous dress code

Facebook in Balduíno reflects the same concerns found offline in the public side of evangelical families. Being an evangelical Christian in the

Figs 3.35–3.36   Photos showing the ties among members of a local church and the congregation singing during a service

settlement is about getting one's Christianity 'out of the closet' – especially considering 'evangelising' is a distinguishing feature of this group. For them, the person's spirituality and morality need to be constantly socially exposed (Figs 3.35–3.36). Clothing is very important in that context as a marker of both socioeconomic distinction and moral evolution (more sober items oppose the exposed sexuality associated with prostitution and infidelity); 'proper clothing' shows an embrace of high culture, taste and Christian values (Fig. 3.37). By following a similar dress code evangelical Christians can identify each other both on and offline, and show their faith and commitment to the church.

Evangelical Christians in Balduíno are more concerned with evangelising than with charitable activities. The act of promoting Christianity happens as they share personal testimonies of the works of God in their lives.

Offline we see this practice during church services and as part of everyday life, through informants constantly mentioning and talking about religion. The same process of expressing and making one's faith visible appears on social media. As well as displaying prosperity and moral elevation, evangelical Christians display their faith on these platforms by sharing moral and religious memes (Figs 3.38–3.40).

It may become easier to perceive social media in its 'lights on' mode by considering that all the photos presented in this section expose elements of the users' personal lives – their homes, relatives, peers, routines, religious practices, etc. – and are posted without content filters to

Fig. 3.37 A photo celebrating romantic bonds between evangelical Christians

be accessible to anybody using the same platforms. The term 'lights on' is a broad label to indicate a pattern that interconnects the images in this section. It does not refer to a specific platform, but rather a disposition to use social media to reach a certain audience, often with the motivation of showing off personal and family progress and values. Although this type of posting is more often shown on public-facing Facebook timelines, other spaces such as WhatsApp groups can also serve the same purpose.

Figs 3.38–3.40 Evangelical Christian memes. Translated, these read: 'Everything that you value so much goes away and finishes. We do not choose to come to the world, but we have the right to choose where we want to spend eternity' (Fig. 3.38); 'If you think that today is a day to THANK GOD, share' (Fig. 3.39); and 'How many times I attended service like that… There GOD spoke to me, and I left like this!!!' (Fig. 3.40)

Figs 3.38–3.40   Continued

Indiretas

We have so far looked at images that work as advertising of the moral self ('lights on') and of images that are exchanged secretly ('lights off') because they refer to aspects of life deemed as backward or morally unacceptable. In this context the *indireta* is a hybrid genre and, as Chapter 2 shows, it offers a way for people to negotiate conflicts.

In visual postings *indiretas* also relate to a practice of communication in which people make conflicts public without directly referring to the other person (the adversary) involved in the problem. The fear of revenge is normally what limits the cases of direct confrontation between people with opposing interests. Offline, people's way of 'sending an indirect' (*mandar a indireta*) is to speak out loud about a subject near the person that is being criticised, but without addressing him or her directly.[40]

One typical situation for *indiretas* on social media is that of two women in dispute over a man. Economic prosperity is also a recurrent motivation for gossip. Locals circulate rumours about how the wealth of others is the product of prostitution or crime, which can escalate into an indirect confrontation. As the person displays his or her prosperity through 'lights on' postings, others dismiss their achievements through rumours behind their back. The person under attack then writes on social media that the malicious gossip is motivated by jealousy. The common argument is that others are circulating lies as a way to attack his or her accomplishments. The *indireta* thus becomes a way of drawing more attention to the person's successes.

For locals memes are a popular method of flagging tensions that exist in their lives, both through humour and moralising content and as ways to promote or reinforce social norms.[41] Taken outside of the context of a specific posting, such memes sound like a pessimist kind of popular wisdom, but locals can connect information and interpret the message they really carry.

Loss of trust

The loss of trust is usually related to gossiping. It refers to the situation of learning or deducing that someone whom a person considered a friend was spreading rumours or lies about him or her (Figs 3.41–3.44).

Becoming someone's friend on Facebook raises different expectations. Many complain about people who 'friended' them, but then never spoke to them (Fig. 3.45). The memes below address this issue. They also display the

Figs 3.41–3.44 Memes expressing loss of trust. Translated, these read: 'Be careful with who you TRUST' (Fig. 3.41); 'People admire your virtues in silence and judge your vices publicly' (Fig. 3.42); 'Let people say bad things about you, as they are fond of criticising who they want to become!' (Fig. 3.43); and 'If I wanted to please everyone I would not have a Facebook profile. I would throw a barbecue party' (Fig. 3.44)

Deixa que falem mal de ti, as pessoas costumam criticar quem elas querem ser!

SE EU QUISESSE AGRADAR TODO MUNDO EU NÃO FARIA UM PERFIL NO FACEBOOK. FARIA UM CHURRASCO.

Figs 3.41–3.44 Continued

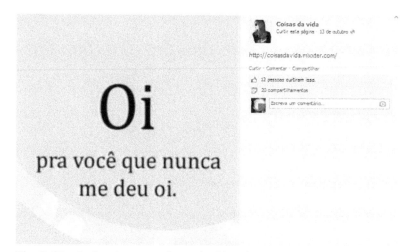

Fig. 3.45 An ironic meme about the idea that Facebook contacts are really friends. Translated, it reads: 'Hi to you that never said hi to me'

Fig. 3.46 A meme criticising the materialism of evangelical Christians. Translated, it reads: 'Evangelicals always practice the love of others… As long as these others are also evangelicals'

perception that Facebook is not as much for building relationships as it is for people to spy on one another.

Religious differences

These conflicts also happen in the context of religious differences. Evangelical Christians are under constant criticism for being 'snobs', for 'thinking they are better than others' and for preaching about the spiritual world while accumulating personal wealth (Fig. 3.46).

Within the church tensions can be seen emerging in Facebook postings when issues arise over inappropriate as well as appropriate behaviours. Tensions are generated among young people, especially

Fig. 3.47 A photo illustrating moral criticism of women's dress. Translated, it reads: 'Moderation!'

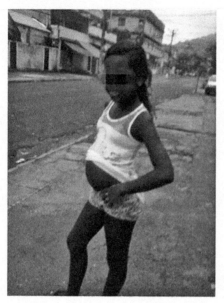

compartilhou a foto de _____ Blessed _____

17 min ·

meu Deus!!

GENTE O MÚNDO ESTÁ PERDIDO .... ! ' MENINA DE APENAS 1O ANOS GRAVIDA ISSO
ACONTECEU NA BAHIA MUITO TRISTE ESSA SITUAÇÃO, VAMOS ORAR PELOS
NOSSOS, FILHOS

Curtir · · Compartilhar

_____ _____ curtiu isto.

F _____ isso nn a nada e so o começo

Fig. 3.48 A photo shared by evangelical Christians reflecting the
supposed 'decadent values' of modern society. Translated, it reads:
(above) 'My God!'; (below) 'People, the world is lost … 10-year-old girl
pregnant. This happened in Bahia. Very sad this situation. Let's pray for
our children'

Fig. 3.49 A photo expressing moral criticism of how partners behave in a relationship. Translated, it reads: 'God does not destroy a family to create another one'; (longer text): 'Think about this: to have an affair is to work for the devil'

Concordo. E vc?

ACORDA BRASIL !!!

Curtir · · Compartilhar

8 pessoas curtiram isso.

 ▦ Eu concordo.
há 14 horas · Curtir

CONCORDO....
há 12 horas · Curtir

Fig. 3.50   A photo displaying the supposedly 'decadent values' of
modern society. Translated, it reads: (above) 'I agree, and you?'; (on the
poster) 'In Brazil, minors can: steal, kill, harass, sexually assault, burn
people, be prostitutes [several other similar offences]; in Brazil minors
cannot: work, be physically disciplined or answer for his/her crimes.
Wake up Brazil!'

girls, who are criticised for uploading photos on Facebook in which they wear clothes (during the service or in public) not considered acceptable for an evangelical person. One image and accompanying message (Fig. 3.47) criticises girls and young women who dress inappropriately, especially when it comes to going to church. Other images posted by evangelical Christians comment upon the state of moral decline they perceive in their country, often focused upon family breakdown, social and domestic issues and crime (Figs 3.48–3.49). Sometimes generational conflicts are the main target, as in Fig. 3.50.

Conclusion

The first element to stress from this chapter is that people are the centre of attention in the settlement. The regard shown for photographing people – themselves, relatives, neighbours, work colleagues or school peers – echoes the interest in using social media as a tool that helps to maintain the dense sociality of people in Balduíno.[42] The subjects that they want to record visually are not picturesque scenery or the angle of aesthetically attractive objects such as food, a pet or flowers. Especially on 'lights-on' social media, their cameras focus almost exclusively on themselves and their close associates. This appears to have been a common practice even before mobile connectivity simplified the act of posting images online.[43]

The main purpose of this chapter has been to offer a framework to analyse the various forms of social exchanges taking place in Balduíno. The analytical tool proposed here separates the visual material that has been collected by contrasting initially two motivations for social media use. Those were labelled 'lights on' and 'lights off'. Another aim has been to show the images they share more frequently through social media interactions.

Looking further at the types of visual content going around the settlement, the difference that emerges immediately relates to intended audiences. Part of the material is shown only to individuals or small groups, and circulates through trusted direct exchanges ('lights off'). Other images should necessarily be shown openly and publicly, associating the person who posts them with shared moral values, aspiration and prosperity ('lights on'). Then there is the *indireta*, a hybrid type that appears both on

Facebook timelines and on WhatsApp exchanges. *Indiretas* usually respond to situations of conflict, scandal or gossip. When it comes to images, memes that express *indiretas* often defend high moral standards and a moral right to prosperity while resenting the loss of trust and solidarity.

Comparing these three types of content helps us to understand the roles these exchanges play in a context of intense social change. Locals are continuously looking back at traditions and contrasting them with the new possibilities now at hand in relation to family, gender, work, religion, sexuality and class. These tensions become more obvious when one considers how the types of images shared change radically as we move from 'lights off' to 'lights on', which might have given the impression that people belong to either one category or the other. However, it is only by considering how these different types of content represent aspects of the same reality, circulating through the same mobile phones and computers, that we can understand both who these emergent Brazilians are and why social media means so much to them.

4
Intimacy: dense networks

It is common in Balduíno to hear locals talking nostalgically about 'the time the settlement was like a family'. This refers to the period before the opening of various roads in the region; a time when – as Chapter 1 describes – their economy was rural and travelling to street fairs and markets in nearby cities involved a journey of several hours, either by sailing or on foot. And as people reflect upon these 'family relations' that connected locals in the past, they mean it both metaphorically – to indicate how residents trusted and supported each other – but also in some ways literally. In the 1950s, when only a few hundred people lived in Balduíno, locals commonly married other locals or people from neighbouring localities, so in most cases any one person could connect the various links associating him or her to the other residents. These relationships could be traced through blood ties, marriage bonds, different forms of child adoption and also fictive kin connections (for instance godparents) – especially important in creating links between peasants and local proprietors and leaders.

Now, although the population of the region is expanding quickly because of work migration, and long-term residents often complain about the growing number of outsiders (*gente de fora*), the people of Balduíno and other settlements in the Coconut Coast still retain dense forms of social relations. These are 'dense' in various ways: in the sense that many have local family ties, because they live in a relatively small area and people thus see each other constantly, and also because of the importance of networks of solidarity that still exist – a response in part to the weak presence of public services – to help individuals and families.

It is commonly believed that new technologies are eroding pre-existing relationships.[1] Given the context in the settlement, this chapter will consider some of the intimate relationships[2] that exist in Balduíno today[3] and examine how these bonds have been strengthened or weakened because locals now use social media. The first section looks at the broad support networks that exist beyond direct family connections. In the cases of these relationships, individuals offer one another material and emotional support, examples of which include looking after each other's children, intervening in cases of illnesses or violence, sharing useful information and constantly helping each other to find work opportunities. Next we consider how social media has impacted on how people find, keep or break romantic partnerships. This is of particular importance given the intensity with which locals discuss social media in relation to infidelity. The last section deals with the effects social media has in the relationship between parents and offspring. Younger people are conscious that they love social media largely because of their parents' precarious literacy and technical skills, an imbalance that means their collective acts and interactions through services such as Facebook and WhatsApp become literally invisible to parents and relatives.

Friends and rivals

As Chapter 2 shows, a very important topic of conversation in Balduíno in recent decades concerns young people becoming less respectful to elders, especially to their parents and grandparents. This theme is often interconnected with the understanding that the state is partially responsible for this situation, as it is now legally forbidden for people under 16 to work and for minors (under 18) to go to prison if they break the law.[4] The logic these informants follow is that young people no longer learn the discipline of work from an early age, as they did in the past, and that parents are no longer allowed to educate them properly (usually a reference to beating), while young people are not properly punished if they do get involved in criminal activities.

From this topic, following discussion of the growing cases of forms of violence associated with the city, resulting in the lowering of trust between locals, the conversation about ungrateful offspring moves towards talking about the increasing population of outsiders (*gente de fora*) now living in Balduíno. Outsiders, the older residents argue, particularly those from cities, bring in bad ideas and attitudes; they teach the local youth to be materialistic, promiscuous and lazy.[5] This has also become a sensitive subject in the settlement. Locals, especially those whose families have been living in Balduíno for several generations, will complain that nowadays they cannot leave their doors unlocked because these unknown outsiders will come in and steal their possessions. Nor can a man resolve disputes in a 'manly' way (*como homem*) any longer, because the current opponent, being an anonymous stranger, has no local ties; he just might have a gun and decide to kill you. The decrease in peace and co-operation is seen as a consequence of the growth into a larger settlement, in which locals are less and less able to recognise one another, or know who one another's families are and where their relatives live.

However, in different contexts, these same locals will still say very naturally about the settlement that 'everyone knows everyone' there (*todo mundo se conhece*). So on one hand they complain bitterly about the loss of trust due to the increasing number of strangers in the locality, while on the other they say that nobody living there is actually a stranger because, even now, 'everyone knows everyone'. This apparent contradiction is useful to start a section about intimate relationships outside of the family domain.[6] In recognising the internal categories that people in Balduíno have to indicate proximity, we can discover at least some of the criteria locals use when adding people to their networks online.

Levels of closeness

Balduíno is a settlement of about 15,000 people, so at first the expression 'everyone knows everyone' seems something of an exaggeration. What exactly do locals mean by this and what kind of knowledge do they actually have of every other person? To find out I invited two of my research assistants to sit at a bar table on the pavement of the settlement's busiest street one day, to see what they could tell me about random people passing. After about an hour my young local assistants had identified nearly everyone that we saw, and yet it is important to clarify the kind of knowledge they showed when it comes to 'knowing everyone'. On a few occasions they knew the passing person's name and details of his or her family history in the settlement. More often they did not know the individual's name, but could give the part of the settlement in which he or she lived, as well as more general information, for example if the person was known to hang out (*tinha amizade*) with 'bad people' or belonged to a certain church. However, the most common type of information they presented were various kinds of associations connecting themselves and people passing. For instance, they would say: 'he is the cousin of the son-in-law of my aunt's former next-door neighbour' or 'she used to be the partner of a man who worked as kitchen assistant at the hotel with my brother'.

Considering the results of this experiment together with the ethnography in Balduíno, it became apparent that 'knowing everyone' did not mean having an active relationship of any kind with most of the other residents. I noted generally three categories of proximity. The most distant was simply knowing someone 'by sight' ('*de vista*', that is, recognising them mainly in terms of common relationships); the next level of closeness was between people who would greet one another as they met in the street;[7] finally the closest connection was between people who enter one another's homes. The final group are thus strongly connected and a more active part of each other's support networks.[8]

However, as I discuss later in this chapter, the settlement does not correspond to a single network. Local relationships are dynamic and constantly being re-negotiated, so two people who were once close associates might now ignore each other on the street. At times this may be the result of a dispute leading to a relationship breakdown, but more commonly this now happens because one of them has joined an evangelical church, and thus stopped socialising in bars or attending events that involve consuming alcohol; essentially he or she no longer wishes to be seen as being on friendly terms with someone who is not also baptised.[9] Greeting is therefore a traditional form of displaying and publicly acknowledging closeness in the region, but speaking or not speaking to each other does not necessarily reflect the level of knowledge that people have about others.

This brief introduction helps to consider the criteria which young people in the settlement use to decide who to add as 'friends' on their social media. The category of 'knowing by sight' is particularly important in understanding why many local users regularly add people from distant places whom they have never talked with, seen or met before – and yet these contacts are not viewed as strangers.

Adding mutual friends

As in other places and socioeconomic contexts,[10] most teenagers in Balduíno believe that having a great number of 'friends' on social media reflects positively on their popularity. Consequently using social media is often talked about with excitement, but it also demands an ongoing engagement: this is a serious matter to them. For example, a mother told me that her 13-year-old son begged her to 'do like the other mums' and punish him with beatings, rather than forbid him from using Facebook. Talking to these local teenagers,

I often had the impression that being on Facebook for them was an obligation similar to working; it consumed time and effort, had to take place regularly and included particular aims, but in exchange produced a certain value that they could use to measure personal prestige. Similarly to people in an office job, they stare at a screen and may struggle with pressures to perform. In Balduíno, one of the consequences that shows teenagers' efforts to outperform others in gaining online friends and popularity is to be temporarily suspended from sending friendship requests on Facebook. This is an automatic restriction imposed on users who send large numbers of requests, many of which are denied. However, teens often talk about these suspensions with an underlying sense of pride. For them the punishment illustrates their dedication to social media – and also suggests that they have access to a private computer, to be able to spend so many hours online.

Wellington is one of these teenagers. Aged 17, he lives with his mother and a younger brother in an area relatively distant from the settlement's centre – which reflects the limited income of his family. He goes to school in the morning and works in the afternoon at a local printing shop. This does not pay very much, but is nevertheless a valued job, as it allows him to be near and have occasional access to social media during working hours. Though obviously enthusiastic about computers and the internet, Wellington does not demonstrate this excitement by talking about a video he saw online, content he downloaded or the friends he has made around the world. Instead he constantly mentions numbers to demonstrate his success online. He has over 2,000 friends and most nights (after pretending to go to bed so that his mother then falls asleep) he socialises on Facebook until it is time for him to go to school. He is proudest of the number of online friends that are active at night – a high number, proportional to the number of his Facebook friends. Between 8 pm and midnight, for example, 'over one hundred people'(!) are simultaneously connected and available to chat with him. Rather than enjoying the conversations he has online, Wellington refers to the experience of daily chatting with his online contacts as a difficult task to be accomplished. 'It's tough! I can barely speak to so many people at once!' His computer screen during these hours shows many chat windows open. However, unless he is talking with a potential romantic partner or with a close associate, the conversations themselves seem mechanical. Wellington does not know most of his online friends personally, and his aim is to carry out as many chat exchanges as possible.

In the settlement there is the category of knowing someone 'by sight', presented in relation to shared connections. On social media, this level corresponds to having mutual online 'friends'. Local teenagers do not have any problem with adding people they have never seen or talked with before. Also, in a similar fashion to the face-to-face version, knowing someone 'by sight' on Facebook is a category of relationship that can entail, but that often does not demand, specific behaviour, such as having to greet each other online. It is generally good enough to be able to exhibit these contacts as 'friends' on their Facebook profile, and also to use them to add new contacts.

However, social media becomes more complicated if it involves local relationships. When it comes to 'friending' locally, there are obviously the peers with whom the young people already hang out, and it is expected that they will use social media to communicate with each other. But then there are other locals whom they know only 'by sight'. Being online allows individuals to reach out to these distant contacts and connect to them, with a degree of privacy that was less available in the past. But while sending a friendship request to someone outside the settlement does not make that an active/participant relationship, locals who receive friendship requests from other locals often interpret it as an act of greeting. Their expectations about future interactions are raised accordingly. Those sending the requests find it considerably more simple and less painful than approaching offline the person they already know 'by sight' and asking if she or he wants to be friends.

If the other person accepts the online request, there are basically two common outcomes. Some informants report that the newly opened channel of communication is followed by an awkward silence. Others explain that the new relationship takes off online: the two actively like each other's postings, leave comments and, above all, greet and chat constantly when they notice that the other is online. The problem arrives when these two people meet each other on the street. Both expect to be greeted (as they now have a new level of closeness), but both become afraid of the other person 'turning the head away' (*virar a cara*). Such a rejection is seen as a public embarrassment, as the rejected individual will be ridiculed and made fun of by his or her associates.

This common situation – waiting to be greeted before reciprocating – tends to produce bitter feelings in the person that received the request. As the expected 'friendship' fails to blossom offline, locals commonly interpret the friendship request as a trick by the other person. They believe it was made to gain access to their postings and online activities, and consequently to spy on and gossip about them.

Rivalry as social glue

I started this section with a schematic view of how locals relate to each other outside family boundaries. They associate with others roughly in three distinct levels: 'knowing by sight', greeting (which implies publicly acknowledging a relationship and sharing of information) and finally the condition of greater closeness between people who enter one another's homes.

Nurturing these closer ties is very important[11] as public services in the region are still precarious. If someone needs to go urgently to a hospital – the nearest ones are about one hour away by car – he or she will most likely travel in a private car driven by a neighbour rather than in a (scarce) public ambulance. Instead of calling the official number for the police, locals needing a quicker response will call friends who work at the police. It is a longstanding tradition in the region for groups of men to gather on Saturdays to help to build a house for a local family (an activity known as 'bater laje').[12] However, relations between locals are not always friendly and supportive, and the boundaries of each person's network of support constantly change. Adult women and their children are known for repelling families of newcomers, sometimes through violence.[13] And belonging to the settlement implies also being constantly subjected to silent informal scrutiny; everyone is constantly paying attention to, and gossiping about, everyone else.[14] The shared assumption in Balduíno is that anything that happens in secret is potentially a threat to everyone else. 'Otherwise, why would the person want to conceal it?'[15] This information (often concerning illnesses, deaths, infidelity and similar topics) circulates not only as a way to display affinity among allies, but also as a means to attack the reputation of foes.

Anthropologist Claudia Fonseca has studied low-income populations in Brazil since the 1980s, and has theorised that rivalry and internal antagonisms represent a key formative element of these particular communities. In other words, for her the social glue that bonds people together in settlements such as Balduíno is not their solidarity against 'common enemies', such as the rich, but rather ongoing disputes and disagreements. 'Under this light, the community appears still with defined boundaries, but what stand out, above all, are the heterogeneous nature and the changing status of its members.'[16] Relationships are forged initially not with the intention of providing help and support to others living in similar conditions, but as forms of protection. People establish alliances because they feel threatened or distanced from other groups, and these ties are constantly re-worked according to changes in contexts and events.

Fonseca's theories reflect the continuous forging and breaking of relationships in Balduíno. I mentioned above how families or individuals who become part of Evangelical churches constantly have to demonstrate publicly that they are behaving approriately. But the social dynamics inside churches are equally tense, with a requirement to have close friends within the church and to attend services regularly. At the local Assembly of God, church members make great efforts to discuss and participate in internal politics. For example, an important current theme that divides the congregation relates to the importance given to financial prosperity (see also Chapter 1). This is debated not only in the abstract, but also in response to the institutional roles that the head minister controls and distributes as he sees fit. In this context, the community gossips about, for instance, the head minister's high salary (comparable to the monthly earnings of a hotel executive in the region) and of the privileges he enjoys, such as not having to pay for petrol or many of his travel expenses. Some also condemn his practice of giving prestigious positions in the local church hierarchy to the most prosperous members of the congregation. This occurs, they explain, because these wealthier people's tithe (one-tenth of an individual's income, which is pledged to the church) amounts to a lot of money. They believe he is less generous in offering positions to those who work hard for the church but are struggling financially; they do not pay a tithe, or have only a little to give away. Such disputes are not obvious to outsiders, but they are an integral part of belonging to the Assembly of God in Balduíno. Applying Fonseca's interpretative framework we could argue that it is the heterogeneous boundaries and internal disputes that make that church a community and bond a certain group together.

'Sandwich living' and social media

As Chapters 1 and 3 show, aspiration and resentment against socioeconomic distinction are subjects important not only to members of a church. The tensions that result from wanting to be part of the local support networks are common among low-income urban Brazilians and prominent in local everyday relations. Recent developments in the region have led to increased possibilities of labour, which attracts large numbers of migrant workers, and these have contributed further to tensions and the desire for support.

One of the field sites Fonseca researched is a low-income neighbourhood in Porto Alegre, a city in the Southern region of the country that has been strongly influenced by the arrival of European migrants in the past 150 years. It is clear that, in spite of the distance and many cultural differences between South and Northeast Brazil, there are important similarities between the field site Fonseca studied and Balduíno. Like the people with whom I was in contact during my research, her informants were neither the most vulnerable (those living in virtual destitution, such as beggars or informal collectors of discarded things) nor the disciplined workers with stable professions and values similar to those of the more affluent classes.[17] Fonseca has proposed the notion of 'sandwiched living' ('*vida em sanduiche*') to represent this group, positioned in between those living in poverty and the level more accustomed to formal labour, and more aligned in values with the country's affluent classes.[18]

Like those who participated in her study, my informants in Balduíno are either employed as low-income manual labourers (cooks, security guards, cleaners etc) or own small businesses such as bars or hair salons. As Fonseca puts it, 'their practices reflected the limited influence of "normalizing" forces', such as schooling and access to banking services.[19] In this volatile, precarious situation, rivalry and antagonism are an integral characteristic of social relations. People are constantly trapped between a desire to distinguish themselves from the even poorer and the risk of achieving too much distinction, which then leads to social isolation.[20]

More than other groups in Balduíno, teenagers find themselves intensely trapped in this experience of seeking distinction while also displaying affinity, showing off prosperity while avoiding being singled out and cast aside as pretentious and arrogant. There are many examples from everyday experiences and routines related to this. A school principal mentioned that her poorest students, who have to work full-time and consequently attend classes at night, have recently been wearing Kenner, an upmarket brand of sandals, to school. She had been struck by this, not just because buying this product means a great investment for the students, but also by the curious visual effect of such posh sandals appearing as part of the school uniform in this poor settlement. Ultimately buying a Kenner sandal is a display of financial achievement that does not make the wearer distinguished – it rather makes them equal to everyone else.

Similar efforts exist through other established practices. For instance, two or three close peers may arrange between themselves to go to school on a given day wearing exactly the same new clothes and accessories (for instance, Nike tennis shoes, a Cyclone shirt and an Adidas backpack). Each pupil gets his or her parents to buy the items, saying that other parents are doing the same for their children. Older teens also often order special personalised T-shirts for events such as concerts or parties, as they want to be visually identified there as a group.

Digital technology and social media are part of these negotiations in 'sandwich living'. People are constantly pointing out their neighbours, saying things like: 'this family cannot even properly dress their children and yet they pay to have cable TV at home' or 'they buy brand name clothes for their children, but don't care if they learn to read or not'. A teacher who was born and raised in a neighbouring settlement told me about a recent meeting he had with the mother of a student. He explained that the family of this student was particularly vulnerable, consisting of a single mother supporting four children from three different relationships. Their home, still under construction, was at a plot far from the centre and did not have doors and windows, 'not even in the bathroom!'. However, the mother, who worked as a cleaning lady and had just been fired from her formal job at a hotel, spent most of the money she received as compensation (R$ 2,000 / US$ 1,000) to buy a fancy mobile phone for her 17-year-old daughter.

This teacher's words reflect the type of criticism that locals use to separate themselves from those socioeconomically beneath them. But he also acknowledges that the purchase of the (perceived) superfluous item in the end does not make its owner distinguished. The peers with which this student hangs out come from similar struggling backgrounds, and all of them own similar high-end mobiles.

These events also commonly happen online. Chapter 3 shows how public-facing Facebook timelines and social media as a whole are used to show distinction and conformity at the same time. Many of the photos posted relate attempts to display 'beauty', and that beauty is also often associated with consumption: wearing makeup, having brand name clothes, going to the gym, having a smartphone, enjoying expensive food and drinks, etc. But the images that go on social media also often include peers sharing the same types of photos displaying consumption; posting such photos is tied with the expectation of receiving endorsement. Showing oneself as prosperous and aspiring while avoiding being considered arrogant ('se achar') is part of the overall strategy and practices to make and break alliances. It is seen as important to display oneself together with some products recognised as prestigious, but local teenagers are so worried about the approval of others that they take down photos that receive few likes and comments.

The next sections consider social media and its effects on different aspects of family life in Balduíno. We start by examining partnership bonds between men and women.[21]

Trust, infidelity and spying

There is a vast anthropological literature about low-income families,[22] gender[23] and race[24] in Brazil, and more specifically in Bahia. This body of literature expands further as it interconnects with other important themes such as religion, media and domestic violence, among others.

If, in general, we need to avoid speaking about the homogeneity of working-class Brazilians,[25] this seems especially important in Balduíno, given the multiple changes that have taken place in only a few decades. Here, different groups of migrant workers have arrived in an old, but also rapidly transforming, country location. Balduíno was a difficult-to-reach rural settlement, largely driven by a plantation type of agriculture now in decline. During most of the twentieth century proprietors and even their direct subordinates had informal rights to have more than one partner, and therefore to be the head of multiple families[26] – a practice that has not completely gone away. More recently, regional economic development began to attract people mainly from the hinterlands of Bahia and from the state capital. In recent squatting areas residents often live side by side with other newly migrant 'strangers', but it is still common to see family plots, or even sections of streets where multiple houses are inhabited by relatives.[27] Those arriving from the Salvador metropolitan area often come from *favela*-like settings. Other new residents come directly from rural areas, experiencing life in urban-like, working-class dormitory settlements for the first time. In respect to family traditions and practices, then, Balduíno today has multiple influences.

Other changes have taken place too. This locality that had very little state infrastructure until the 1980s now has three public schools, a health centre, a police station, a mail office and a branch of the national welfare service. Institutional relations – that is, public servants providing government services – did not formerly exist, but are now close to people. Transportation and communication are part of nearly everyone's everyday lives, so travelling to Salvador, the state capital, speaking on mobile phones and now using mobile internet is not a privilege of the well-off local families. These, plus different forms of media channels including cable TV and internet, as well as the large presence of evangelical Christian organisations, also influence how relationships within local families are now formed, maintained or broken in the settlement. So in short, although I will refer to various cases and characteristics of family relations in these next sections, they do not form a model that is necessarily homogenous in the settlement.

Sex and marriage

Sex is a constant subject of conversation in Balduíno.[28] Both men and women joke, brag and gossip about it conspicuously. I was once participating in an afternoon-long Catholic festivity that started with a procession and soon turned into drinking and dancing. There I overheard Antonia, a 50-year-old woman well known in the settlement, and the mother of seven grown-up children, talking at a bar table about her young boyfriend's voracious sexual appetite and of the three dildos she owns and uses while watching porn. Evangelical Christians from the Assembly of God have special retreats meant to strengthen the intimacy of couples, and its participants said I'd be surprised at the conversations they have aimed at spicing up their sex lives. Yet sexuality is also constantly being controlled.[29] Men and women categorically avoid being seen publicly interacting with a non-relative of the opposite sex, as such interactions quickly fuel rumours about illicit affairs. Parents often forbid their adolescent daughters to have boyfriends, and only agree to premarital relationships if they take place under supervision.

Marriages are common among evangelical Christians,[30] but outside of such religious circles similar unions can be represented by the act of moving in together.[31] In spite of the contradictory morals, it is not uncommon for local women to get pregnant as a consequence of casual relations during their teenage years.[32] Particularly until the recent past, the girl's partner and/or her family would build her a house for them to use; after the first partner left,[33] this house would then shelter various subsequent partners with whom she would have children. These temporary relationships would help to cover the household expenses while the partner lived there. As the woman's earlier children grew up and began to work, her dependence on other men for protection and money would decrease; but prior to that, mother and children acted in alliance to ensure her current partner worked and provided for the household.

Such patterns still continue in the settlement. Loriana, for instance, a 24-year-old mother of five, lived in a squatting area with three of her five children. Whenever her partner found a temporary job as a builder, she sent her eldest child, an eight-year-old boy, to follow him to work to make sure that he did not drink during the lunch break and that he brought back his wages at the end of the shift. Yet children can be manipulated by either partner in a relationship – having children is seen as a way for men to ensure control over their partners.[34]

The expectation of infidelity[35]

Non-evangelical men generally perceive infidelity very positively, speak about it recurrently and are proud both to have established lovers and engage in casual adventures. A visiting friend of mine from São Paulo was bathing at the beach near the settlement when a man arrived to flirt with her; when she said she was married, he did not look convinced and asked if her husband was around (implying that 'otherwise, that was not really a problem'.) Armando, a 29-year-old taxi driver, is now married to his former lover, but he also has a new lover whom he protects and helps with money. He has two daughters by previous relationships, the older one now aged 16 years. André, a fisherman, tells me proudly of his love for his partner Helena, adding that after 30 years together they still have good sex. But he adds that every time his partner finds out about him having a new girlfriend he sleeps 'with one eye open' as he is scared that Helena will take revenge and throw boiling water on his face when he is sleeping. Luiz, another taxi driver, talks without inhibition of affairs he has with single mature women whom he meets through his work and of his adventures with 'novinhas'[36] (young women, often in their teens). But he does not consider breaking up with his long-term partner because, as he says, these other romances are temporary and young girls today are only 'piriguetes'[37] (materialistic and promiscuous). 'They don't care for love.' His partner, he explains, will be there to care for him when he is old.

Women in Balduíno often talk about their partner's infidelity as being mainly the responsibility of the other women. The understanding is that men 'have their needs';[38] women use their bodies and sexuality to manipulate men and 'steal' them from their families, so they can benefit from their support.[39]

Although during the ethnography I heard considerably fewer cases of infidelity from women, the reason is probably because this topic is not discussed as openly[40] and, outside evangelical Christian circles, my main informants were men. Pedro, a schoolteacher whose parents moved to Balduíno in the 1970s from the hinterlands, says that none of his seven siblings married 'nativos' (people from local families). None of them believed that either the women or the men born in that region make trustworthy partners.

Just as local men are praised and respected for their infidelities, however, they are haunted by the possibility that their partners have made them a cuckold (corno).[41] Locals often associate female infidelity with a curse or with a transmitted disease, and it is considered a family matter when men decide to punish physically the women who have these affairs. I was told of a house in the settlement that is empty because the owner's wife betrayed him; people are afraid the same might happen to them if they move into this house. There are many jokes about this topic and being called a '*corno*' is highly offensive. It is also common to hear that alcoholism or other forms of drug addiction result from this type of public dishonour. The term 'infidelity' may also be applied to a woman leaving the household and only later beginning a relationship with another man.

Romance, infidelity and social media

One of the clear perceptions about social media in Balduíno is that it represents a rich mine for romance. Several reasons contribute to this perception: the sheer increase in the number of people who can now be reached, moving beyond former constrains of time and space; the possibility of contacting people privately and communicating with them discreetly; and the access offered to users of services such as Facebook and Orkut to navigate others' friends lists.[42] In an environment where people are acutely aware of, and exposed to, social control through gossiping and rumours, being able to reach potential new partners easily and cheaply explains the perception that social media is – for good and for bad – a playground for romance. These perceived advantages represent an important reason why locals learn to use computers and spend money at internet cafés, and why they are now buying smartphones. Given the social importance that having a prodigious sex life has for men, it is perhaps less surprising that functionally illiterate (older) men engage in writing to flirt and co-ordinate secret meetings with lovers using texting and now social media.[43]

This interest in romance through social media is a topic in itself, but also relates to different subjects people of the settlement talk about. These include social media being a catalyst and promoter of infidelity, social media offering alternatives for new forms of distant relationships, social media enabling the distribution and consumption of amateur porn, social media being the means of publicising 'revenge porn' and other types of public shaming (such as students uploading and sharing videos of school fights) and social media becoming a new hunting ground for sex predators (*tarados*).

The perceived advantage that WhatsApp has in relation to flirting and infidelity is that the service automatically accesses the users' mobile phone contacts and adds them as WhatsApp contacts. Similarly to texting, WhatsApp is used, among other things, to broadcast messages to different groups. These messages are often religious stories with moralistic conclusions, humour and announcements considered to be of public interest. This practice can then become an icebreaker between people who know each other only 'by sight', and these exchanges may eventually lead to secret romances. In addition, young unmarried locals are now creating WhatsApp groups populated by people that they know but who are not necessarily friends, or who know each other only 'by sight'. An informant added me to these groups and they seem like a variation of speed dating events: individuals are added to a chat group with a few dozen strangers and subsequently publish greeting notes and selfies so that others in the group know them visually. On this basis, they can decide whether to begin private conversations. The intention of the creator is to gather enough active participants so that they will constantly add more people (thus displaying the popularity of the group creator). However, many of such groups have interactions only in the first few days.

Social media and spying

When asked to say what they think about social media, some locals' initial reactions display frustration. They say using Facebook and WhatsApp brings a great deal of stress to their lives. In this case they are referring to the problems they experience when personal profiles are accessed by people close to them, not an uncommon experience. Adults with limited computer skills need the help of young relatives or friends to create, and sometimes to access, their accounts on Facebook, so the passwords of adult relatives are often known by others. Since these situations often produce tension, both men and women talk about closing their Facebook accounts when they enter more serious relationships, as social media is normally seen as a driver of infidelity. Being off Facebook means that they do not have to worry about contacting and being contacted by other people, or that their partners will attempt to spy on their lives by secretly accessing their profiles to look at direct exchanges.

It is not that people failed to spy on each other prior to social media. As Chapters 2 and 3 show, locals are constantly aware that they are being observed. This interest in the private lives of others becomes more evident when we consider the sophistication and audacity of these acts now that social media is available. Clarissa, a 16-year-old evangelical Christian, had been dating Allan since she was 12 and he was 15.

They are from the same church and most of their social lives take place in religious contexts. So when she ended the relationship with him, two things happened. Firstly, many of their shared church friends sided with him. Secondly, her friends in general were curious to learn the true reason for the separation. Since both are active evangelical Christians, other locals wondered if the end of the relationship was due to infidelity on either side. It was in this context that she noted her peers were asking to see pictures on her phone (a common request) and then, with the phone turned away from her sight, they would open her WhatsApp to look at who she was talking to and what the conversations were about. This happened repeatedly until she installed an app to lock her WhatsApp. After that she could still hand her unlocked phone to people, knowing they would not be able to spy on her private exchanges.

This type of tension relating to social media and infidelity is the subject of a particular comic video clip[44] that circulated widely in Balduíno. It enacts a situation in which the boyfriend is having a heart attack, but the battery of his girlfriend's mobile has run out. The boyfriend then chooses to die rather than give her the password to unlock his own phone and call an ambulance.

Many partners successfully guessed and secretly saved their partner's Facebook password on the web browser in order to monitor private conversations. Roberta, a 29-year-old teacher, kept in touch with me through Facebook because she proposed to take me to see a group performing folk dances from a neighbouring settlement. Our exchanges were only occasional, consisting mainly of her apologising for being busy and not yet having had time to find out the dates of the group's rehearsals. However one day, several months after we first became friends online, I received a message with several misspellings and grammar mistakes (which her previous texts did not have) saying she did not want to speak to me again. A couple of weeks later, the sender wrote a more direct message saying: 'Hey partner, this woman is married, so you better stay away from her or things will get ugly.' Then, a few days later, Roberta herself contacted me, also using Facebook chat, to talk about the rehearsal. Apparently her partner was accessing her Facebook profile while she was away. He made threats to every man he did not know, then erased the messages so that she would not discover his spying practices. In this way he could carry on monitoring her conversations.

Spying constantly resulted in violence against women.[45] The typical case people talked about involved the woman putting her phone down and leaving the room to do something else. The partner, who happened to be near, picked up the mobile before it automatically locked itself and looked at the conversations she was having. Ronaldo, a moto-taxi driver, told me about his sister-in-law; she had been beaten by her partner as he thought that she was sharing 'intimacies' (*intimidades*) with another man on WhatsApp. He also confiscated her phone and kicked her out of the house. After she had stayed at Ronaldo's house for a couple of weeks, he accepted her return and she received her phone back.

Men can also be the target of spying. Luis, a 36-year-old evangelical Christian, was harshly confronted by Samanta, his stepdaughter, because of a conversation he was having through WhatsApp. She found out – probably by spying on his mobile – that Luis was having 'very friendly' and continuous exchanges with a young, good-looking sales representative from a motorcycle shop in Balduíno. Samanta and Luis had a very heated exchange through WhatsApp (as they did not want this situation to be known and gossiped about). He told me in his defence that the interaction with the sales rep was motivated by his efforts to evangelise and bring new people to their church, and went on to complain about his stepdaughter, claiming she 'behaves saintly in the settlement, but has a boyfriend in Salvador and spends whole weekends alone with him there', in an attempt to portray her as the sinner, not him.

Sharing passwords and social shaming on YouTube

Before ending this section about social media, romance and infidelity, two unrelated phenomena are worth noting: the popular practices of exchanging social media passwords with the partner and of recording and sharing videos of women fighting.[46]

Evangelical Christians frequently share social media passwords as a sign of mutual trust and commitment to the relationship. In Balduíno this happens mainly between couples, but it can also take place as a family agreement ('no secrets in the house') or a demonstration of religious commitment between teenage individuals and their leaders in a particular church. The obvious intention is to allow the other person to access one's private exchanges, so they can check the people they are chatting with as well as the conversations. As the practice has disseminated outside the domain of evangelical Christian circles, some teenagers explain that such agreements can provoke a necessary preparation: both members of the new couple first delete conversations that took place before their relationship started and that should not be seen, as they are unrelated to the present romance. However, the overall perception about exchanging passwords is that this creates more problems than it resolves. Locals say that it will not keep a person who wants to cheat from seeking out other relationships; he or she will simply have more than one Facebook profile or use other less popular platforms, such as Skype or texting, to flirt secretly. People can also have conversations on Facebook and immediately erase them. The arrangement can also add tension to the relationship, as any friendly conversation can be interpreted as a discreet form of flirting.

Another topic that is common in the settlement and has links both to romance and social media concerns shared videos of women fighting. As Chapter 2 shows, 'indiretas' (indirects) are an integral part of local ways to negotiate conflicts, and thus are popular among social media users. The most common type of online indirect in Balduíno happens between two women in dispute over one man. To speak indirectly in this case means that the post mentions the situation without referring to the name of the person accused of being involved. Such conflicts sometimes lead to physical confrontations, often in or near a school, with the events being videoed and then shared on social media.

There are pages and groups on Facebook dedicated to gathering and sharing this type of material. It may be said to combine violence and eroticism, as these fights often result in the participants removing items of clothing. For example in a clip circulating on WhatsApp, three young women catch another girl, beat her violently, undress her and release her in the streets. Such videos not only record students participating in violent acts in or near their schools, they also have shaming consequences similar to revenge porn.[47] The student who is humiliated by the beating is further humiliated by the video of the event circulating online; the audience of the event increases and the file can stay perpetually available to be re-circulated.

Such material raises tensions between parents (those whose children are beaten) and makes the school vulnerable to administrative punishment for not safekeeping their students' wellbeing. At one point the circulation of such content on social media became so common in the settlement that the head teacher of one of the schools told students that he would suspend anyone who uploaded or shared this type of video.

Parent–child relations

The literature about parenthood[48] in low-income Brazil is also considerable, given the importance of this topic in anthropology and the wealth of experiences researchers commonly find. In this region of Bahia, for instance, not too long ago a pregnant woman who did not wish to keep the child would informally announce this in the settlement in order to find an adoptive mother.[49] This other woman, often better off economically, could be childless or someone who did not have children of one specific sex – or she might simply be willing to raise the child. In Balduíno the local adults I met who were foster children (*filho de criação*) often show real pride and gratitude to their foster mothers, even as they know who their blood mothers are and also display some respect for them. Another common practice was to give up a child temporarily,[50] typically when parents decided they did not have the means to support the household and their children were not yet old enough to work outside the home. These children were 'given' to better off families for a year or more, to be fed and eventually have the chance to go to school while learning how to work as a cleaner and cook (for girls) or as a general servant (for boys). Many of my adult female informants and some adult male informants had had this experience at some point between 5 and 13 years old. Such topics, which have been well studied, are now at a stage of transition in the settlement as locals become more exposed to institutional rules and procedures.

This brief introduction to the topic of parenthood and parent–child relations is to indicate that this is a complex issue. In a similar way to the previous section about partners, the cases presented below cannot be applied to all families living in the settlement: the place itself is in a process of transformation, and the population includes people of different backgrounds. However, as a rough pattern, we can say that blood ties[51] between mothers and offspring tended to be strong and long-lasting in opposition to precarious marital ties,[52] and that, in relation to social media, the opinion of parents has broadly two extremes.[53] On one side, the poorest families tend to see their children's interest in technology positively, as an indication of a promising future working with computers. On the opposite side are the better-off and often, but not exclusively, evangelical Christian parents. Many of them purchase computers and install internet connections in their homes because they fear the consequences of their children coming into contact with other locals at internet cafés.

Maternity, work and social media

Many of today's young people in Balduíno live only with their mothers, or with their mothers together with a stepfather.[54] Women's work in the region was traditionally in or around the settlement, enabling them either to carry their children with them, while teaching them how to work, or to be close enough to home to monitor them. These women often also gathered in groups to collect shellfish or worked in the settlement's stores. As the region developed into a leisure destination for affluent urban families the number of affluent visitors rose, and local women started to cross the road to attend casual informal jobs cooking and cleaning for visitors at weekends.

In this context, it is relevant to note a change taking place with the growth of tourism-related businesses. As Chapter 5 also discusses, more and more women are leaving their children behind for several hours, both on weekdays and weekends, to reap the benefits of regular formal employment.[55] Women make up the majority of the stable, low-income workforce in hotels and managers confirm that women are more optimistic than men and try harder to keep their jobs. While these jobs provide greater financial stability for the family, however, it is still the mothers' responsibility to care for the children. Mariana, aged 22, got a job at the region's prestigious five-star hotel resort. In her initial months there she dreamed of receiving a prize given to the most dedicated employees. But then her two-year-old daughter got ill and, because her partner does not consider child rearing his responsibility, she had to stay at home for nearly two months. Stressed by the situation and saddened by being away from her job, she also forgot to take her birth control pills and is now pregnant with her second child.

While the better-off families in Balduíno talk about absent parents being morally corrupted or lazy, and thus unable to impart or teach respect to today's young people, these local mothers who are either alone at home or who have temporary partners are the ones who often participate in street protests.[56] They go to meetings with political candidates and representatives, both in the settlement and in Camaçari city, often attending such meetings to complain about the lack of state-sponsored activities available for young people outside school hours. With the perceived rise in crime-related violence in Balduíno, they are also increasingly concerned that the frequent absences of teachers (most of whom commute every day from Salvador) generate further opportunities for children to be alone. Teachers fail to attend classes for a variety of reasons, and the result is that pupils are often left unsupervised for parts of the school day. Chapters 5 and 6 discuss this problem in more detail.

To reduce the consequences of this lack of state infrastructure, some parents, especially better-paid mothers who are employed outside the settlement, pay local adults to watch over their children. Some women with more years of formal education are opening their homes to small groups of students, whom they look after and assist with their homework after school. Digital technologies are also part of the solution used by these parents. Offering internet, video game consoles and cable TV is a way to attract children and teenagers away from playing in the streets, encouraging them instead to stay longer at home. Mobile telephony, social media and, particularly, WhatsApp are intensively used by mothers to monitor their teenage children while away from home. This is not ideal, however, especially as older children also use the same social media to avoid the surveillance of adults.

A place parents do not control

Relationships between parents and offspring are one of the recurrent topics of this book. In Chapter 2 we began by describing how adults increasingly complain about young people's lack of respect for older relatives. According to teenagers, adults have been showing enthusiasm for social media, particularly so that they can see what their children are doing there. Although adults have been using Facebook and WhatsApp regularly in the past few years, however, young locals are not really worried about that, conscious of the literacy gap between the current generation and that of their fathers, mothers, uncles and aunts. As Chapter 5 describes, in the past couple of decades the number of years of schooling available in the settlement has jumped from 4 to 12, and the number of students has risen from only a few dozen to around 2,000. In this context, parents want to find out what their children do online, yet they are usually functionally illiterate and depend on their children to navigate computers and social media.

Although they use the same platforms, therefore, one generation behaves completely differently online to the next. Locals under the age of 30 tend to include writing in their everyday use of social media. Older adults, in contrast, have more restricted forms of participation. On Facebook they mostly share content, 'like' posts and add short comments such as "kkkkkk" (a Portuguese version of 'LOL'). On WhatsApp, besides sharing visual content, they tend either to exchange audio messages or to use the service as a telephone.

Consequently young people are far more worried about their peers on social media than their parents. In Chapter 2 16-year-old Margarete was the one who created her mother's Facebook account and helped her to set up the computer to use social media. When she wrote on public-facing social media about the romance that her mother was trying to discover, she knew that adults will only check for incriminating photos and not attempt to read long posts. In Chapter 5 Marina, an evangelical

Christian, explains that one of the reasons why young people use social media is because parents are not there to control them. Although Marina would never risk being seen in the settlement talking to a person belonging to an Afro-Brazilian religion, she felt at ease to have such connections through social media.

My final example to support this argument about how the online domain distances people of different generations is from a long interview I conducted. It was with a 22-year-old university student called Debora, at her house. While her mother paid close attention to all our conversation (as she was unsure about my intentions), Debora explained to me in detail her experiments in creating sophisticated fake Facebook accounts to then 'friend' her foes in the settlements and find out about their 'dirty secrets' (i.e. who they were sleeping with). I asked her at the end, in front of her mother, if she thought her mother understood what she was saying. 'Not at all,' she replied calmly, and the mother confirmed. The implications of a fake Facebook profile are not something that her 43-year-old illiterate mother would appreciate.

Social media, parenting and sexuality

There is one more concrete instance of conflict between some parents and their children regarding the use of social media. It relates to teenagers using digital media to flirt, and occasionally becoming pregnant as a consequence. An earlier section of this chapter explained the importance locals give to using social media with the intention of having affairs or starting relationships. Social media is not changing this practice or introducing a new desire: it is simply broadening the possibilities for secretive communication. But while partners tend to be of similar ages (and to have similar literacy levels), this is not the case for parents and their children. As a result parents tend to be at a disadvantage when they try to spy on their children using social media.

Teenage pregnancy is a topic commonly discussed among some – predominantly male – adults. As Chapter 2 explains, in general they point out 'the lack of respect' that young people now display towards older relatives. However, a common theme during these conversations is the growing number of teenagers trafficking and consuming drugs in the settlement and, in association with this, the increasing number of young, unmarried teenagers who are pregnant. Yet such conversations often ignore, or are silent about, the fact that the more underprivileged women in the region have traditionally had children in their teens (as have low-income women in the country as a whole), often beginning to cohabit with partners only after having two or more children. So today's teenage mothers tend to be the daughters and granddaughters of women who themselves started having children in their teens.

The parents who attempt to control most strictly their daughters' secret romances are mainly evangelical Christians, but they face a difficult challenge. As we saw on Chapter 1, these Christians tend to have higher literacy levels and consequently better technical skills for using the computer, especially the younger parents. For many, the greatest difficulty they face consists in watching out for children while being away at work. Lorenço and his wife Nívea, both in their early thirties and active participants in the local Assembly of God, were caught in precisely this situation, having to leave their children behind every day. This couple decided to sacrifice their stable incomes as formal employees at hotels. Instead they rented a little store space in the commercial centre of Balduíno and offered services: he fixes mobiles and she is a seamstress. They explained that it was a necessary choice: they have two young daughters and want to be near them when they are not at school. Despite such precautions, Lorenço admitted to a problem that they had experienced. Recently the parents had learned that their 12-year-old had been speaking secretly on her mobile to an adult man she had met online. They only found out because one day the daughter sent a text message mistakenly to Nívea. Her parents confiscated her phone, and when the person called at midnight they answered it, threatening to take the matter to the police.

Lívia, aged 14, was involved in an extreme example of the tensions that occur within some families. She was only a toddler when her parents split up and José, her father, remarried, since when she had been raised by him and his new wife. Recently, José had beaten Lívia violently after he discovered she had photographed and videoed herself naked to send this content to a lover – a practice known in English as 'sexting'. José acted according to tradition: in Balduíno educating through violence is not only acceptable but also perceived to be a demonstration of one's parental concern (see Chapter 2). However, in contrast to what is expected from an errant child, Lívia did not just confront José, hitting him back and promising to 'get even': she also screamed, 'I know my rights!' Then the following week the situation got more complicated as she, apparently out of a desire for vengeance, accused him of sexually abusing her in the past. José was arrested, but acquitted because of lack of evidence. The situation in their house improved only over a month later, when Lívia decided to move to another city to live with her mother.

Social media was the direct trigger for this event, as the offending video was found on her mobile, ready to be sent via WhatsApp. Social media is also part of the context in which young people such as Lívia now live: one in which teenagers constantly interact and exchange information, including details about their rights. Cases of sexual abuse inside homes are not uncommon in the region, although most still go unreported. It is also possible that Lívia invented the accusation against her father, in reaction to what she perceived as unfair treatment. Ultimately Lívia's sexting is a tragic case: it epitomises a broader phenomenon of the rejection of family hierarchy in the context of migration to cities in Brazil. Writing about youth criminality in a *favela* in São Paulo, Feltran refers to a case in which a young offender replies, when asked about the alternative of working: 'Why work? To be like my father?'[57]

What stands out from this case, however, is how Lívia's action fits into the local script about the corruption of family bonds mentioned above. Similar stories and anecdotes of children confronting parents circulate widely, mainly in daily conversations – not just in the settlement, but also among other low-income people I met. In the most common versions of this situation, the child speaks to a policeman (representing the law and expected to assert their 'rights'). Instead, the child receives a lecture on how the law is far more cruel than the parent.

Teenage sex and pregnancies were common long before social media, and continue to be common today, in some ways assisted by social media. Yet not all parents react to the topic in the same way. Márcia, aged 33 and a casual cleaner in the region, used social media to play down the unexpected pregnancy of her 15-year-old daughter Carla, presenting it online as a celebration for her debut as a grandmother. In private Márcia told me that although the pregnancy was unexpected and 'a fright' (*um susto*), she realised 'the important thing is that the baby is born healthy and that it's a pregnancy, not a disease. So we have to keep moving'.

Márcia has a boyfriend who is not the father of her two daughters; although the couple consider themselves partners, they choose to not live together. After learning about Carla's pregnancy, Márcia used WhatsApp to organise a baby shower. The group was opened during the 20 days before the birth, and while Márcia constantly fed practical information (such as what size of nappies guests should purchase), other participants used it as a regular WhatsApp group, as discussed on Chapter 3. They shared large numbers of memes and videos, mostly relating to faith in God, with sexual jokes for entertainment. After the birth of her granddaughter Márcia sent images of the child through WhatsApp to her friends and family members.

Fig. 4.1 A selfie announcing pregnancy. Translated, it reads: 'My little girl'

Finding a middle ground

In Balduíno social media mostly helped teenagers rather than the parents who tried to control them. Teenage pregnancies are not uncommon even in evangelical Christian families, but I have also seen examples of social media becoming a tool for evangelical teens and young adults seeking to maintain a middle ground; they have to navigate between control from their families and churches and the local peer pressure to engage in premarital sexual relationships. Through social media these evangelical Christians could build a sense of identity together, drawing on elements of the faith they embraced, but also modernising and updating their beliefs to move beyond the stereotype of religious fanatic.

One group that I followed consists of young adult females from the local Assembly of God church. They grew up together, and now keep in touch and support each other during the intense years as university students. Together they resist the pressure from the church's minister, who insists that evangelical Christian women should dress respectfully and modestly, for example by wearing skirts, never trousers. However, the young women ignore him in this matter, as wearing only skirts at university reinforced the prejudices of other students that evangelical Christians are close-minded, backward and subservient to archaic values. During weekdays, Facebook and WhatsApp is key for these women; they remain in continuous communication as they follow individual but equally intense schedules, including long daily bus trips to and from the city. Through this communication, and when meeting for Sunday activities, they also closed ranks against the minister's desire to invigilate people's social media. The women say the minister is wrong to publicly shame teenagers from the church during services because of things he finds on their Facebook timelines – generally girls and young women posting photos wearing 'less respectful and modest' clothing.

In short, this group of young adults used social media chat and also Facebook timelines to present themselves – both to conservative adults from their church and to their 'more liberated', non-evangelical peers elsewhere – as achievers who are progressing in life, have interesting careers and futures ahead, are acquiring sophisticated training and knowledge at their university courses and have loyal and supportive boyfriends whom they plan to marry when the right time comes.

Conclusion

The sections of this chapter about intimacy and social media refer primarily to cases related to teenagers. However, as the ethnographic evidence suggests, the online social relations of teenagers and young adults generally differ from adults (in relation, for instance, to infidelity) only because of the time they have available to use social media and their subsequent level of experience. Their online presence reproduces experiences that previously took place in the context of face-to-face exchanges. The apparent modernity of social media can make it difficult to see the effects online communication has on local social relations. At first we might be tempted to see the novelties of computers and the internet being quickly adopted and incorporated into the daily routines of these low-income Brazilians. However, the everyday use of social media in Balduíno shows similar results to the ethnography Fonseca produced during the 1980s and 1990s, discussed in the early sections of this chapter. In my Bahian field site, the presence of government services has expanded noticeably in the past few decades in terms of health services, schooling and police, among others. However, support networks are still intrinsic to living there; social media has been incorporated often not as a driver of change but rather as a means to reproduce the possibilities for creating and cultivating alliances.

As the initial sections of this chapter also indicate, locals bring to social media the values that their community has traditionally held for many years. The way in which teenagers 'friend' people from outside Balduíno follows a similar pattern to a local form of relationships offline. These online 'friends' are just like the people in the settlement whom they 'know by sight'. But as social media users move to 'friending' inside the settlement, a conflict develops between tradition and new technologies. Locals try to establish new connections independently of face-to-face networks of relationships, and yet these new relationships tend not to evolve. The desire to meet this other person known only 'by sight' is insufficient to challenge the fear of greeting a person who might not greet back. The actual relationships that prosper online are often those of previously existing networks, established through face-to-face interactions in the neighbourhood, at work, at school or at church. Once these face-to-face relationships exist, online becomes yet another medium for the person to create and nurture his or her position within networks of mutual help that expand beyond direct family bonds.

The middle part of this chapter focuses on romance and infidelity, showing the sophisticated and creative use of social media when it comes to cheating on one's partner or to reducing the possibilities for being cheated on. No topic is more closely related to conversations about social media locally – particularly among men – than the many ways in which these platforms help with flirting and also spying on others. Sometimes couples agree to exchange their social media passwords as a sign of trust, so that each one can see to whom the other is speaking and the conversations they have, but the outcomes of these experiments are not considered entirely satisfactory. Traditionally in the region both men and women tend to have several partners (sometimes simultaneously) during their lives. Social media does nothing to make people more faithful to their relationships. If anything, it makes them more excited about the possibilities of having secret lovers, and also more stressed as a consequence of the expected acts of spying and social control.

From the perspective of affluent, middle-class values, it is often tempting to classify relationships outside the nuclear family as problematic or less structured, possibly the result of 'corrupted' family morals or practices driven by their inferior socioeconomic situation.[58] However, the way that locals in Balduíno use social media today suggests that at least part of the population, both men and women, want to keep the possibility of having more than one relationship during their lives. With regard to this subject, therefore, we conclude that social media is popular for channelling many people's choices to retain established norms and practices concerning romance.

The final sections, in which we explore parent–child relations, show that there is a lot going on between generations through social media. In the region, low-income women have historically been in charge of the family house and of their children. They now face a difficult decision in relation to raising and protecting their children. The settlement is a volatile place for teenagers to live these days, as drug dealing and other forms of crime provide access to new and more exciting possibilities of consumption. Traditional forms of entertainment such as going to the river or the beach are not as safe as they once were, nor as enchanting as modern alternatives such as going to the gym, having an ice cream at the fancy fast-food joint, going to the mall or playing video games. To try to offer some of these opportunities while keeping one's child out of danger (often without support from his or her father), these mothers often work formally outside of the settlement, leaving their children on their own for some hours of the day. The arrival of WhatsApp means that such women can quickly send and receive text and audio messages to and from the children, and attempt to monitor their whereabouts. In the following chapter we further examine the accumulation of their roles as both mothers and formal employees who spend most of their days away from the house.

Even if their mothers now have smartphones to keep in touch with their children, however, the latter are not easily giving up their traditional freedoms. The relatively peripheral areas of the settlement have long been used by teenagers to meet up away from the control of adult authority. The issue here has different, and complex, layers: teenage pregnancy is not the consequence of a new means of communication, nor is it responsible for locals using it to flirt and to spy on each other. As the book has shown so far, the changes taking place in the settlement relate mainly to the possibilities of having formal employment and the radical increase in the presence of evangelical churches.

Parents who belong to evangelical organisations are making greater efforts to promote a structure of family very different from local traditions. In this ideal, the same two people meet and stay together, are faithful to one another and have less distinct roles: both should study, have careers and contribute to caring for children and household expenses. However, in general evangelical parents (especially when mothers are also working outside of the settlement) struggle to control their offspring and impose these strict values; today's teenagers will always know more about social media than adults and can circumvent attempts at monitoring. And yet, as the last case shows, social media is also becoming a space in which these evangelical teenagers can craft identities that retain certain aspects of their faiths, such as avoiding drinking and premarital sex, while at the same time presenting themselves as modern in terms of aspiration for, and access to, education and careers. Viewed from this perspective, religious beliefs do not make them appear backward: they make them seem advanced and proud.

This chapter has mainly shown how social media has not significantly changed personal social relations in Balduíno. The way in which people use social media is broadly informed by forms of sociality that derive from face-to-face interaction; these follow norms that regulate relationships in families and inside broader networks of support and help. Social media is popular largely because it provides opportunities for people to embrace external processes of change and modernisation while retaining many traditional social values. However, social media is not just being widely used; it brings the chance to employ alternative channels to communicate and form alliances, and also poses new situations of conflict. The argument is that the people of Balduíno are using technology to be more like themselves. Yet technology is not a 'neutral agent': even as locals use social media, they are also reshaping social relationships and values.

5
Education and work: tensions in class

Education is a common theme used to illustrate the advantages – but also the problems – that digital communication brings to society. Framed in a positive light, social media provides underprivileged populations, such as those living in Balduíno, with access to information and knowledge that was previously confined to the socioeconomic elites. But the cases presented below show that the consequences of digital communication in the settlement are not easily interpreted. Talk to local teachers and they will probably say that social media is a 'tragedy' that makes teaching and dealing with students more difficult. What they mean is that local schools have already fallen behind compared to the infrastructure and the higher quality staff available to the middle and upper classes through private institutions; unlike the families of students from affluent backgrounds, parents and relatives in Balduíno are mostly functionally illiterate and unable to assist their offspring with their homework. On top of these problems, teachers complain that students are now spending not only their free time but also their classroom time monitoring conversations and interacting with peers through Facebook and WhatsApp.

To address these complex issues, it is important to see how schooling has evolved in Balduíno. By all possible measures, students today have much better educational conditions than their parents did: the number of years of mandatory education available in the settlement has increased from 4 to 12 and, while in the past many families prevented children from going to school, today literally every child attends classes and receives the necessary resources to study. However, in general students in Balduíno are not interested in formal education. Many finish high school only because a diploma increases their chances of competing successfully for similar low-income manual jobs to those their parents do.

And yet, while teachers are right to say that schools have become 'facebooked' (turned into a meeting ground for young people to socialise when they are not on social media), the ethnography shows that digital communication has improved locals' literacy and is often used as a source of information to deal with everyday issues. Furthermore, social media has also become instrumental for people – especially women – to pursue formal work or university degrees, which demand that they leave their homes and spend part of their days away from their local support networks. The relationship of social media and education in Balduíno is complex, therefore, and needs to be explored further.

The chapter is based on a variety of case studies, some featuring teenagers still at high school, others young people starting their professional lives and yet others involving adults who left school years earlier. Some of the stories are of people who, like many in the settlement, are not particularly convinced of the advantages of formal education, but we also examine instances of locals who have made strenuous efforts to go to university. The perspectives of men are important because they are in general more resistant to formal arrangements, including employment, that demand submission to schedules and bosses. But the views of women are also relevant, as traditionally in the region they have been responsible for homes and childcare; the prospect of formal employment has shifted priorities for many, who now perhaps delay their plans to start a family and invest time in studying and building a career. Finally we also consider how evangelical Christians use social media to further their educational and professional aims. Throughout this book evangelical Christianity has constantly been associated with literacy and aspiration, and not surprisingly a significant number of local university students are evangelical or have evangelical parents. Having to spend long hours commuting every day, these students count on social media to co-ordinate their classroom activities. However, the online domain is also used to cultivate relationships outside of established religious boundaries.

Schooling in the settlement

Like other nearby settlements, Balduíno has had a public school since the first half of the twentieth century, but these institutions offered very limited services. The school building in the 1980s had four classrooms and its teachers (always female) either moved from Salvador to take the position or were the educated daughters of distinguished local men (property owners). Classrooms had few material resources and students were often barefoot, wearing old, used clothes. Teaching methods, which included routine physical punishment using spanking paddles,[1] were relatively primitive.

While the state has now strengthened the incentives for underprivileged children to be sent to school, until the late 1980s and early 1990s many parents preferred to have their children available to work and to help at home. The children allowed to take the school's four-year programme were taught to read and write; they studied basic maths, science and history and were lectured in a mandatory discipline called 'Education, moral and civic'. However, the difficulties these adults have today in reading, writing and performing basic calculations suggests that they ended their schooling as functionally illiterate,[2] not then a problem considering their work prospects. During pre-teenage years boys often helped other male relatives (for example as builders, fishermen, some traders), while girls assisted their mothers at home, helping to raise younger siblings and also participate in productive group activities in the locality such as gathering wood and foods from the forest, weaving straw (to make hats and other products) and fishing for shellfish, crabs and shrimp in the river.

Ricardo, a geography teacher in his late thirties, is one of the few people of his age in Balduíno with a university degree. His family owned a small shop in the locality, but their business did not provide them with a better lifestyle than families of fishermen and builders had then. So Ricardo grew up as a local boy, doing what all others of his age did: fishing, stealing fruits and goats, chickens or fish for fun, playing football, helping at home and going with peers to festivities in neighbouring settlements. However, Ricardo's father had more formal education than most people in the settlement. Born in Salvador, he read newspapers, could write messages and notes on paper, and performed algebra calculations in his sales work. Ricardo says that it was to honour and impress his father that he decided to step away from the everyday routines of other children in order to carry on studying.

Supporting Ricardo remaining in school from the age of 11 (his fifth school year) was expensive for a family of their income level. A variety of costs were incurred by keeping him studying. Firstly, because he was away or doing homework during the day, he was not around to help with the shop. The family had to pay for his daily travel to school, a journey of 30 km, and back; they also had to purchase books, notebooks and other necessary equipment. Seven years later Ricardo was finally accepted at a free public university in Salvador, but his financial difficulties continued. For lack of money, during a long period of his four-year course he had to spend nights secretly in the students' common room (after everyone else left at 11 pm), eat only one meal a day, consisting of bread and butter, and go home only at weekends.

At home he could eat and sleep properly, but his weekly visits to the settlement were nonetheless stressful. His peers were then beginning to make a little money (for example by catching and selling fish and lobster to affluent visitors, or by working as builders); they could purchase new clothes, shoes and, very importantly, develop relationships and buy gifts for girlfriends. Ricardo still remembers with bitterness one girl who dumped him because she, like everyone else, could not see the point of studying when easier money could be made without leaving Balduíno. Because of his insistence on pursuing a university degree, Ricardo was also commonly treated as arrogant.[3] This became apparent when his peers would say provocative things such as 'no, you won't like this music. You only like city music now', and generally make him feel an outsider.

Only one generation later, the Coconut Coast is a different place when it comes to education. Instead of the four-year basic programme, today Balduíno has two schools providing foundation-level education (years 1 to 8) and a secondary school offering middle-level education (years 9 to 12); schooling is compulsory.[4] The number of students in the settlement, just a few dozen when Ricardo started studying, is now over 2,000. Elementary schools are in better shape: their buildings include proper offices for administration, a staff room, telephones, internet-connected computers (used by staff members only, though students often find out the password), toilets, an industrial kitchen to cook meals for students and staff, areas for students to gather outside of classrooms and, in one of the schools, a sports court. On top of all this, students now receive everything needed to go to class for free: uniforms, transport to and from home, textbooks and other classroom material, plus extracurricular activities to help students with academic difficulties.

However, the presence of this infrastructure is not always sufficient to encourage families to embrace formal education programmes. The following case presents some of the difficulties faced by local students who attempt to move away from traditional gender roles through education and work.

'I lived on a different planet'

When Maria was growing up, she accepted various invitations from evangelical Christian schoolmates to visit their churches. She tried several and spent longer periods of time attending services in some of them, but, like other locals, during her teenage years she gradually lost interest in spending time in church activities. Maria explained that she grew progressively disillusioned by the 'hypocrisy' of evangelical Christians: 'they talk so much about God, but what really matters for them is money'. Although Maria has now rejected this form of religion, her choices concerning work as an adult look similar to the path often taken by evangelical Christian women, in terms of delaying motherhood to focus on their careers and looking for better paying jobs that offer security.

Aged 22, Maria works as a bar assistant at one of the region's upscale tourist resorts. Although this is a relatively less prestigious job in these businesses (viewed as being more 'manual' in comparison with a reception desk or an office), it has been a tough journey for her to arrive there. As she explained, during most of her teenage years she 'lived on a different planet', but relationships formed at school with other female students of similar background made her realise there were new paths for women to follow in the region. Her peers talked excitedly about taking short-term professional courses[5] in Camaçari city to enhance their employment prospects, and she decided to do the same. But Maria's family, particularly her mother, did not agree with her decision. For them it had already been unsettling that Maria, a girl, stayed to finish secondary school while her older brother did not. In their view, her priority should be becoming a mother and caring for her home (cleaning, cooking and bringing up her children), so she should take on only an informal job at some shop in Balduíno to help with the income of the home.

Family resistance towards Maria's desire to follow a different path had two consequences. It created distance between Maria and her mother, to the extent that they now barely talk, and it made Maria more determined to pursue a more professional career path. Like many others of similar age and background in Balduíno, she signed up for the 'Jovem Aprendiz'' (Young Apprentice Programme), a training scheme paid for by the region's large hotels. At these courses 'apprentices' have classes on working practices, standards and etiquette related to the leisure industry. They learn, among other things, the levels of hygiene that have to be maintained in industrial kitchens, ways of interacting with clients and how to use standard spoken Portuguese. Together with classroom activities, the scheme provides temporary employment to young locals to acquire work experience. After the 'trainee period' ends, some candidates are selected for formal employment, based on their performance on the scheme.

Given the difficult relationship Maria has with her mother, she eventually decided to move in with her long-term boyfriend. She says that it is now too late for her to go to university considering the limitations of her income and her age, but she views her current work status as a step up from the ('locked-up-at-home') life women such as her mother have had to accept in Balduíno. Having a formal job gives Maria a sense of independence and autonomy, as her wage, career prospects and benefits are similar to those of her partner. However, like other working women in Balduíno, when she arrives home she is still responsible for cooking, cleaning and childcare, if she has a family.

Like almost everyone in her age group, Maria is at ease with social media, but being online was not as important as being at school from the point of broadening her career prospects. She took a step in a new direction because she had seen other local girls sharing their enthusiasm for new work opportunities. However, social media has been important to consolidate her transition from a situation that felt like being 'locked up at home' to having formal employment away from the settlement. Though Maria managed to overcome her family's resistance and was successful at pursuing formal employment, the mobile phone, and now WhatsApp, became instrumental for her to manage this new experience. These are technologies she now uses more intensively, as they allow her to remain part of her support networks by keeping in touch with close friends and family members. She is also able to support them and participate in the circulation of gossip that, as Chapter 4 explained, is an important part of her life.

So far we have considered the transformation that has taken place in Balduíno since the 1990s when Ricardo decided to pursue a university degree. Schools have improved considerably, so people such as Maria have all the resources necessary to finish 12 years of compulsory education. She has been using social media since her teens, initially through internet cafés, as other locals did. Yet when she describes the experience that changed her professional path, she does not mention social media or her teachers. Rather she speaks of how she felt encouraged to pursue a different career because of her relationships with peers. So before examining the effects of social media on learning and education, it is useful now briefly to examine why teachers are not particularly mentioned when local students discuss their education and careers.

Better schools, new problems

When Balduíno had only one school with four classes, parents were accepting of, and often encouraged, teachers physically disciplining their offspring. Until the early 1990s the spanking paddle was just as much part of the teaching equipment in local classrooms as the blackboard. But now things have changed, and not only for the better. Students have better facilities and more teachers; they do not have to travel to finish compulsory education and receive all necessary material free from the government. However, problems between students and teachers, and more broadly between locals and local schools, are rising in the settlement. Maria's case starts with her family's opposition towards her determination to finish high school when her brother did not. In the following paragraphs I will present some of the factors that have made schools become disputed spaces in Balduíno.

One of the basic issues with today's local schools has to do with many teachers being strangers to Balduíno. Schools prefer to hire people from the region, but there aren't enough qualified teachers living there to take these positions, so most teaching staff commute daily from the city. This creates new anxieties. Some parents and relatives complain about the high rate of absence among teachers, which happens for a range of reasons including lack of motivation and problems with commuting. This recurrent situation means that students are often unsupervised during class hours, and so more likely to get themselves into trouble with drugs, leading to unintended pregnancies, etc. However, another reason why parents complain is their fear of what these teachers can do to their children. The private lives of teachers not living in the settlement are beyond the reach of the local gossip networks so parents often worry that some of these strangers are paedophiles and sexual predators.[6]

The tensions between staff and students also increase because schools are overcrowded. In the era of compulsory education local head teachers are obliged to accept anyone, with the result that spaces initially planned to be libraries or computer rooms become classes.[7] The growing number of students reflects the effects of two economic-related factors. One factor is that more low-income families now benefit from certain welfare schemes under the condition that their offspring are registered and attend school regularly.[8] The other is that, with the expansion of the formal job market in the region, parents – and increasingly mothers – are taking advantage of these opportunities to work and make money, but they have also to deal with the criticism of 'leaving children behind' and concerns about drug addiction and crime. These people see schools as places that will take care of their children for at least half of the working day. These two new situations are important to understand the increase in the number of students. Children should attend schools regardless of these issues, but the reality is that the school system, though expanded, is not able to manage the size of the influx and the challenges that these new conditions have created.

Furthermore, while these families send their children to school, they are not necessarily interested in pushing them to study. They may lack the knowledge to assist their sons and daughters with lessons in maths or biology, but they may also often be sceptical about the advantages of 'having an education' for their children. To local families on the lowest incomes, for instance, the amount of time young people spend in internet cafés using social media represents a clearer indication of a promising future than going to school;[9] knowing how to use a computer looks more like a specific skill that can help young people make money. So many parents who make their children attend classes do not stimulate or motivate them to do their homework or to study for tests, which makes the work of teachers more difficult and frustrating. As a consequence, teachers not only have to look after a growing number of students, but they are also, in general, the only ones concerned about educating these young people.

It is not just a matter of students having academic limitations to follow up with classes: it is rather that they are often not interested. I experienced this first-hand when I took care of a class of around 30 seventh graders (aged about 13) for two consecutive 50-minute classes. Since I only had to make sure they stayed in class and behaved, I proposed we spent the time having a conversation about things they were interested in, such as WhatsApp or gaming. After several attempts, I realised the only activity that more or less kept them busy and quiet was dictation. Otherwise, most children were both excited and entertained by undermining my attempts to interact with them. As the following case argues, many young people may actually want to finish high school, but learning has little to do with their choice.

A high school diploma to be 'tranquilo'

Diego had both parents at home when he grew up and enjoyed a comfortable life in comparison to most in Balduíno. His family home, located at a premium spot near the main street, has a DVD player, an X-Box game console, a laptop with broadband service and a 25-inch flat screen television that receives cable TV programming, including the more expensive movie channels. This high-tech environment results in part from Diego's fascination with technology. He is the family nerd. His father, an illiterate fisherman, speaks very proudly of how Diego helps him to access online information about weather conditions before he sets sail. Diego is also constantly asked to resolve issues related to smartphones and computers – not only for his family but also for friends and neighbours. Most of these issues include uploading files to a phone, downloading and installing apps or changing equipment settings. And when it comes to more challenging problems, he resolves them using Google, studying threads of exchanges on forums, watching YouTube videos and also talking to friends who are equally into 'messing around and geeking out'[10] ('*fuçando*' or '*bulindo*') with digital equipment.

Diego says his parents did not push him to do well at school, and that his only aim with finishing secondary school was to take advantage of the symbolic value this diploma holds in the region's leisure job market. Five years ago, when he joined the staff of waiters of the upmarket tourist resort, he was not just the youngest in a large team (waiters at this hotel attend guests in four restaurants and eight swimming pools); he was also the only one with a high school diploma. Given the lack of local workers with better literacy, hotels have to transport employees back and forth from Salvador – even some of those working in positions that do not need specific training or accreditation, such as waiters or security guards. So these businesses appreciate a candidate for a low-wage position who has spent 12 years at school.[11] Diego, seeing this potential, got the position at this hotel. He has benefits that include health and dental private insurance, as well as food stamps (*vale refeição*) that his family can use at supermarkets.

Despite having the curiosity and talent to deal with electronic equipment, Diego did not want to spend another three or four years studying in a university or on professional technical courses in order to become an independent technician or an IT person at local businesses. Another option for him was to be trained with his father and eventually take over his boat – an expensive item – and still make good money as a fisherman and taking tourists on fishing trips. Instead, at 17 years old, Diego began working as an assistant waiter at a hotel resort. He acknowledges that if it wasn't for the internet he would be a '*tabareu*' (hick, an ignorant person). However, his plans for the future consist of having money to afford his bills (*pagar as contas*), go out with his friends and play his beloved video games. He wants to be '*tranquilo*' (at ease) with regular working days and hours, to have good benefits and to enjoy the security of getting paid at the end of each month.

Some young people in Balduíno turned their passion for computers and the internet into a profession by becoming local technicians and servicing computers, or opening businesses such as internet cafés. However, cases such as Maria's and Diego's represent the ambitions of many local young people. They see formal employment as advantageous for the consumption of goods (especially those they have seen on television); it also brings them greater legal protection as workers (with consequently less chance of being fired) and access to private health care. Neither is among the more vulnerable groups in Balduíno, who consider formal employment to be 'modern-day slavery' and declare they prefer to work autonomously as builders or as motorcycle taxi drivers. To Diego and Maria, the important thing is to be sure that their wages will be available to them at the end of the month. In the following section we will consider what is keeping young people like them from also taking more advantage of formal education. As things stand today, the school is mostly a hurdle one needs to overome to reach formal employment.

Class separations[12]

The lack of discipline in school and constant challenges to the staff's authority is mainly visible in the form of a generalised rejection of the mandatory uniform (shirt with school logo and blue denim trousers). Instead students arrive in the morning wearing part of the uniform together with a variety of other items (usually associated with hip-hop culture): expensive caps, thick golden necklaces and earrings, branded sandals or tennis shoes, mini-skirts, colourful shirts and bermuda shorts. This aspect of school life has become such a difficult problem that in one of the schools the head teacher now sits at the entrance gate every day before class starts and inspects each of the pupils personally, 'because they will not respect and obey anyone else'.

This growing 'insubordination' relates to the lack of concern displayed by some families towards formal education, and also the problem of teachers coming from outside the community, as noted above. However, the ethnography indicates that this confrontation of authority is also an issue of social class. While part of the younger population is more open to the constraints and advantages of formal work, in general work relations are a sensitive issue. The uneasiness felt in classrooms appears similar to that experienced by local adult employees, also commonly insubordinate in a workplace structure. They express their unease in a variety of ways. They may openly reject any type of subordinate employment, collectively or individually boycott certain bosses, deliberately choose temporary jobs instead of formal contracts or accept formal employment temporarily, only to force a situation in which they are fired and can then collect unemployment benefits. Like Diego's father, other adults often talk about formal work as being a type of 'modern-day slavery'.

Such resistance to formal structures of work by low-income groups has been previously analysed as being a strategy of self-preservation.[13] The argument is that the individuals belonging to the more marginalised (often referred as sub-proletarian) strata in Brazil are constantly being shown that the best work available to untrained manual labour depends on 'good appearance' – a criteria that refers to having a certain taste (shown in one's choice of clothing and hairstyle)[14] and that also relates to skin colour. Those coming from underprivileged rural backgrounds (usually of African descent and with little or no schooling) learn that the only regular employment to which they can aspire in cities is that in which they need to 'break their backs' serving younger and less experienced affluent bosses – who in turn will often use their position and social class to justify abusive behaviour. Unsurprisingly they prefer ways of making money that are independent and informal. In Balduíno this translates to a range of informal activities. Driving a moto-taxi is a popular option among the young, but others include working as an independent builder, a fisherman or selling products on the streets.

Like managers in work environments, teachers often come from urban backgrounds and may get impatient when students from a rural family background do not follow academic programmes that also reflect middle-class values.[15] In a similar way to their parents in work situations, young locals at school are constantly made aware of their inferior socioeconomic status because they are 'hopelessly ignorant'.[16] If some employers in work environments talk openly about how their employees cannot be trusted and are dirty and lazy (even if the individuals are nearby at the time), in schools teachers similarly talk about the 'serious deficiencies' that their students face and point to how many 'have been in school for five years or more but can barely read and write'. This identification of teachers with employers adds to the various other factors to complicate the unfortunately marginal position schools have in young people's lives.

As Chapter 2 shows, parents and other adult family members are themselves often critical of 'young people's lack of respect today', expressed in the form of a lack of discipline, materialism and what they perceive to be an aversion to hard work. But when it comes to problems that their children have in such institutions these people, instead of supporting schools to put pressure on students to behave, become their children's advocate, deploring what they consider to be 'discrimination', 'harassment' and 'unfair treatment'. While at work low-income people understand themselves as being the ones with the least institutional power, when it comes to school the relationship changes: they are acting as clients of a service, so they feel more at ease to complain.

Finally, while parents act to defend their offspring, schools in the settlement are also increasingly becoming part of the territory belonging to drug gangs. The regular absence of teachers means that students are constantly hanging out outside classrooms or in the areas next to schools, where they are easy targets. Yet situations related to drug consumption and trafficking also happen in the day time, during normal working hours and while teachers are in class. I was present at a local school when a teacher arrived nervously in the staff common room saying that three girls (aged between 11 and 12) had just been trying cocaine during his class. He did not see it happening because they were behind other students, but after the class dispersed another student told him what had happened. Confronted with such pressures, the principal of the largest local school went from classroom to classroom announcing to students he was giving up his 'sovereignty' inside school grounds. He had decided to bring the police in to deal with events and matters that he and his staff saw as beyond their scope and responsibility.

How school staff see social media

The background presented in the previous section is necessary to then consider where the staff of local schools are coming from when they talk about social media, which is mainly associated with a lack of discipline. Their view often divides the internet into the good and the bad.[17] In their reasoning, one of the benefits is that it can provide an invaluable advantage to students lacking favourable material conditions and family support for studying, and could consequently open a path to better opportunities and socioeconomic evolution. The best representation they have of the 'good internet' is Google, which they refer to as an online library with all sorts of useful educational content that local students can now access. Yet despite this unprecedented variety of resources being available to them through the 'good internet', students choose to indulge in the 'bad internet' represented by social media.

As one head teacher explained, social media consumes the little attention that these students once devoted to classroom work. Her perspective is that before internet-connected mobiles, the school was firstly a place that provided formal education and secondly – only as a relatively unimportant outcome – a place where students got together and socialised before and after class. Now the order of priorities is the opposite. She explains that it is not just a matter of using mobiles during class, but of how students now interact with each other continuously even while they are away. 'They talk and talk and talk using their phones while they are apart. Then they meet at school and the conversation goes on! I really do not understand what subjects are sucking their attention this way,' she says, sounding frustrated but resigned.[18] Her conclusion about this recent and evolving scenario is that local schools have been 'facebooked': they now exist as a space for a daily social gathering of young people to expand conversations circulating through Facebook and WhatsApp.

Though this argument is not new, and indeed echoes the perceptions of parents and teachers in other parts of the world,[19] it needs to be relativised and contextualised to the Coconut Coast. The position of teachers and school staff as 'outsiders' in Balduíno is mainly responsible for their pessimistic view of social media. As a whole, they blame social media for the failings of a poor educational system. As other ethnographies from the 'Why We Post' project have shown, social media is many different things with different consequences, some of which are forms of formal and informal learning.[20] Locals as a whole say that they are better informed of things happening outside the settlement as a consequence of using social media, and young people refer to it as something that has broadened their personal experiences drastically, in contrast to the limitations of their older relatives. A teenager observed that without the internet he would be a 'vegetable'. This contrasts with the generally pessimistic perspectives that teachers have about digital communication.

The following pages describe how the constant use of social media – contrary to what the teachers say – can actually help teenagers and young adults to learn, and particularly to improve their literacy skills. It thus makes university education and professional diplomas more attainable for the new generation living in Balduíno.

Social media as a school

For teens and also for interested adults in Balduíno, Google and especially YouTube represent a repository of information about practical things they want to learn.[21] Mainly YouTube, but also some other specialised forums, provide information about even highly complex procedures. For example, I saw teenagers at an internet café looking up videos to teach them how to install a small hardware item called Gevey that they had successfully imported from China. At the time Gevey was a solution to bypass technical locks that prevented an iPhone 4 originally used in Europe from being unlocked to operate in other regions. Nor is this an exceptional case of learning taking place with the help of digital resources. YouTube, often described more abstractly as an online video platform, is used routinely as a source of tutorials for different demands.[22] Locals use it often inside social media to share video content, but they also use it independently when it comes to resolving practical matters (Fig. 5.1), as in the following examples.

Fernando, a 38-year-old builder, is functionally illiterate, but wanted his children to be able to access the internet at home. However, they live in a squatting area, where the electricity they use is illegally channelled to the constantly varying number of houses in that area. Fernando and his teenage son thus went to the internet café to learn how to install a certain brand and model of a no-break system, in order to protect the family computer from fluctuations in electricity. YouTube is crucial for them because they can see and hear the instructions instead of having to read text and follow diagrams.

After having safely turned on the computer, a friend of Fernando offered him free access to broadband. This friend wanted to test a recent experiment he had made to install an antenna at home, together with equipment to broadcast his broadband signal through radio. He then hoped to provide this service to other squatters interested in having a home internet connection.

Fig. 5.1 A local man learning how to fix a car engine using YouTube

The internet is also a source of other kinds of information and knowledge. It is used, for example, to fulfil needs relating to the weak government services available in Balduíno – another practical reality of living there. Luciana, a 35-year-old mother of three, uses both Facebook and YouTube intensively to gain information. Her family moved to Balduíno from Salvador in the 1970s, seeking to escape the growing violence in the city's *favelas*. She worked as a daily cleaner for affluent families, but since she had a nervous breakdown[23] ten years ago – when a nephew was murdered while serving a prison sentence – she has struggled to find regular employment: her confidence is low and her emotional state uncertain. Though she has the support of her family (most of her brothers and sisters live in various houses in the same street), Luciana and her partner have scant resources to get by. He does odd jobs as a cropper and she mostly stays at home. But he managed to barter for an old computer in exchange for a plot of land he had acquired years earlier at an abandoned farm, and they also sublet the broadband connection from a neighbour. Since then they have been intensively using this new opportunity for communication.

Luciana has specific health issues that the health facility in Balduíno cannot accommodate. In contrast to schools, which have evolved considerably in the last two decades as described above, local health services remain precarious. Aside from a broad lack of motivation among nurses and other employees, general practitioners are available only on certain days and within certain hours, meaning that people have to queue for hours in the morning to schedule an appointment. Luciana's mental condition is currently stable, but she cannot schedule to see a specialist in Balduíno. So when the circumstances demand, she asks friends or family members to accompany her during the long commute by bus to and from the county's public hospital. Now, though, access to the internet allows her to obtain information without having to undertake such a strenuous journey.

Being a long-term evangelical Christian, Luciana reads and writes better than the average person. So to her and other literate adults, Google has become a sort of 'house doctor'. YouTube is valued for specific and often practical situations such as those described above, but it is not as useful when it comes to medical issues. Luciana accesses the internet constantly to find information, from the possible diagnosis of a group of symptoms to a check on whether certain conditions she has experienced could be side-effects of medicines. This type of information is abundantly available in textual format online and Luciana is becoming increasingly experienced in making these searches. However, self-diagnosis and self-prescription of medicines can cause new complications for her and other locals in Balduíno.

Social media is also part of the strategy Luciana created to earn money when she does not feel confident enough to leave her home. She searches on YouTube for video tutorials showing how to make party food and also subscribes to different Facebook pages which specialise in cooking tutorials. She gathers these recipes and now earns money cooking and selling food for birthday parties, weddings and other celebrations. Luciana also photographs and uploads the results of the various orders she has cooked as a way of advertising her activity.

Being an evangelical Christian puts Luciana in a better position than most locals of her age because she has been a reader for many years. However, as the following section indicates, social media has made reading and writing an integral part of the everyday practices of the settlement's young people.

Spellchecking and the public display of literacy

Until the growth of interest in social media, and with the exception of evangelical Christians, people in Balduíno were not generally interested in reading and did not practice writing. The perception of most in the settlement until the recent past was that (as Ricardo's case shows) studying was a waste of time. As a local elderly man summarised, explaining his father's decision in the 1940s not to allow him to go to school: 'the literate get by, and the illiterate get by just the same'. This low regard for literacy appears, for example, in the local library, which is indefinitely closed, and with the general lack of interest for consuming printed media in Balduíno. The only places that sell newspapers and magazines there are the local pharmacies, as these are businesses where affluent travellers stop by as they enter the settlement, to shop for provisions on their way to other locations.

Social media has changed this disregard for textual communication, particularly among young people, because literacy combined with online communication opens up a social domain that adults in general cannot reach, as explained in Chapters 2 and 4. Since internet cafés began to operate in the late 2000s, reading and writing moved from being something taught and used only in classrooms to becoming a cool skill that expanded one's possibilities for social interaction and the exchange of content.[24] From 2013, when inexpensive smartphones began to flourish among young people, an inversion happened. Before that date they rarely practiced reading or writing, but after it reading and writing became about the only thing that they do continuously: at home, out with friends, at school and, especially, during long bus journeys. The change impacted, for instance, on family relationships, with illiterate parents and other adults suddenly finding themselves socially isolated and alone while children and younger relatives devoted hours to conversations through social media.[25]

But social media is not just a place for practising literacy skills. Part of the improvement in writing results from locals becoming more aware of their poor literacy, and the public nature of their resulting embarrassment. Now any mistakes they make on the posts they upload to Facebook or on WhatsApp exchanges can be seen by all. As young people began using social media, the more learned used writing to display achievement (similar to wearing brand name clothes) and the least literate became aware that what they posted needed to be correct in order to avoid public ridicule.[26] With regard to this second situation, a phrase occasionally seen on Facebook comments among young people was: 'You think so much of yourself and yet you cannot even write correctly.'

In a nutshell, young people found themselves trapped between having to participate in social media exchanges, while at the same time having to worry about the accuracy of their written language. Their generation could not hide behind the simple practices of sharing or liking, as their parents and older relatives do (see Chapter 3). Because young people are identifying themselves in contrast with previous generations through digital technology, they need to use it more capably and proficiently, including writing correct posts (Fig. 5.2). Teachers in the settlement, themselves in general less knowledgeable about social media than their students, apparently disregard the anxiety that using social media brings to young locals. Yet I found that, based on 15 months living in the settlement, the one common experience all young people in Balduíno had was the fear of writing incorrectly on social media and being subjected to public shaming as a result.

This context – of having the pressure to write correctly to be respected on social media – led locals to embrace all possible technological solutions within reach to improve the standard of their writing. Some have spell-checking apps on their mobiles and computers, and use them thoroughly. Others with less capable phones, or those lacking technical literacy, will 'google' the word to see whether the autocomplete feature[27] points to an alternate spelling. This Google search functionality is also useful because the person can look for a certain phrase to confirm whether verb tenses and plural forms are correctly applied. But finally, if after using these resources they still do not feel sure about the spelling and cannot find a synonym, most decide not to post, to avoid the possibility of being laughed at by peers online.

As my research happened during the period in which WhatsApp and mobile internet became popular, I followed the change in the quality

Fig. 5.2   A Balduíno local using social media at a bar

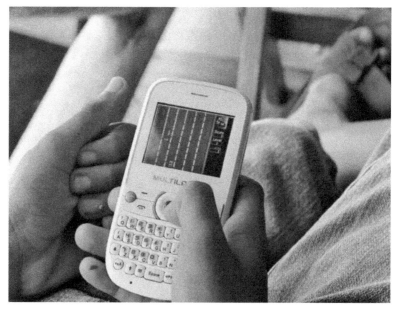

Fig. 5.3   A child playing an online game using a smartphone

of texts locals sent during personal exchanges or posted on Facebook. The movement to WhatsApp is important in the sense that previously locals depended on internet cafés or home computers to interact on social media. As they embraced WhatsApp, they also started to use pay-as-you-go plans to access the internet at any time and from anywhere.

When I arrived in the settlement, their writing was similar to speaking:[28] people spelled words as they sounded, and many found full stops and commas vague abstractions that they used almost randomly. Also, like their spoken Portuguese, their writing disregarded the often confusing grammar rules concerning verbal tenses and the use of singular and plural. So in the beginning of my field work I could see some serious language mistakes, even among university students. Gradually this changed, however, and as I finish the writing of this book in late 2016, it is impressive to see the evolution of the textual content that young people currently post online. Many of the formerly recurrent misspellings and grammatical errors now appear only rarely on Facebook and WhatsApp exchanges. The common mistakes that remain are the indiscriminate interchanging of words with similar sounds such as 'mais' and 'mas' or 'me' and 'mim'.

The effect of social media upon teenagers and young people is also having an influence on children, largely as a consequence of their interest in online gaming. The next section gives an idea of how being able to access the internet and play online has become not just a common leisure activity, but also a prestigious practice leading to the acquisition of knowledge that improves literacy.

Children and gaming

Balduíno still does not have the same types of social hurdles as cities in Brazil. For instance, the settlement does not have 'street kids' who have run away from home or been abandoned by their families. Even the more vulnerable children have a home and a parent or relative, so I was surprised one day to see a child beg for money near the cashier of the local bakery. However, as the baker quickly explained, the boy was not homeless. He lived with his mother, but she worked all day and he (at the age of eight) was left behind by himself. The money that the child was collecting was not, as was the begging that we saw in cities, to be used to buy food or drugs. As his classes were only in the morning,[29] the child spent many hours during his afternoons in the internet café across the street from the bakery; since he did not have money to pay for the access, he would come to the bakery and collect a few coins before going back again. The money was not used to access social media, as this does not particularly interest local children of that age, but to access game portals. He played these games to pass time, but also because this is something that enchants children of his age (Fig. 5.3).

Local children rarely have mobiles with an internet connection, so they either play more primitive games on their phones or rely on using computers. At a local NGO, created to provide complimentary classes to students with low academic performance (*reforço*), teachers take advantage of children's interest for gaming to negotiate deals to ensure they co-operate during class (Fig. 5.4). Namely, the teacher offers time in the computer room in exchange for successfully answering questions on the topic being taught. However, teachers tend to talk about this situation with the same pessimism described above in relation to their peers working in public schools. When we chatted about children's fascination with gaming, one of the teachers commented that 'before the internet, all they wanted was to be outside playing football…' She paused for a moment, then added sadly: 'At least playing football meant they were exercising…'

This view often stresses the negative effects of gaming (such as having less time to do homework). This may sometimes be true, but it disregards the other consequences that result from the effort local children put into learning how to use digital media to play computer games.

As video game consoles are not as available to children as computers, those aged five years and over play simple action games provided at certain portals.[30] As instructions and other information are often written in English, they learn by watching others play and exchanging tips with peers.[31] However, the consequences go beyond gaming. In order

Fig. 5.4   Children playing games at the computers of a local NGO

to operate the computer, they are constantly using the keyboard to type words, names, URLs and passwords, which means that they are continuously using the alphabet and other written symbols indicated on the keyboard to form words. Far more quickly than adults in general, younger children become proficient at using these machines: turning them on and off, navigating the visual interface using the mouse, opening and running software and managing digital files.

As the last sections argued, locals with few literacy skills now have new opportunities and motivations to learn. As we approach the end of the chapter, we will examine social media and learning in relation to evangelical Christianity. Together with being helpful to locals who are pursuing university degrees, social media is also promoting cosmopolitan tastes and experiences. To see how it does that, we turn to the personal trajectories of a 52-year-old mother, who works as a temporary cleaner, and her 27-year-old daughter, a university graduate in psychology.

Pentecostalism, education and social media

Following the economic development of the region, especially since the arrival of international hotel companies in the 2000s, Michelle (aged 52) found employment at an industrial laundry. Gradually she acquired knowledge of the work, eventually gaining the trust of the owners sufficiently to be offered the position of manager. She accepted the offer and welcomed the increased income, but eventually decided to quit because 'that money became too expensive to earn'. By this she meant how much of her day the job consumed, as well as the emotional toll of anxiety and insomnia that it brought. She says it was a difficult decision to leave that job because of the things her family could achieve thanks to this salary; not having the same income made it challenging to pay her daughters' monthly university fees, for instance.[32] But as a casual cleaner she has more control over her time, and can earn extra cash when there are opportunities to do so. Otherwise Michelle uses her free time to visit and care for friends and relatives, and also to travel (sometimes nationally) as a guest preacher in branches of the Assembly of God.

Michelle only developed her ability to read thanks to a prolonged effort to comprehend biblical texts. Even today, after many years of daily reading, she still finds it difficult and tedious to read other books. Her uneasiness regarding reading appears in her reluctance to use social media by herself. At home the family has a computer and broadband, which are mostly used by young people: sons, daughters and other friends and relatives who are frequently there. Her daughters created a Facebook profile for her (she has over 600 friends), but Michelle accesses Facebook only through their mediation. Each time one of the daughters is online she logs in to her mother's page and goes through the notifications, reading them aloud so that Michelle can respond verbally; the daughter then types her replies.

As it is more and more common in the region, the literacy gap between Michelle and her children is wide, reflecting the relative importance social media has in their lives. At the age Michelle was starting to going to night classes to learn how to read and write, her daughter Marina was finishing secondary school. In contrast to her mother, Marina's career depends on her using social media for many hours every day.

Marina's working week for the three years of her psychology degree was not easy. She was employed on a paid, part-time internship programme. In order to manage both study and work she travelled twice to the city and back every day, leaving home first at 5 am and going to sleep around midnight. Because of the distance and of city traffic, Marina reached her university almost at the time the first class started and had to leave soon after the last lecture to catch the last buses back home. As a result she had little time to enjoy the social aspect of the course or to hang out with peers with similar interests, ambitions and curiosities.

In this complex context of long daily commutes and limited time available outside of the classroom, email, Facebook and, more recently, WhatsApp became an essential part of Marina's life as a student. She – and other locals in the same situation – use these intensively for personal and group communication in relation to studying and other university activities, for example co-ordinating group assignments, sharing information about work opportunities and communicating about traffic disruption that could affect their journey to and from class. Marina also managed to follow what happened among students thanks to social media. She was both part of groups with hundreds of participants (bringing together wider social circles such as all undergraduates from her university, or all psychology students) and also a member of smaller WhatsApp groups, connecting people on the different courses she took. Finally, she also belonged to some very private groups, featuring just her closest friends at university.

Being a practising evangelical Christian from an austere evangelical church represented a social challenge for Marina when she started her university degree. Being an 'evangelical', she says, made it harder to win the respect of some colleagues. She felt undervalued and dismissed as narrow-minded because of stereotypical views, such as evangelical Christians believing in creationism over scientific evidence. The problem was actually twofold. As an active member of her church in Balduíno, she does not feel comfortable in the settlement interacting with people with other religious affiliations – particularly Afro-Brazilian religious groups, which are demonised by evangelical Christians. In this regard, Marina attributes to Facebook and WhatsApp the solution to remaining part of both worlds. In university she was able to develop friendships with people whom she admired independently of their religious backgrounds; although she was mostly physically absent, she was able to participate in their conversations and to show that her faith did not blind her critical thinking.

Marina sees this effort to socialise beyond the circles of religious affiliations as a contribution to the evangelical community. She successfully presents herself outside of church circles as an 'open-minded evangelical', and in doing so helps to reduce the prejudices associated with evangelical Christians. At the same time – and in a similar way to the case of Maria, discussed above – Marina also used social media to keep in touch with her friends and the community from her church in the settlement. She followed their everyday conversations and remained respected and admired in her local social groups. Because of this capacity to interconnect these two groups, she confronted a deep-rooted local tradition of women straightening their hair (often using dangerous chemicals and hot iron tools). Her proximity to black pride advocates who were studying at the same university made her aware of the consequences of colonialism and segregation in Brazil, and she gradually adopted a new Afro look. She posted the transitions as selfies on Facebook, and the support she received online helped her to face up the resistance she experienced in the settlement.

Although Marina went to university and Maria only finished secondary school, both used social media to support an effort to spend part of their days outside the settlement. The final case of this chapter analyses the use of social media by someone who does not want to live in Balduíno.

'I want to have my own place'

Jonas's father is an accountant whose family came from São Paulo, and whose mother, born in the settlement, is an experienced maître at the region's five-star tourist resort. Their home is located only a couple of blocks from the settlement's commercial centre. It is a small but cosy two-bedroom house that is constantly being improved – as his father explained humorously – because Jonas's mother 'doesn't want to look bad' in front of her church friends. In contrast to most others in their street, therefore, their home looks new: it is nicely painted, with sophisticated tiles and a nicely kept flower garden. Jonas, aged 16 years and only one year away from finishing secondary school, has a bedroom similar to many stereo-typical, middle-class teenage bedrooms shown on television programmes. At the bedroom entrance is a doormat with the image of the iPhone's unlock slide button, while on his bed is a red and pink pillow that his girl-friend gave him, featuring a selfie of them together surrounded by red hearts.

Jonas is a popular and friendly teenager. He likes hanging out with his neighbours and school peers, but at the same time being in the set-tlement is not helping with his plans for the future. He is still not sure whether he will go to university to study biology, engineering or law, but he is certain that in a few years time he will have a university degree. New private institutions now offer undergraduate and graduate programmes more attuned to the budgets, interests and educational deficiencies of working-class students. In addition, government scholarships are now available to students from low-income backgrounds to pay for university fees. University students living in the Coconut Coast also have free trans-port, facilitating a daily commute to and from Salvador where universi-ties are located. However, because he attends public secondary school in Balduíno Jonas's prospects for the future are reduced. His teachers regu-larly do not show up for class, and many of his peers like it that way; for them, being in class (as in Diego's case) is a necessary drag. This is where social media comes in.

Jonas and his closest friends are constantly a step ahead of his peers in their online habits. He started using WhatsApp earlier than most and, while locals tend to prefer to be in the same online places as everyone else (see Chapter 2), Jonas likes to explore.[33] When celebrities such as the footballer Neymar started publishing photos on Instagram, he also became a regular user and was excited when another Brazilian 'living in the United States(!)' started liking his photos and interacting with him. Recently he has been one of the first locals to use SnapChat. In short, social media helps Jonas to cultivate relationships with people who are not necessarily living in the same place as him, but who share his inter-ests and ambitions.

'Networked individualism' is a concept describing how digital com-munication becomes an alternative for those living inside 'small, densely knit groups such as households, communities, and workgroups'.[34] Instead of being 'embedded in groups', digitally mediated social relations allow the person to become the focus of networks of sociality, 'not the family, not the work unit, not the neighbourhood, and not the social group'.[35]

Just like Jonas, networked individuals use their online connections 'to find support, solve problems, and improve their knowledge and skills'.[36]

Jonas estimates that only three out of ten of his peers will enter a university undergraduate programme, and fewer will be able to start a career using their degrees. As success stories he mentions a woman from the settlement who finished a law degree and is doing well after she opened Balduíno's first law firm, a dentist who also has his clinic there and a nutritionist who now works at a physiotherapy clinic. But although he acknowledges that (especially as the country's economy slows) few people with university degrees can achieve work opportunities in their field of study, they still have better prospects of being employed in more prestigious office jobs in hotels. As he says, these people are going after their dreams; they are not simply 'acomodados' (people who are laid back). *Acomodados*, he explains, are content to live in a home on top of or next to those of their relatives. Instead, he wants to afford his 'own place' (*meu espaço*) – not on top of his parents' home, not even on the same street. His use of social media mirrors his intention: to achieve financial independence through a career and probably to move away from Balduíno.

Conclusion

The main question that this chapter intended to answer was whether locals are using social media for educational purposes and, if so, how this might be influencing their chances of improving their socioeconomic situation. This seems a tough objective considering how education itself is a complex and sensitive issue in Balduíno. While schools have improved radically since the 1990s, they also have become a disputed space in the settlement. Like Diego, most students see the advantages of finishing secondary school in order to have the diploma, but they are not particularly interested in paying attention to what teachers have to say during classes. However, despite the complexity of this issue, as the various cases presented show, the answer to the question raised by this chapter becomes straightforward after we clarify what we mean by 'education'. So below are the three main consequences of social media in Balduíno, based on the analysis presented.

If we take the view of education being the outcome of attending public schools as they exist today in the settlement, social media is both a threat to education and is increasing the visibility of the stresses of a poor system. Maria says that her aspiration for formal employment outside of the settlement resulted from her contact with peers, rather than with teachers. Diego sought to finish secondary school only because of the symbolic value of the diploma in the regional job market. For Jonas the local school is a demotivating place, with frequently absent teachers and peers (dismissed by him as *acomodados*, or laid back) who are actually quite happy if teachers are not there. As social media has become more popular, and young people now have 24/7 access to the internet in their pockets, it becomes increasingly evident that students are not interested in school as an institution. Such a situation lies behind the complaint from staff that social media has a negative impact on students' work. In fact, as they have alternative ways of exchanging information and interacting with each other, it is harder now to convince students to engage and participate in classroom activities.

However, if we ask whether social media has helped people in the settlement to learn and to develop themselves professionally, the answer is clearly yes. Diego may not have chosen to pursue a career in technology, but this does not keep him from 'messing around and geeking out' to solve practical software and hardware problems. Even more apparent is the evidence that locals with no previous interest in reading and writing are now practising these skills as they use social media. They have learned not only through the experience of communicating using textual posts, but also because they are anxious about writing such posts correctly. Similarly children from lower-income backgrounds arrive at school with a greater awareness of the alphabet and of words, and of how to operate computers.

Finally, social media helps with the social aspect of transitioning to new possibilities of work and employment. This chapter showed how, in the cases of Ricardo and Maria, relations can become difficult for those with personal ambitions that differ from local norms and traditions. In the 1990s Ricardo was ostracised and ridiculed for choosing to pursue a university degree, and Maria's choice to prioritise a career over family still has the effect of distancing her from her mother. Even today many locals from impoverished rural backgrounds resist formal employment, and are at best ambivalent about education for their families.

WhatsApp and Facebook were used by both Maria and Marina so they could be present in the settlement and nurture their local relationships while they were away. They kept their social networks, remained part of the flow of gossip and continued to display attention and support to their family and close friends. Jonas's case is similar but also complementary to theirs. He spends most of his days physically in the settlement, and yet his plans include a univrsity degree, which will hopefully open up new career opportunities. Though he still inhabits 'small, densely knit groups', through social media he becomes the focus of his individual network, surrounded by others more attuned with his aspirations. In short, social media has become both the settlement one can keep close to when away and the wider horizons of city life that one can experience while still living in Balduíno.

6
Politics: dangerous words

Politics may seem like an odd topic to appear in a book about social media in a low-income settlement in Brazil. To some extent this is true: locals in general dismiss politics as a topic, sharing pessimistic views on government politics with comments like 'politicians only show their faces here during election campaigns' and that they 'always forget their promises after they are elected'. It is not a subject people enjoy, hence the general absence of political dialogue on and off social media. Some discussion does take place, mostly during election campaigns, when locals use social media to show support for a candidate or to share an opinion regarding a national debate – or, mostly, to post humorous memes that reflect their scepticism and pessimism about politicians. But although campaigning parties and candidates bombard the settlement with leaflets, posters, slogans on walls and loud jingles, this does not seem an especially relevant topic here (Fig. 6.1).

However, this is not the usual type of scepticism found in middle-class conversations about corruption in public offices. Locals recognise that politics is vital to people's welfare in places such as Balduíno where most residents are constantly struggling. They represent the social group that relies most on government help. In contrast to the affluent population the inhabitants of Balduíno mostly go to public schools and depend on the public health system; many cannot rely on private security schemes and look for formal employment because of the public benefits that it entails (such as job-seekers' allowances and pensions in retirement). And on top of this, the most vulnerable people in the settlement receive money from welfare programmes. The fact that conversations about politics are not particularly present in their everyday exchanges (whether on social media or in face-to-face exchanges) is therefore interesting in itself. However, in order to examine political disputes we need to broaden the definition of politics to consider it in terms of how individuals and

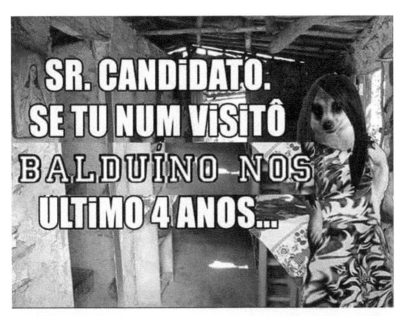

Fig. 6.1 A pessimistic meme about politics. Translated, it reads: 'Mr Candidate, if you did not visit Balduíno in the last 4 years ... you will not do it now. Get out, plague!'

groups negotiate their interests in society.[1] From this perspective we can investigate how social media plays a role in mediating relationships that are not based on personal ties.

Once we adopt this wider conception of politics we realise that, far from being an irrelevant topic, politics appears as a key subject which has also featured in all previous chapters. For example, Chapter 2 examined how locals learned the advantages of acting 'invisibly', including online, such as when they use language strategies to encrypt their conversations so that others around cannot understand. Chapter 3 contrasted the highly moralised and controlled central spaces in the settlement with more peripheral spaces that allow insubordination, and explored how this context influences posting on social media in terms of 'lights on' (everyone is watching) and 'lights off' (only some are watching). Later chapters analysed more specific domains involving power relations in intimate alliances (Chapter 4), or in school and work (Chapter 5). In this chapter we consider relationships beyond these previous spheres, including those that are mediated or associated with evangelical churches, police and organised crime.

Since most disputes examined in this chapter are not related to government politics, it is useful briefly to contextualise the different forces driving change and influencing relations in the settlement today. As Chapters 1, 2 and 4 illustrated, Balduíno is a place that still has only a shadowy presence of the state; living there is still largely associated with participating in networks of mutual support and extended families.[2] Yet there are also other forces currently interfering in the settlement's social relations, given how the Coconut Coast has developed in the past decades into a touristic variation of a gated community,[3] and so attracting some of the tourism previously focused on the city of Salvador. These new economic pressures reflect on locals, who have to deal with the growing institutional presences of '*agentes de saúde*', akin to UK district nurses, a police force and educational services,[4] formal and informal businesses and evangelical organisations. All of these have now arrived in Balduíno, along with migrants seeking new employment opportunities.

The chapter has two parts. The first examines various events that attracted collective attention in the settlement, including crimes (deliberate and accidental), and shows how some of these events mobilised locals to organise public acts of protest. In this context we will consider, for example, the differences that exist when people discuss a certain violent event online and offline: do they repeat online what they say when they meet others in the streets? In most cases the conversations in the streets and on social media are very different, and it is useful to analyse what this difference says about local social relations.

The second part of this chapter assesses situations in which locals use social media to influence public opinion. We will see, for example, how and why a former drug dealer used Facebook to publicise his conversion to evangelical Christianity and how this act may reduce his chances of being killed by former rivals. Church communities, groups of drug distributors and the local police also take advantage of social media to influence society.

In this chapter I aim to answer whether social media actually empowers vulnerable individuals and groups, and also whether the local enthusiasm for social media means that people are gaining more independence from their traditional support networks.

Vulnerability

Violence is a common part of everyday relations in Brazilian low-income localities.[5] Although violence is now increasingly associated with crime, it also featured prominently before the recent economic development of the region (see Chapter 2). Social media provides a useful opportunity to compare the conversation about these violent events that happens online, on both public- and private-facing domains, with face-to-face exchanges or public demonstrations offline.

This part of the chapter includes analysis of disputes that attracted attention and motivated locals to engage in days or weeks of discussions. These cases are about conflicts of interest, some caused by the robbery or murder of locals and others by accidents (unintended situations) with victims. As the first cases show, violent conflicts are intensely debated as people move around the settlement and meet face to face. However, these conversations either disappear or are highly self-censored when they are mentioned on public-facing social media spaces such as Facebook timelines.

Talking about crime on Facebook

One winter morning in Balduíno the brakes of a middle-size truck parked at the top of a slope somehow came unlocked. The vehicle ran freely down the main street, where it struck two eight-year-old girls. The event visibly transformed how people moved and communicated in the settlement for the following weeks.[6] Instead of moving along chatting in pairs or small groups of friends, as people usually do, they moved much more slowly, constantly stopping to form or join small groups with people they were not necessarily close to, simply to exchange information related to the accident. This new pattern, which reflects the high interest produced by the accident, lasted for three weeks following the crash.

The noteworthy aspect of this event is the discrepancy between the interest that this accident raised offline, shown in face-to-face conversations, and the way in which locals mostly avoided discussing the event on public-facing Facebook. On the streets people displayed intense curiosity about its causes and consequences, inquiring after the condition of the two girls and also discussing the responsibility of the owner of the truck. On Facebook timelines, however, it was as if nothing of significance had happened in Balduíno. It felt as if the people using social media were different from those walking the streets. Locals in general did not mention the story online, while those who did framed it only in relation to religion, never clearly discussing it as a criminal matter.

Here is an example of a rare post about the occurrence. Two days after the accident had happened, a young evangelical Christian, owner of an air-conditioning business near the site of the crash, posted the following message:

> GOD IS VERY GOOD! Look at the damage the truck did in the gate and fence of the site opposite to my shop. Had it come to the other side I would have had a great loss of money. The truck went down the street driverless for about 100 metres, 2 children were hit and [the truck] caused this damage you see. I am sorry for the children, but I'm glad they lived thanks to God.

His post included the photo of the place where the truck hit the wall (Fig. 6.2). It was taken from the front of his business in Balduíno.

Fig. 6.2 A photo posted online that refers to the accident with the truck

Later in the week the mother of one of the girls began to use social media to send updates from the hospital in the city to Balduíno. Her name is Lúcia and she is 26 years old, owns a smartphone and is experienced at using Facebook. After the accident Lúcia received many direct messages, including from people not close to her family. Those were, among others, neighbours, work colleagues and members of her church, as well as teachers and the parents of children in her daughter's class at school. These messages were generally wishing the family well and asking about the girls' health. Lúcia realised that by sharing updates online about her daughter, she would not need to respond to every person individually.

Being also an evangelical Christian, Lúcia presented the event on social media as God testing her family's faith (comparing it to the biblical story of Job);[7] she also thanked God that her child was otherwise well. On her first post Lúcia uploaded a photo of her daughter, showing the bandages around her forearm, part of which had had to be amputated, and adding the message: 'Thanks very much everyone for your prayers. I am all right. God is faithful. Believe in that. These were the words my daughter asked me to share together with this photo so you will not worry about her.'

Looking at how the event was presented and discussed online and offline, we see that people on Facebook followed the outcomes of the accident with attention. One of the early photos Lúcia uploaded was shared 126 times in the same day, and it also received many 'likes' and short, positive comments. However, locals were cautious when it came to discussing the event on social media. They showed interest (as seen by the number of shares, 'likes' and comments), but avoided associating their profiles with the critical opinions they themselves expressed during street conversations.

What the use of social media makes evident in this case is how people in Balduíno feel vulnerable, particularly to violence through revenge.[8] The day the accident happened, for example, a police investigator met with a friend of mine who works at a shop near the place where the truck had been parked. She told him that she had not seen anything that morning. After the policeman left, however, she confided that even if she had seen something, she would have given the same answer to avoid becoming involved. She argued that these investigations are only superficial, an opinion shared by most people in the settlement, and that suspects are rarely arrested or brought to trial. 'I am sorry for the girls,' she commented, 'but things won't change now. The accident cannot be undone whether he is found guilty or not. Plus the police investigation is just a formality. They have to do their work, but they don't care about us. Each family has to look after itself, and this man [the truck driver] can take revenge on me, or on my family. We have to be silent. That is how it works here, unfortunately.'

Locals know by experience that the police are understaffed. They are also conscious that the attention and service they receive is different from that displayed towards affluent families. Policemen generally are thought to show unwillingness and arrogance when low-income families and individuals need help. Locals say that unless the media picks up a case and promotes it to reach larger audiences, investigations undertaken into common accidents and fights that result in victims are mostly quickly archived.

Such feelings of vulnerability do not affect 29-year-old Cássio. He is a business owner of affluent background who studied in a private school in Salvador, then came back to Balduíno to manage his family's local restaurant. After a friend of his from the settlement was killed, he posted a message on Facebook that, compared with the previous case, is very explicit. He wrote:

> PLEASE, stop asking me questions (especially through the chat) about the death of Antônio; I am not from the police and am not investigating the case. All I know is that my friend was killed! I am 100% sure that he was not doing anything wrong… He probably fucked the woman of a coward cuckold and got into a fight in the street, or something else equally banal… The reason (for me) does not matter. I lost my friend and nothing will bring him back… I only wish that the bastard who did it pays for the crime he committed.

This post also contrasts with another murder case that circulated on social media. Robson, a 23-year-old driver living in the settlement, used his motorcycle to follow the daughter of another local businessman one afternoon. Robson heard she was going to the bank to deposit a large sum of money and, as she parked the car in a neighbouring settlement (there is no bank in Balduíno), he stopped by her window and, pointing a gun, forced her to give the money to him. As Robson left the woman called her father, who immediately took off in his car and identified Robson – by his clothing, helmet and motorcycle colour – parked at the side of the road on his way back to Balduíno. The father made a quick U-turn and drove into Robson and his motorcycle with the car. As Robson laid unconscious on the floor, other people arrived on the scene. One of them, from Balduíno, made a video using a smartphone showing Robson and all the surroundings (Fig. 6.3).

Fig. 6.3 A screenshot from the video about Robson's case

The three cases presented so far relate in the way they circulated on social media. Typically this kind of content does not appear on public-facing Facebook. The criminal aspect of the accident with the truck had to be neutralised, so the event was described as a test from God. Robson was not an evangelical Christian, however, and he had been caught committing a crime using a shotgun. The video made of him was widely seen in the settlement but only through Bluetooth direct exchanges, as locals were careful to not share it outside of their trusted circles. Nothing about Robson's armed robbery and subsequent death surfaced on Facebook timelines.

Locals used the same direct exchanges to contact Cássio and ask whether he knew the reason why his friend was killed. Cássio's message makes it clear that many people were contacting him on chat and asking if Antônio was involved with drug dealing. Because of his affluent background, Cássio was not afraid to talk directly about a crime on his Facebook timeline, but he also dismisses the event as quite likely to have been the result of a banal situation, and definitely not caused by a more serious offence.

The following section further examines the pattern of how social media is used locally in situations about the discussion of crime and violence. The next story studied has different components: the victim belonged to a family who had been in the settlement for many decades and was therefore embedded in the local support networks. Also, although this is a serious case of murder that probably happened in the context of gang violence,[9] many references to it appeared on locals' Facebook timelines.

Protesting and social media

One night in April 2014 Rafaela, a teenage girl, was chatting with a friend near the settlement's football field. There were other people in the vicinity, but not really close to where they sat. It was a little past midnight when a car approached and stopped in front of the place where the two teenagers were. A back door then opened and there was a brief conversation. Rafaela's friend ran, and a person inside the vehicle shot Rafaela three times in the chest before the car took off. Rafaela died on the way to the hospital.

Rafaela's being from a poor but respected family in Balduíno resulted in the event gaining more public visibility. However, like the first story of Lúcia and her daughter, a clear gap emerged between the circulation of information through face-to-face chats and the type of content that locals risked showing on Facebook.

Whereas people mostly ignored the accident with the truck on their Facebook postings, Rafaela's face appeared on many people's timelines the morning after the shooting. Her closest circle of friends, as well as other teenagers that she went to school with, changed their profile photos to images that represent mourning ('*luto*'), for instance flowers with dark petals (Fig. 6.4). Many of Rafaela's friends and relatives shared photos of her, adding messages to display solidarity with her parents and siblings:

> Today I only want to ask God mercy. Father, these days are difficult. Please have pity on your children. Comfort the hearts of everyone from her family and friends.

The murder of Rafaela filled social media with posts, but again no references are made to the situation that led to her death. What people posted did not include the information related to the murder that they shared when they met face to face in the streets.

The day following the murder, relatives of Rafaela decided they needed to organise a demonstration. Privately people talk about the

Fig. 6.4 A meme used to illustrate mourning

growing influence of drug gangs, arguing that local young people are being attracted to making money by selling drugs – then, as these groups compete with each other, young people get killed as a consequence. However, these protests related to crimes bear close resemblance to the self-censored material shared on social media. For example, the march was promoted without a mention of these gangs: it was described as a 'protest for peace' – though in private conversations locals talk about intending to press the authorities to increase the police presence in Balduíno.

As the day and time of the march was announced, locals found themselves in a delicate position. Many felt under social obligation to show solidarity by walking with Rafaela's family, and most in the settlement agree that having more police there is a good thing. However, just like posting something on social media, participating in a public event indicates the person is taking a side. In Rafaela's story the march was a gesture of public condemnation towards the person who murdered her or ordered the crime. Because of the march, then, locals not particularly close to the family intensified their efforts to check whether Rafaela was 'involved' (this is the expression they use) with these gangs. They wondered if she was unjustly shot dead or if she was taking part at some level in drug-related activities, and thus bore some responsibility for what happened.

The rumours circulating about this case were not uniform. People closer to Rafaela and her family were quick to say she had 'friendships' (*amizades*) with drug dealers, but that she was not 'involved' with the operation. Others presented a mixed scenario: Rafaela was a consumer as well as a friend, but she did not sell the drugs. Yet another rumour explains that Rafaela was shot by the leader of the group she had ties with. She had been a consumer and also active in the 'business', but had recently decided to stop working for them. The third rumour is probably the most convincing because it explains why a person not particularly prominent in the context of drug groups had been murdered.

In the end only about 200 people attended the 'march for peace' in Balduíno, a number considered disappointing in comparison to the intense mourning that happened online. The absence of many locals did not represent a moral condemnation of Rafaela's supposed involvement with a criminal group; it showed rather than many in the settlement were concerned for their own lives. When such cases happen, the police come and follow the legal procedures, but afterwards each family is again responsible for their own protection. Attending a march or becoming a witness in an investigation is a conspicuous political stand, with risks that locals often decide are not worth taking (Fig. 6.5). In Rafaela's case it would have been all right to attend the march if she had been an entirely innocent victim, but the general interpretation was that she was 'involved'. The solidarity for the family translated into publishing neutral content about her death, but only the family's closest friends and supporters showed their faces at the demonstration.

Other protests happened in the settlement between 2013 and 2014. One in particular was nationally associated with the use of social media. Throughout June 2013, and into the following month, millions of predominantly affluent Brazilians took to the streets in large cities, protesting against corruption in politics.[10] During this period these events, which were largely discussed and co-ordinated using social media, saw Brazil included on the global map of places being shaken politically through online activism,[11] including Iran, Egypt and Turkey.

Social media had an important role in the 2013 protests in cities as participants resorted to online media to promote their opinions and organise actions. But whereas in cities the news about protests began on Facebook and only gradually appeared on big media outlets, in Balduíno people's Facebook timelines, as well as everyday conversations, indicated that these large-scale street demonstrations did not particularly matter to them. Salvador, the country's third largest city, staged various protests that literally blocked the flow of people and vehicles in large areas. Although this was taking place only 100 km away from Balduíno, and locals constantly travel back and forth to do business in the city, the intense news coverage did not interest locals beyond its immediately dramatic visual aspect (large numbers of people facing police repression).

Fig. 6.5 A meme referring to the growing violence in the settlement. Translated, it reads: 'My son, all this is Camaçari.' 'And that dark spot over there?' 'There is Balduíno, a place that cries for peace.'

At first it seemed that for locals these gatherings might as well be happening elsewhere in the world, not in their own country at all. Considering how unconcerned people looked, this could be news related to the Arab Spring, the Indignados movement in Spain or the Occupy Wall Street campaign in the United States. Eventually, however, after about a month, a few locals began to upload and share memes about these national events. Local university students, who travel regularly to Salvador and saw some of their peers discussing the marches, started to declare their support for the protesters. As more content referring to the marches appeared on local timelines, Zulmira, a 37-year-old evangelical Christian, formed a group on Facebook scheduling a date and time for locals to join a 'Peaceful demonstration in Balduíno'. Students added their local friends and the group quickly gathered over 1,200 participants. An invitation meme followed:

> Everyone, come! We have to demand our rights. Balduíno is abandoned. We want change [including] a health centre [that stays] open 24 hours, a post office. High school students do not have a [proper] school.

At the day and time the demonstration was scheduled to start, the gathering place was empty except for a television crew from a small cable television channel and a couple of other journalists from regional online news services. A few minutes later, however, a group of four mothers and pre-teenage children arrived, blowing noisy party whistles and carrying protest signs, handwritten on cardboard. Since it was a regular working day, many local adults were in their jobs at that time, but soon after the march started a group of about 30 people formed, composed mainly of students, women and children. As they moved, more people gradually joined. My informal assessment was that in total up to 300 participated – a number which does not include the many locals who watched the protest from the side of the street. After the march had progressed round the settlement participants dispersed, and the Facebook group was not used to schedule other similar events.

During the 15 months I lived in Balduíno locals protested for various other reasons, but in general these events had little consequence. The demonstration in July 2013 was no exception. Participants expressed legitimate concerns as they marched – mothers spoke about the bad quality of the health centre and of how teenagers are getting into trouble because there was nothing for them to do in the settlement after school. However, participation did not progress to organising more activities.

Aside from this particular case echoing a larger movement, protests in Balduíno happened in relation to specific local events, such as the murder of Rafaela. Most also did not appear on social media, nor did they use social media as a particularly important tool to co-ordinate participation. In terms of practical outcomes, they were not successful. For example, the cases described below did mobilise people to demonstrate, but none achieved their intended aims.

- A group of about 40 locals twice demonstrated in front of the mayor's office to demand the construction of an alternative route for the heavy trucks that pass through Balduíno. The vehicles currently break the settlements' pavements, making some areas difficult to reach because of the mud and also causing locals to develop respiratory problems.
- The families of two men murdered by the same person also organised a march because the (known) assassin had not been arrested.
- Some secondary school students closed part of the road to Salvador to complain that their school was closed indefinitely because the Education Secretary stopped paying the salaries of the outsourced staff.

Locals justify their lack of interest in politics for various reasons, including lack of time, fear of revenge and scepticism that these movements will achieve the desired consequences. As the following section explains, however, locals also avoided sharing opinions online because of the support networks to which they belong.

Avoiding politics on Facebook

Pedro has been actively using computers since the mid-1990s, about ten years before the first internet cafés opened in the settlement and locals began to know about social media. He owes this opportunity to the education he had.

His father, Antônio Carlos, had little schooling, but for some years he became one of the richest and most powerful men in the settlement. Thanks to the 'blessings' of an influential politician, Antônio Carlos profitted from selling costal land in the settlement to development companies and rich urban families. While his family had money, Pedro was sent as a teenager to live in Salvador, where he could study at affluent private schools. But when Antônio Carlos's business slowed, and as he routinely

spent money partying, his son had unwillingly to move back to the settlement and help take to care of his siblings. Since then, and thanks to his
years of schooling, Pedro managed to find employment in better-paying
office positions in hotels and other tourist-related businesses. Because
of having held such positions in offices since the mid-1990s, he began
using computers and accessing the internet relatively early – at around
the same time as young affluent urban families were doing so in their
work and at home.

Other locals see Pedro today as a sort of 'local-foreign' and in a way
he prides himself on having this distinction. While other men in the settlement (like his father) spend a lot of their money drinking and partying,
Pedro sits at home after work and watches lectures from eminent intel-
lectuals on YouTube. He is also privately pleased that others, including
his wife, consider his choices of profile pictures on social media 'weird'.
As we saw in Chapter 3, locals use public-facing Facebook to display personal beauty and prosperity, but Pedro disregards this normative practice
by constantly changing his profile picture to ('totally uncool') close-up
pictures of cats and monkeys, ('strange looking') faces of indigenous people from different parts of the world and famous (but locally unknown)
artwork from artists such as Duchamp and Dali. However, there is one
aspect regarding the use of social media in which Pedro resembles his
neighbours: he rarely discusses politics online.

Reading and debating politics has become in recent years (especially since the 2013 national demonstrations) an important part of what
educated Brazilians do online. Pedro follows the often passionate posts
shared by his affluent online friends, but he avoids sharing and debating
his own political views – unless they are about cases unrelated to local
politicians. In many regards, he has more reasons to be upset than affluent people who have private health insurance and send their offspring
to private schools. Pedro's 14-year-old twins, for example, are missing
classes every day at the local high school. At the beginning of the school
year he was angry with the teachers for their 'lack of professionalism', but
the situation subsequently got more complicated as the state, because of
budget deficits, stopped paying the salaries of the outsourced contrac-
tors who drive school buses and clean the facilities. Students and their
families collected groceries for a period of three months to help these
employees, but the local high school eventually had to suspend classes.

As I explained at the beginning of this chapter, locals in Balduíno
are pessimistic about politics. In everyday conversations they will repeat
that politicians 'show their faces only during election campaigns', but
the reality is more complex than that. Here local political leaders win

votes by exchanging favours inside extended family groups.[12] This is a time-consuming activity that includes providing job positions in public service to close associates and their families, and also helping local voters confronting everyday difficulties to bypass state bureaucracy. Some of these locals need to speak to lawyers to help release a relative who has been sent to prison; others ask for samples of expensive medicines, available in public hospitals under the control of doctors; mothers may seek to have their children admitted at drug treatment facilities. Political leaders in the area use their contacts and influence to help the families of voters access public resources, such as doctors and medicine, but these demand time and literacy to access. In Balduíno the patronage of these local leaders supplies these necessities as a gift in exchange for loyalty and political support. For example, their contacts inside the government machine can access the medicine destined initially for hospitals, so supporters do not need to buy these often expensive types of medicine in pharmacies. Health is an area that illustrates the importance of all forms of support network in the settlement. In the case of medical emergencies, for instance, people have to be driven privately to the local hospital, as public ambulances take too long to come.

In personal conversations Pedro says he wishes he could talk more freely online and use the internet as a podium to criticise people responsible for these problems, such as council representatives, the mayor and political parties (as his affluent friends do). 'It is not that I am afraid of these politicians,' he explains, 'the problem is that I have many family members who either work for or owe their jobs to local political leaders'. These family members would thus 'not be pleased to see me being ungrateful' to these people. Pedro, like other locals, has to take care of these networks of mutual help so that, when or if his family faces problems, he will be assisted in turn.

Influencing public opinion

The sections in this second part of the chapter have one key thing in common: they show the various ways in which locals use social media to interface with public opinion. We will assess the use of Facebook, photographs and personal online networks as means to influence situations of conflict, such as a former drug dealer presenting himself to rival groups as an evangelical Christian and an evangelical Christian wanting to be baptised in her church against the wishes of the head minister. The first case indicates that when it is convenient or considered necessary, police as well as criminal groups use their private WhatsApp contacts to disseminate certain types of content by releasing them to local contacts.

Promoting anxiety

Both police and organised crime groups in Balduíno use WhatsApp intensively and in comparable fashions,[13] as their operations demand speed, group communication and confidentiality.[14] While WhatsApp can be described generally as a sort of 'Swiss army knife' – an all-in-one communication tool to connect to groups and individuals – police and criminal cells in Balduíno exploit all these uses and possibilities of the platform, making it a crucial part of their work. The platform helps them quickly co-ordinate among close peers, but it also interconnects individual participants inside broader networks of relationships concerning their professional networks and affiliations. In addition, WhatsApp is also used in a strategic, 'political' way – to influence public opinion to favour causes that benefit them.

It is worth remembering that this is a new technology at the settlement – WhatsApp became popular in Balduíno only at the end of 2013 – and both the low-ranking military police in the settlement and local criminals belong to the same low-income working class. This is perhaps more obvious to affluent outsiders in regard to the young people in poor neighbourhoods, who perceive organised crime as a viable career path: it offers a more adventurous life and the chance to earn more money than would ever be possible for manual, unskilled, under-educated workers.[15] Yet the ranks of the military police are equally segregated, with separate career paths available for people of different socioeconomic backgrounds. While candidates to commanding (officer) positions are tested on university-level disciplines such as law and history, exams to enter in the force as constables require only compulsory-level education. The personnel selected for this 'second rate' group can, in theory, eventually take new exams to move into the hierarchy of command. However, most retire after a career spent working on the streets, in which they are routinely exposed to life-threatening situations related to crime prevention.

The following section describes the use made of WhatsApp, first by the local police and then by local crime groups.

WhatsApp has become important to police officers working in the settlement as a tool that increases their protection as a group – both when they are together and for individuals off duty. Before WhatsApp, they were limited to using police radio installed on cars and in unit buildings, but they explain that radio communication is not as nearly as efficient as

WhatsApp, considering their needs and the context in which they work. In places such as Balduíno there are 'shade areas' where radio equipment does not work but phones do. Also they say radio exchanges are overly hierarchical and bureaucratic because messages are transmitted vertically: they need first to reach the police department, then to be assessed, and finally to be broadcasted to other units. The immediacy of WhatsApp is useful because it bypasses these technological bottlenecks.

WhatsApp interconnects the 14 policemen and women of the local unit 24/7, whether they are working or off duty. The platform is not used just in moments of need. The unit's group provides a form of ongoing report log, in which each participant posts what is currently happening – shootings, accidents, requests for ambulances, bodies found, etc. With this communication, off-duty police (who tend to be more vulnerable, as they are alone) can request immediate assistance directly from their peers, from any place; they can also, depending on the circumstances, be summoned to action. Together with these more intense exchanges centred on the group's unit, local police are also individually in contact with people from other units; they thus circulate information to co-ordinate support depending on the requirements of each situation. Even as these inter-unit communication exchanges take place, individuals continue to forward information to keep commanding officers aware of developments.

Local criminal groups, like the police units, are in continuous contact internally between each other using WhatsApp. Individually they can also reach other similar groups and organisations with whom they collaborate. Social media allows criminals to co-ordinate activities as a group with privacy, speed and efficiency.

Both police and local criminal organisations also use WhatsApp on occasion to broadcast information to society to influence public opinion. During the 2014 Bahia state police strike, the police that adhered to this political movement judged that media channels were boycotting their action by failing to report their demands and to cover the supposed many disturbances in the unprotected city. They responded to this situation by using WhatsApp, distributing photos of bodies found in crime scenes to personal contacts. These actions increased public anxiety and fear, raising the pressure on government officials to reach an agreement with the police.

Similar content has been circulating in Balduíno lately, with similar results, but this time the sources are local criminal groups. As rivals compete for the control of the local drugs market, and for the channels for distributing drugs to wealthy visitors in nearby tourist resorts, they have turned to social media to intimidate each other (Fig. 6.6). For example, a criminal group may record video messages displaying guns and making

Fig. 6.6 A screenshot from a video shared on WhatsApp by a local criminal group to intimidate a rival gang by showing their guns

threats to their rivals (challenges such as 'Show your faces!' are common). They also use the sounds of a surprise attack in the rival area, recording their threats followed by the sound of shooting, then circulating this material through their contacts in the settlement using WhatsApp.

If police and criminal groups both use WhatsApp to influence the public domain, the following example explores a different but equally dangerous situation. One person, a former drug dealer, now uses his profile on Facebook to publicise his new status as an evangelical Christian.

Facebook and religious conversion

Today 18-year-old Patric lives with his 17-year-old partner and her mother, who is retired on medical grounds. He works as a builder when there are opportunities available and also receives money from the state because his father, who worked as a policeman, died in action.

Their home is only a few metres away from an open area, located more or less in the middle of the street where they live. A couple of years ago children in the vicinity could not be seen playing freely outside as they do today. That open area across from his home was the 'office' where Patric, his brother and other peers formed and managed a local cell to deal drugs. Even Patric's relatives – grandparents, uncles and aunts – avoided approaching them to give advice as the boys both were violent and refused to listen, but they still helped continually by hiding them when necessary. During day and night, the doors and windows of local houses were kept closed because at any time people – this group, their rivals or the police – might arrive carrying guns. When shootings did erupt, families lay on the floor to protect themselves and hoped for the best.

As the situation worsened and neighbours felt under constant stress, one of Patric's aunts approached other evangelical Christian women in the street to form a 'praying circle' (*círculo de oração*), through which they would display their devotion to God 'in exchange for a miracle'. Their agreement was that for one day every week each of them would pray for one hour during the full 24 hours of the day, asking God 'to change the lives' of these young men and bring peace to the street. During the following months, things changed. Patric's brother was arrested and later killed in prison, and other members of the gang ran away or were arrested in turn. Patric survived and himself converted to evangelical Christianity. Today the street is no longer considered a dangerous place.

Similarly to what I heard from other evangelical Christians, Patric explained that many gangsters are very religious deep down and fearful of God. They may on occasion become protectors of local evangelical people, especially those considered to live honourably. Patric said during his time as a criminal he constantly toyed with the idea of quitting crime and 'following Jesus', and that the turning point occurred one particular day, during a close-range shoot-out with police. He found himself surrounded and running out of ammunition; he thought he was going to die. At that moment he made a promise to God to give up crime and 'surrender his heart to Jesus' if God protected him and allowed him to stay alive. Patric did escape the situation alive, and he quickly chose a church to fulfil his promise.[16]

Patric's story comes alive when you visit his Facebook profile. As a cover photo he uploaded an edited image (Fig. 6.7). On the left this shows a photo of him from his gangster years, while the right portrays his current identity as a well-behaved and active evangelical Christian, regularly attending the local Methodist church. In his former guise Patric looks directly to the camera, hands pointing forward (simulating guns); his reformed image shows him holding a smartphone in one hand and a Bible in the other.

This image relates to a common practice among evangelicals. During services or in personal conversations they tell their own miraculous stories of conversion, to give testimony of God's power to change

Fig. 6.7 The 'before' and 'after' selfie from a former drug dealer who abandoned crime to live as an evangelical Christian

lives. However, simply quitting his crime activities is not enough for Patric and others in the same situation to stay alive. He explains that gangsters sometimes turn to the church while they find themselves in difficult situations, so his former rivals will not be easily convinced about his conversion. As his retirement from crime is still recent, Patric's action in uploading the image disseminates his new self to the settlement, moving beyond the circles of people whom he regularly meets. The montage in itself makes his transformation more convincing; it adds visual evidence to information circulating on local networks of gossip and rumour. The image is a public statement in which he appears to everyone formally dressed as an evangelical Christian, wearing the typical 'uniform' of shirt, tie and Bible. Symbolically this effort can help to impress his rivals, though Patric adds that he does not fear for his life. His rationale is simple:

> God controls everything that happens. Next to God, a gun or a person are nothing but dust. He is "the God of the impossible"[17] and without His acceptance, no one can touch me. So I do not worry.

To Patric as well as the other evangelical Christian in the next case, Facebook becomes the platform to display the evidence that God is on their side.

Social media and church politics

Evangelical Christians now form nearly one-quarter of the Brazilian population, according to the 2010 census data.[18] As previous chapters have shown, they are an influential group in Balduíno because of the number of locals who belong to, and regularly participate in, church activities. These churches are important because they also promote literacy, and evangelical families often experience greater socioeconomic mobility than non-evangelical ones.

In this context, evangelical Christians are particularly interested in social media and computers. Working parents use digital technology to stay in touch with their children;[19] they also use it as motivation for younger family members to spend more time at home, rather than in internet cafés with 'bad company'.[20] As Chapter 3 has described, social media is also used as a 'window' for neighbours and relatives living elsewhere to see the family's growing financial achievements and strong family bonds, displayed through photos of the interior of their home, their holidays and activities such as dressing up to attend church.

Finally, social media is an important space for local evangelical Christians to maintain relationships with others from their religious social circles who live elsewhere. It also offers the opportunity to access an endless source of evangelical content, mainly on YouTube. This includes not only videos of preaching and gospel music, but also news and literature of interest to this sector.

However, the elements that I mentioned above often produce a narrative of evangelical Christians that is flat and does not include conflicts. Viewed from the outside, often these stereotypical evangelicals represent uncritical but financially ambitious people with conservative family values (they are generally opposed to abortion, gay rights, etc.) and who more recently, in some cases, have been incorporating neoliberal values about individualism and prosperity. This section, however, discusses politics and social media while also acknowledging the conflicts that occur inside a church. Social media plays a role in the negotiation of conflicts between groups representing different values and ideologies, especially regarding the recent incorporation of meritocratic views that are not a key element of Pentecostal organisations.[21]

Sandra is 34 years old and moved to Balduíno from a *favela* in Salvador as a child.[22] She is among the few locals I knew who does not just read well, but actually enjoys reading as entertainment. However, she has no interest in or intention of turning this valued training into a better paying job. She works part-time at a shop in the settlement, does not have children and treasures the fact that every day she has half a day just for herself to watch television, listen to music, pray and write in her diaries. When others press her to stop being 'acomodada' (laid back, lazy), she replies that she has done her share of hard work in life. By this she is referring to the ten years that her parents 'gave her away' – to be cared for while working for a family as a child servant.[23] This began when she was only five years old. Together with the load of daily work she was given, Sandra also suffered several situations of violence and abuse.

Evangelical Christianity is an important part of Sandra's identity, and she treasures the moral respect that belonging to the Assembly of God gives her. Her life constantly revolves around talking about the Bible with fellow members of the church and family members, and in participating in religious events. Like other devoted Christians, she knows countless literal quotes and stories from the Bible by heart.

However, because Sandra joined the church as an adult she has encountered difficulties in becoming a full member. To do that she needs to be baptised, but the current head minister has strict rules. He will not marry individuals who are currently living or have previously been living with partners, on the grounds that religious marriage should only happen once. And because she holds the status of 'together' (*juntada*), in his view Sandra cannot be baptised.

Since she did not marry her partner and has not been baptised, Sandra cannot sit in the prestigious 'married women' section of the church during services. Nor can she participate in some church activities, which are restricted to full members, or hold prestigious positions such as teaching children at Sunday school.

Like others in her congregation, Sandra resents the growing influence inside the church of people who, in her view, are distorting the purpose of the Assembly of God by making superficial things such as clothes and cars seem more important that one's personal faith and practices. In Sandra's case, her wedding became a key political right she fought to acquire. In this battle Facebook played an important role, allowing her achievement to be seen and recognised among her peers at the church.

Sandra says her wedding happened because of the 'grace of the Lord, as a recognition of my faith and devotion'. She also adds that God has appreciated the merit she has by rewarding her with 'a beautiful wedding party that people with much more money than her did not have'. However, another way of describing her ceremony is as an example of the importance mutual support networks still have in Balduíno. Sandra did borrow some money to buy some of the ingredients for the food and to rent the dress she wore that night, but everything else was the result of weeks of collaboration by her networks of friends and relatives, many of whom belong to the same church and hold similar views to Sandra. Their assistance included providing material gifts such as flowers and fruit, volunteering to help on the day by singing or playing music, cooking, driving or taking photographs, and exploiting political relationships so the party could be held at a local public school. The previous head minister of the church, still an active participant of the Assembly of God, came to Balduíno to conduct the ceremony, making it religiously official.

Sandra's marriage gave her political capital, as its success is framed through the internal logic of evangelical Christianity as resulting from the will of God. The head minister had refused Sandra's request for him to marry her and consequently created greater difficulties for the wedding to overcome, since she could not use the local church for the ceremony and had to hire another venue. Facebook has been a strategic weapon in this political struggle. The photos of Sandra's wedding were uploaded on to the platform the day after the ceremony and, because it was an impressive party, these photos circulated inside and outside the church community.

While gossip would have also disseminated the wedding's success to the settlement, Sandra's family saw Facebook as an important ally to promote her achievement further. The images on Facebook attracted shares, 'likes', and comments not just from Balduíno, but also from extended networks outside the settlement. The photos alone count as symbols of success, but the display of approval from her social circles enhances their value.

Conclusion

This chapter began by considering the point of discussing politics and social media when in Balduíno politics is a topic that most people have little interest in posting about. This apparent disregard for the subject needs to be contextualised, however, as residents here belong to precisely the strata of Brazilian society most dependent upon government services such as public schools and hospitals. The principle aim of this chapter has therefore been to examine their use of social media in order to understand better this paradoxical lack of interest in politics.

The cases presented in the first part of this chapter show how the population resents a lack of commitment from politicians, such as candidates for mayor and state representatives (*deputado estadual*). 'They only show their faces during campaigns' is a phrase repeated in the settlement like a pessimistic mantra. Besides this, however, there are other reasons for not wanting to show an interest for politics. Locals are also associated, directly or indirectly, with local political leaders and often find themselves indebted to them for favours given in exchange for loyalty and support. Locals and their families rely on people in positions of influence to bypass state bureaucracy. They avoid discussing government politics on social media because they cannot criticise local politicians and local political leaders directly without appearing ungrateful to local leaders.

This absence of discussions about politics is also reflected in people's caution in addressing situations of conflict, especially in publicly exposed ('lights on') situations. Locals do not discuss sensitive issues outside trusted groups because of a shared perception that they are vulnerable to violent acts of revenge. They discuss situations of conflict with a wealth of detail through face-to-face communication in a 'lights off' context, but sensitive subjects either do not appear on public-facing social media or are stripped of any references to conflict. Such situations are often presented as a religious issue, but evangelical Christianity provides only a partial response to people's sense of vulnerability.

In Balduíno the police do not have the infrastructure to service this population. The choice to refrain from talking about conflicts coincides with the locally shared pessimistic perception that 'things are the way they are': they do not change, and standing up against injustices only increases problems in the settlement. The cases reported in this chapter thus support a conclusion that social media has done very little to change the situation, or the perceived state of vulnerability. Locals depend on personal networks for protection and, in general, they choose the safer strategy of keeping quiet about sensitive issues. Social media helps locals to retain contact with their networks of relations even when they are away from the settlement, as they have to be more often these days – but it is not being used to strengthen individualism or individual expressions.[24] As Chapter 4 shows, it is constantly used to nurture local bonds through interactions, displays of affection and exchanges of help – and by engaging in the circulation of gossip and rumours.

Public-facing social media carries only very censored versions of what goes on by way of direct exchanges online and offline. As Chapter 2 argues, it is the logic of acting invisibly that is generally preferred in practice. Locals occasionally organise or get involved in forms of protest, but these demonstrations reflect what we see on social media. Collective acts happen without much planning, relatively few participate and the (lack of) successful outcomes only reinforces the sense that standing up to complain is pointless.

It is not that locals do not discuss these situations of conflict. As the initial cases show, some events do capture collective interest and people discuss them endlessly for weeks through direct (usually face-to-face) exchanges. This further attests to the fact that the intense engagement the locals now have with social media has not transformed their social relations. Gossiping – in these face-to-face exchanges of information and opinion – has long been an important aspect of the organisation of low-income communities in Brazil,[25] with significant influence on people's reputations. Cases such as Sandra's and Patric's began with uploading content to Facebook timelines, but they intended this content to be shared through personal networks actually to increase its impact on public perception. Patric wanted to let his gangster rivals know that he was now working for God, and Sandra wanted to be married in a religious ceremony against the will of the head minister. Their use of social media aimed at feeding networks of gossip to increase their own personal reputations.

Finally it is important to consider how and why posts on Facebook timelines about situations of conflict are often framed using religious narratives. In the first case Lúcia, the mother of the child whose arm had to be amputated, talks about the accident, comparing what happened to her family with the sufferings of Job. However, the conversation is not always passive nor always about receiving comfort. For example, on one occasion Lúcia replied on Facebook to some gossip she had heard about the accident in which her daughter's accident was perceived as a punishment for Lúcia's 'past sins'. Lúcia responded indirectly,[26] without mentioning the person she was addressing:

> It drives me crazy that these types of Christians go around talking shit and mixing that with God. But my God is strong and he gives me the strength to face any battle. I will not deny him…

During the months after her daughter had left the hospital, Lúcia posted on Facebook photos of the daughter on holiday, eating out, playing with her new Barbie doll and her new smartphone. Similarly to Patric and Sandra, social media became a tool to shape public perceptions. Lúcia portrays her daughter as 'blessed' and as 'victorious', as the illustrated examples of wealth should attest.

The religious framework not only provides a background in which conflicts can be made public. Evengelical Christianity also enables locals to position tragic events as challenges that may yet lead a person to victory. Sandra is someone who cannot afford to come to services wearing fashionable clothes, yet her wedding and the photos of it that she shared on Facebook are discussed as instances of God's blessing and reaffirmation of her devotion to Christian values. This framing of positive redemption and 'victory' over difficulties is different from the traditional Catholic discourse, which refers to poor people as virtuous for accepting their condition and the consequent suffering that it may cause.[27] Social media has thus formed a powerful channel for such a reshaping of public perception.

7
Conclusion: why do they love social media?

In Brazil as a whole – and Balduíno is no exception – the low-income population has shown great enthusiasm for social media. Despite the many limitations they faced, without government support or the money to purchase computers, they supported flourishing internet cafés in poor neighbourhoods,[1] and overcame limitations in writing and reading. Initially locals joined Orkut, the most popular social media platform at the time in Brazil, only to be publicly ridiculed and exposed by affluent users because of their 'ignorance' and 'bad taste'.[2] As the interest in social media increased and the national economy prospered, during the transition from the 2000s to the 2010s, many low-income families used bank credit paid over many instalments finally to get their own computers at home.

In places such as Balduíno, a settlement evolving out of a fishing village, there were other barriers to social media inclusion. Before mobile connectivity became so widespread, the lack of cable infrastructure offered an opportunity for small entrepreneurs to re-sell internet broadband connection transmitted through radio signals. When in the late 2000s computers began to appear in the homes of locals, teenagers assumed the responsibility for teaching older relatives how to operate them and to navigate the internet. As Chapter 3 on visual posting explains, even the generally low levels of literacy did not prevent many adults from eventually embracing the possibilities of social media; now they too could explore the lives of people online and 'Skype' with relatives living away. This involvement with social media finally consolidated in the second half of 2013 when teenagers learned about WhatsApp – a social media platform that runs well even on less expensive Android smartphones. Now most people under 50 in Balduíno have acquired a good enough smartphone to take advantage of this service.

This book has aimed to examine different perspectives on this phenomenon, including the possible relation between the interest in social media and Brazil's period of economic prosperity. Many analysts and scholars choose to refer to the emergence of a 'new middle class',[3] presented as a positive symbol in a time of falling inequality – although in reality this is more like a new working class.[4] Using social media could be, and often was, considered to be an effort by these Brazilians to emulate the affluent. However, one of the questions this book examines is whether the interest in social media has other motivations. On one hand we usually associate social media with modernity – high tech, fibre optics, innovation, instantaneous access to information – but social media's popularity may also reflect how it strengthens traditional values and practices embedded in social organisations. Key among these in Balduíno are extended families and networks of mutual support, now even more necessary given the radical changes that this population has experienced in the recent past.

Emerging population and social media

This book has a different title to any of the other books in the 'Why We Post' series. It does not refer to a region, but instead uses the term 'emergent class'. The word 'emergent' was chosen because it encapsulates so much about this particular project that links the rise of social media to this specific population. To be emergent implies both a dynamic, a sense that people are becoming something that they were not, and also an increased visibility, a sense that they are becoming more conspicuous, moving from background to foreground. These are exactly the attributes we also ascribe to new social media: they potentially represent profound changes in society and also make these more visible than before.

The key to this book was thus always going to be its ability to help unpack a highly complex encounter, in which there are clear parallels between the impacts of social media itself and the transformations in the society that create this particular manifestation of social media. For this reason we are constantly shifting from a top-down to bottom-up, public-facing to private-facing, forward-looking to backward-looking focus, because all of these are implicated in this situation. In a way the issue of making these entanglements clearer is the conclusion and task of this book.

As the comparative volumes of the 'Why We Post' project emphasise, the point of conducting 15 months of ethnography in settings that deliberately differ from typical researches conducted among affluent, educated, young urbanites is to show how the internet can mean different things to different people. For instance, news articles and books commonly discuss social media in relation to politics, empowerment of the individual or the end of privacy. People in Balduíno, on the other hand, often refer to social media's effects on personal relationships. Conversations may focus upon the 'addiction' to being online that locals are experiencing, reflecting the new possibilities of contact with relatives living away. Young people extol the advantages of having a domain of interaction in which adults cannot participate as freely. Men relentlessly talk and make jokes about Facebook in terms of its facility for secret communication with potential or actual lovers. People in general refer to Facebook and WhatsApp as platforms used by others to spy on their personal lives. And parents, particularly mothers, refer to the new difficulties of having to earn money and leave their children behind – a situation helped by social media, which allows them to maintain responsibilities to home and family while working away from the settlement for long hours on most days.

The book's structure is also intended to address the requirement of multiple perspectives. The three initial chapters describe the 'landscapes': of the field site in which the research was conducted, of the social media that locals use and of the visual postings on social media. They are generic in the sense that they consider a broad spectrum of social relations (in terms of gender, age, etc.) rather than focus on particular contexts or domains. The aim of these early chapters is to put the reader in a position to understand the challenges faced by locals in Balduíno, and to show how they see the possibilities of communicating online. The first chapters thus provide the foundations, the initial climb uphill to a vantage point in order to see as far as possible in all directions across the settlement and their social media. In doing this we can gain a holistic perspective of the various contexts – historical, economic, cultural – that need to be considered in an analysis of how and why people choose to be online. Such a move is also chronological, exploring from the time before the internet became available up to the present.

The last three chapters then take us down the hill to look at particular domains of social relations. They also take the reader from the present back to the past, to examine the ways in which social media is contributing both to changes and continuities in established forms of social relations. The domains considered are the house (Chapter 4), the environments of school/work (Chapter 5) and the street outside (Chapter 6) – not exactly these specific places, but the types of relationships that are embedded there. These connections are represented respectively by the family, the relationships between teachers/bosses and pupils/employees, and finally of locals dealing with each other through the mediation of the state, of government politics and of churches.

Class-based preconceptions

The final parts of Chapter 1, concerning research methods, and the initial sections of Chapter 2 discuss the difficulties I experienced arriving in Balduíno as a Brazilian of affluent background. In the first six months of field work I was troubled by several practices that constitute the way locals use social media. In 2013, before WhatsApp took over as the most important social media platform there, I was a stranger in the settlement, but everyone I met gladly accepted my friendship requests. Young people seemed very proficient at using Facebook and knew how content filters worked, but they consistently did not understand the reasons other people might have for using them. So 'friending' people, I learned, was not really necessary in Balduíno: everyone's Facebook timelines are public, revealing to anybody interested the inside of their homes, the faces of their relatives and friends, the places where they work and the celebrations in which they participate. As I tried to make sense of this lack of restrictions around the display of what appeared to be intimate aspects of people's lives, I concluded initially (and wrongly) that locals did not appreciate the dangers of using social media. I assumed that they knew no better because they were inexperienced users and had had little education.

The problem with this early interpretation, as Chapter 2 also explains, is that it relied firstly on an only partial access to locals' social media and secondly on my own understanding of the terms 'private' and 'public'. Yet these did not correspond with the views of my informants. As Chapter 4 explains with reference to intimacy, in a general sense 'everybody knows everybody' in the settlement, but there are nonetheless differences in the levels of intimacy that are shared. My perception about locals' use of social media changed after establishing bonds of trust that eventually led to my seeing something of the large amount of content which does not circulate on Facebook timelines. These timelines are actually meant to be seen outside of homes (not particularly by close friends and family members); they may be compared to a smart jacket or dress worn for a party or in church on Sundays. Far from being perceived as personal or intimate, what is presented on Facebook timelines often represents a way of displaying one's moral values and achievements.

After returning from the field, I made another assumption that later proved incorrect. For some months I struggled, trying to fit the evidence I had gathered into a common narrative that describes the internet as a democratising force.[5] I wanted to claim that the enthusiasm shown by my low-income informants for using social media expressed a desire to overcome the legacy of segregation inherited from Brazil's colonial past. (The general background of global events such as the Arab Spring or the Occupy Wall Street movement followed similar narrative lines: multitudes using social media to circumvent political challenges.) The 'problem', however, is that this vision of social media as a meritocratic place for activism and personal development disregards important practices happening in Balduíno: they simply did not fit into this existing narrative.

As Chapter 3 shows, a lot of what circulates among people in Balduíno is porn, crude violence, politically incorrect humour and loads of dancing, even extending to photos of murdered people found in the settlement. Chapter 4 explains, in terms of actual interactions and conversations, that the excitement surrounding social media is largely associated with having new methods of finding lovers or spying on each other, especially on one's partners. In addition, young people celebrate platforms such as WhatsApp and Facebook because their parents, generally with lower standards of literacy than their children, cannot follow their children's communication on that space. As Chapter 5 argues, social media is definitely helping people to learn, but this is often not the type of learning that motivates students to go to university. And as we see on Chapter 6, party politics is the very last thing that people in Balduíno discuss on social media, nor does social media assist people who protest there.

A bit of theorising

The first clue to understanding the specific ways in which the people of Balduíno use social media came together with the development of bonds of trust between myself and locals. I was shocked to disover that the endless selfies displaying enjoyment, faith and achievement that I saw on everyone's timelines (see Chapter 3) were but a fraction of the content (including porn, violence, bizarre 'humour' and dancing) that people continuously exchange and talk about – but only through direct exchanges.

The notion of polymedia[6] offers a way to interpret this disparity. It posits that, because now there are abundant possibilities and alternative digital platforms available for people to use, the choice of communication channel follows a moral understanding of these platforms and their function. Applying the concept of polymedia started by considering what type of content locals want to show to everybody and what type is circulated inside trusted networks, and the moral understandings thus associated with one and the other. The broader conclusions of this analysis will be highlighted in the following paragraphs, but initially polymedia indicated that local uses of social media might be following traditions of communication that existed prior to digital media. The locals were thus neither naïve nor inexperienced in their ways of using social media, but their understanding of the concepts of 'private' and 'public' was specific to that context.

Polymedia relates to the key discovery used for this book, as presented on Chapter 2. This is that people in Balduíno have moralised perceptions about different spaces in the settlement; they traditionally learn through everyday practice how to hide certain conversations according to where these take place. This practice of 'encrypting conversations' has been studied in anthropology under the name of 'indirection'.[7] During face-to-face conversations locals learn how to extract the context of the information to talk about sensitive matters when surrounded by different people; they can thus be sure that only some will understand what is being said. Chapters 2 and 3 argue that this type of communication informs how locals use social media, with sensitive information often circulating in incomplete form purposely to restrict the reach and the consequences of referring to such information. This is the case, for instance, of a genre of posting discussed in Chapters 2 and 3 that locals call 'indirect'. In essence this consists of blaming someone publicly for a certain situation but without mentioning the name of the person responsible.

Chapter 3, then, extrapolates from this idea about the circulation of information, arguing that it is problematic to classify content and conversations happening in Balduíno as 'public' or 'private'. Instead it proposes two alternative spaces, one described as 'lights on' and the other as 'lights off'. Since the chapter is about visual posting, the many images shown contrast the types of visual material that are often uploaded to Facebook timelines and those shared only through direct interactions using Facebook chat or WhatsApp. However, as the chapter also explains, 'lights on' is where people often show themselves, their personal lives and the inside of their homes, while 'lights off' is the channel regularly used to discuss topics of broad public interest such as local violence. Some examples of the latter are examined in detail on Chapter 6.

The notion of indirection also indicates a particular aspect of how people in low-income neighbourhoods and settlements in Brazil understand social media. Often the modernistic images associated with social media make reference to a technology that reduces distances. Complex engineering allows for fibre optic cables immersed in the ocean to interconnect people living in distant continents. However, a central concern for people living in Balduíno is not excessive distance but excessive proximity. The problem of communication, as the continuous use of indirectness suggests, is that people live in an environment of dense sociality and often seek ways to restrict the reach of their conversations. Offline the closeness of relations reflects the physical closeness of lives; homes are often interconnected or separated by thin layers, and neighbours are often relatives. Locals constantly observe, gossip or spread rumours about each other's behaviour, actual or presumed. In such a situation social media is useful because it represents new frontiers both for speaking secretively and for spying on one another.

A final bit of theorising draws from the extensive work conducted by anthropologist Claudia Fonseca into low-income populations and class relations in Brazil.[8] She vividly describes the actual class distance separating the poor from the affluent, positing that 'to many Brazilians, the only moments of interclass contact are during conversations with domestic servants or during robberies. The barriers of three meters erected in front of affluent homes are like a metaphor of the almost insurmountable pit'.[9] The brief discussion on race presented in Chapter 2 describes the particularity of Brazil's segregationist society, its hierarchy of prestige based on criteria such as formal education, place of birth, gender, family background and socioeconomic class.[10] Fonseca argues that affluent Brazilians tend to interpret cultural differences common among the poor not as cultural diversity, but as examples of social pathologies.[11] Chapter 4 describes matrifocal homes, often framed by affluent bosses and teachers in the region in terms of a 'culture of poverty', implying that the nuclear family represents the solution to socioeconomic ills. That is why, for example, the vice-principal of one of the local schools related the poor performance of students to the fact that very few had fathers living with them. Difference in family arrangements, in this case, is not accepted as a diverse possibility, but analysed as a cause of their condition of poverty.

Such a perspective relates in turn to social media because of the ways in which low-income populations were – and are – continuously attacked online on the bases of taste. There is often an underlying assumption, discussed in Chapter 5, that the poor have not been capable of taking advantage of the internet and social media to improve their education; instead, as a local teacher explained, they have 'facebooked' the school to turn it into a place for 'pointless socialising'.

Why is social media important?

The following sections draw on the various cases presented during the book to respond to the important question of why social media is important to low-income Brazilians.

Social media is economically convenient

It is perhaps easier to explain the interest low-income people display in social media in relation to the economic advantages the internet brings – considering that using social media often also helps to reduce other expenses, namely often costly mobile phone calls. As most of these families (if not all) have relatives living away, social media has become a cheap and efficient way of keeping in contact with them, including people in neighbouring settlements or nearby towns, as well as those living in distant parts of the country. Furthermore, the book demonstrated in Chapters 4 and 5 that younger adult women now spend increasingly great amounts of time away from the home, whether for work, study or simply running errands. Social media is also economically convenient in allowing them to communicate with family members and other close peers while they are physically distant.

As the section in Chapter 2 on mobile phones and the internet shows, the people of Balduíno can be very sophisticated when it comes to finding (and sharing among themselves) solutions to being online. They discover and share Wi-Fi connection passwords at work and at school; they share or rent their local Wi-Fi services at home to neighbours; they regulate their mobiles to upload larger files only when connected through Wi-Fi; and they are quick to assess the advantages and disadvantages of various alternative data plans available in the market. The possibilities of audio and video conversations facilitate communication for those who have difficulty in reading and writing. Social media is different from phone calls: when it comes to local communication it allows for more prolonged exchanges and for simultaneously speaking to various individuals and groups.

Social media represents socioeconomic distinction

Brazil experienced a period of political stability and economic growth during the 1990s until the mid-2010s, bringing positive consequences for low-income Brazilians in general. As Chapter 1 shows, the national government's efforts to control inflation provided a background of prosperity that benefited the very poor in various ways, including through the implementation of successful welfare programmes. Coincidently or not, this period of economic evolution coincides first with the arrival of commercial connectivity services (mid-1990s) and second with the popularisation of Orkut (mid-2000s), an early social media platform that became a national phenomenon among young Brazilians.[12] This second moment is precisely when my informants in Balduíno first describe internet cafés opening in the settlement, and talk about the discoveries and experiments they began to have online.

In this context, it is not difficult to understand how the symbolism of social media, representing as it does modernity and progress, is one of the reasons locals have for adopting it. Working-class families in the settlement are able, for the first time, to use credit money from banks to purchase things that previously they only saw on TV or in the homes of affluent people. The modernity of social media relates first to the price it has, like a new flat-screen television or a motorcycle. Informants talk about the effects of having a television in the 1980s, describing how local children would follow the delivery truck to the owners' home. Becoming involved with social media certainly projects a similar status of socioeconomic distinction that, in Balduíno, relates to parents or relatives having bank accounts, another consequence of formal employment.

In this regard, a computer is yet another expensive item that locals have been finding ways to acquire in the recent decades. Teenagers especially talk constantly about certain objects of prestige, such as clothing of a certain brand, but using social media extends beyond that. The prestige of being online reflects, in part, a certain appreciation for education. Chapter 5 brings evidence that improved literacy has been an unexpected consequence of using social media, precisely because locals are under pressure to show online that they can write correctly. Education has thus become an element of distinction through social media, and a standard by which people are judged.

A close informant once told me she would have doubts about cultivating friendships with people of her age who did not have Facebook accounts. To her, being on Facebook was not a matter of money, as anybody in the settlement could afford to spend time at an internet café. To her and to other teenagers and young adults, the ability to use social media indicates that someone has a modern mindset and is not 'backward'. It also means that the person has the free time to play with social media. This availability of time reflects that the family has reached a certain socioeconomic level which, in contrast to tradition,[13] allows teenagers not to work while they are in high school.

Social media is a particular element of social distinction to the evangelical Christian groups in Balduíno. Although in the past adults talked about social media as a problem (related, for example, to the exposure of children to pornography), this pessimistic view was not prevalent among local evangelicals in Balduíno during my field work; digital technology was rather related by them, in various ways, to personal progress and achievement. For example, during a special event in the presence of a popular artist who had adopted Pentecostalism, few of the hundreds attending the ceremony were not using their smartphones and tablets to record videos and take selfies during the service. These devices exposed the economic status of their owners, who were often prospering owners of local businesses or employees in better paid positions.

Evangelical Christian parents openly discuss new media as part of a strategy to protect their children from being in contact with non-evangelicals after school hours. Families spoke about making the effort to purchase a computer and subscribe to a domestic broadband service precisely to keep their children at home, rather than risk them getting into 'bad company' while out of sight at internet cafés. Nor is it a coincidence that the majority of the men who had businesses related to digital technology (printing shops, mobile repair shops, etc.) were evangelical Christians.

Various cases presented through the book refer to the expectation that evangelicals should be able to read, and have incentives within their social circles to go back and finish high school. In Chapter 5, which describes the current status of public educational services in Balduíno, we see how locals in general either despise going to school or treat this obligation pragmatically – a means of securing a diploma that enhances one's chances of finding employment in the best-paying businesses. Evangelical families are the ones who more often find the means to support children interested in pursuing a university degree. At this stage locals begin to use social media to communicate with people beyond one's traditional networks and beyond the physical limitations of the settlement. As the final section of Chapter 4 reveals, young evangelical women are able to curate relationships and information mainly through the use of social media. In so doing they have sought to reshape the stereotype of evangelical Christians as materialistic, backward and fanatics, presenting themselves instead as intellectually and personally successful women.

Social media helps people to accommodate rapid change

Despite these arguments, and the evidence upon which they are based, it is misleading to look at social media's popularity only as a consequence of its practical advantages and of the economic improvement experienced by low-income Brazilians. Chapter 4, for instance, applies the notion of 'sandwich living' to describe the stratum that currently represents most people living in Balduíno. This level is effectively 'sandwiched' between the very poor, marginalised groups and the type of industrial working class that has already adopted 'affluent' values, such as investment in education as a path for moving upward in society.[14]

I continually heard people in the settlement making comments such as: 'that family has cable TV in their homes, but the children at home don't have food on the table'. Observations like these position the speaker on a higher, more responsible and knowledgeable level, displaying their own standards and achievements. At the same time, looking at the visual posts in Chapter 3 reveals the importance locals attribute to displaying their social connections. This echoes a certain practice local teenagers have (described in Chapter 4). Two or three friends arrange to go to school with exactly the same combination of clothes and fashion items (for example a Nike bag, a Cyclone T-shirt, an Adidas tennis shoe and a cap of the New York Yankees). As the 'sandwich living' framework suggests, locals at the same time are keen to distinguish themselves from the poor, but are also afraid of being perceived as snobs and consequently cut off from networks of support. In short, locals have experienced new levels of prosperity, but they still want to retain links with, and take advantage of, extended families and established support networks.

A possible explanation of 'sandwich living' may be that, despite the various forms of material prosperity people now enjoy, they do not feel secure outside of these networks. As Chapter 1 described, change is perhaps the most constant aspect of life in this settlement. Anthropologist Gilberto Velho refers to the 'gigantic growth of the populations that live in urban centres' as a key social phenomenon in contemporary Brazil, and the largest migratory pattern during this period is of families leaving the semi-rural regions of the Northeast for large cities, both in the Northeast or elsewhere.[15]

During most of the twentieth century Balduíno was a rural village inhabited by no more than a few hundred people (including peasants); it has grown in recent decades to a working-class settlement with a population of 15,000. Old-fashioned farming methods, together with traditional fishing, cropping and a collectivist economy, started to change in the 1950s, when a road opened that enabled wealthier city-dwellers to build second homes here for use during weekends and holidays. Locals started working professionally as builders. Affluent visitors also purchased local seafood and hired cooks, cleaners and housekeepers. Money, previously seen only rarely in the settlement, began to circulate more commonly. A daily bus route opened in the 1960s, a paved road to the capital began operating in the 1970s and a growing number of tourism-related businesses have been established there since 1980s. These include five large-scale international tourist hotels and facilities owned by foreign business groups.

The impacts of such changes need to be considered not only in terms of the absence of urban infrastructure to welcome migrants to the region (both in Balduíno and elsewhere), but also in relation to how such migrants are integrated. Many arrive with little or no formal education and come from different sociocultural contexts. According to census data and the report of its inhabitants, people in Balduíno lived up until the 1950s under socioeconomic conditions in many regards similar to those of medieval Europe.[16] The changes that Europe experienced over the course of many centuries, and particularly during the last two, have occurred in Balduíno within roughly one generation. The consequences for urbanisation, transport and telecommunication have been profound. In barely 30 years locals have gone from not having piped water or electricity to being connected to the world through cable TV and broadband internet. For those with formal employment, payments arrive in a bank account, which also means access to easy credit. Locals today consume goods and services that were until recently exclusive to affluent consumers, from air travel and cable television to sending children to university. Chapter 5 describes how four years of optional basic education has now become 12 years of compulsory school attendance, during which time students receive government incentives to study. Though far from ideal, services such as public healthcare and police do at least exist in Balduíno. Yet perhaps the most drastic change concerns religion. Balduíno has experienced a 'Protestant revolution' which transformed the religious landscape in a few decades.

From having one Catholic chapel, the settlement now has over 20 differ-ent denominations of evangelical Christian organisations.

Many of these changes are welcomed, especially by younger locals, but they come together with new challenges. Social media has become popular among low-income Brazilians for helping locals to improve their situations and become to some extent more secure. As Chapter 5 (on work and education) and Chapter 6 (on institutionally-based rela-tions) indicate, institutions such as schools, police and healthcare cen-tres often provide inefficient services in the face of new challenges. Organised crime (Chapter 6) has become the most discussed subject in the settlement, mainly because of its attraction for young people, and locals constantly use social media to share information about crimes and violence. Schools (Chapter 5) have countless deficiencies and are often viewed as day-care centres for teenagers rather than as institutions that can enhance professional opportunities. Political protest (Chapter 6), though it may take place occasionally, seems to bring no real conse-quences online or offline.

What the ethnography shows over and over is that locals still depend upon their extended families and support networks within the settlement. These forms of mutual assistance (based on family, tradition or religious ties) have existed for generations, but have now acquired new possibilities of reach and scope thanks to social media. So we see how social media helps people to remain participants in their networks during breaks from work or long hours of bus travel. By gossiping, advising on problems, sharing jokes and religious stories, members of these groups demonstrate their mutual interest in, and availability to, each other.

So if we look at the symbolism associated with social media, it relates to the display of economic achievement – and in some cases socio-economic class distinction – that is often accompanied by the adoption of evangelical Christianity, the choice for nuclear family unities and invest-ment in education. However, the practices related to social media are predominantly an extension of the forms of communication that existed prior to the arrival of digital media. The actual use of social media is not so much to interact with people that are distant, but more generally to remain in touch with locals while away from the settlement. It also pro-vides new solutions for enjoying secretive conversations while also spy-ing on others.

Such consequences are very far from the common assumption that social media extends only individual-based networks, as argued in much of social science literature.[17] Actually social media is more important in helping people preserve the social relations and support threatened by other modernising forces, which are concurrent with the advent of social media. Through exploring and analysing such consequences, this book comes to conclusions similar to other books in this series, for example Costa[18] and Miller et al:[19] that social media is often used to bolster forms of conservatism.

Notes

Chapter 1

1 Barros, R. P. D., Henriques, R. and Mendonça, R. 2001. 'A estabilidade inaceitável: desigual-dade e pobreza no Brasil.' Henriques, R., ed. *Desigualdade e Pobreza no Brasil*. Rio de Janeiro: IPEA. 1–24.

2 Costa, E. 2016. *Social Media in Southeast Turkey: Love, Kinship and Politics*. London: UCL Press.

3 Miller, D. et al. 2016. *How the world changed social media*. London: UCL Press. Chapter 2, 9–25.

4 Fonseca's seminal work on low-income Brazilians points to the increasing of the distance between the affluent and the low-income population of Brazil – a distance that appears also in the limited interest that (middle-class) social scientists show towards the urban poor. Instead these academics tend either to adopt a pathological perception of the poor or to choose to study more exotic groups, such as *quilombolas* (communities formed through the gathering of runaway slaves) and Amerindians. See Fonseca, C. 2000. 'Epílogo: A Alteridade Na Sociedade De Classes.' *Família, Fofoca e Honra: Etnografia De Relações De Gênero E Violência Em Grupos Populares*. Porto Alegre, RS: Editora da Universidade Federal do Rio Grande Do Sul. 209–28.

5 I refer here to personal social networks as defined by Wellman and of how these form, in the words of Rouse, 'media circuits'. See Wellman, B. 1996. 'Are personal communities local? Dumptarian reconsideration.' *Social networks* 18(4): 347–54.

6 Miller's study of an English village recorded teenagers using six different social media platforms to connect to different audiences and groups. This and other ethnographic cases from the 'Why We Post' project lead to the adoption of the term 'scalable sociality' to define social media. See Miller, D. et al. 2016. 1–9.

7 The categories of 'public' and 'private' are problematic as their meanings are often not carefully considered. See Weintraub, J. and Kumar, K. 1997. 'Preface.' Weintraub, J. and Kumar, K., eds. *Public and private in thought and practice: Perspectives on a grand dichotomy*. Chicago and London: University of Chicago Press. xi–xii.

8 Locals use the expression '*escancarado*' ('out in the open'), commonly applied to refer to a practice that is accepted with 'lights off' but rejected with 'lights on'. An informant explained that it was OK to be a homosexual, for instance, as long as one's homosexuality is not 'out in the open'.

9 See Yelvington, K. A. 2001. 'The anthropology of Afro-Latin America and the Caribbean: diasporic dimensions.' *Annual Review of Anthropology* 30(1): 227–60.

10 See Rainie, L. and Wellman, B. 2012. *Networked: The new social operating system*. Cambridge, MA and London: The MIT Press.

11 This is not surprising considering the importance of extended families for these low-income groups as networks of solidarity and mutual support. See Fonseca, C. 2005. 'Concepções de família e práticas de intervenção: uma contribuição antropológica.' *Saúde e sociedade* 14(2): 50–9. Duarte, L. F. D. 1995. 'Horizontes do indivíduo e da ética no crepúsculo da família.' Ribeiro, I. and Ribeiro, A. C., eds. *Famílias em processos contemporâneos: inovações culturais na sociedade brasileira* (vol. 10). São Paulo: Edições Loyola. 27–41.

12 Rainie and Wellman talk about 'networked individualism' as an advantageous evolution from the limitations imposed by local-bounded relationships. Turkle refers to new communication technologies furthering loneliness and breaking solidarity networks. And Morozov turns around the argument that the internet expands individual freedom. See Rainie, L. and Wellman, B. 2012. Turkle, S. 2012. *Alone together: Why we expect more from technology and less from each other*. New York: Basic Books. Morozov, E. 2012. *The net delusion: The dark side of Internet freedom*. New York: Public Affairs.

13 Neri writes: '[…] about 39.6 million joined the ranks of the new middle class (Class C) between 2003 and 2011 (59.8 million since 1993).' Neri, M. C. 2011. *A nova classe média: o lado brilhante da base da pirâmide*. São Paulo: Editora Saraiva. 237.

14 The classification of this group as a 'new middle class' has been criticised by sociologists, such as in Souza, J. 2013. 'Em defesa da Sociologia: O economicismo e a invisibilidade das classes sociais.' *Revista Brasileira de Sociologia-RBS* 1(01): 129–58. Instead this population is now referred to as working class. See Souza, J. 2012. *Os batalhadores brasileiros: nova classe média ou nova classe trabalhadora?* Belo Horizonte: Editora UFMG. See also Pochmann, M. 2012. *Nova classe média?: o trabalho na base de pirâmide socail brasileira*. São Paulo: Boitempo Editorial. 123. Almeida also explains how this definition of a 'new middle class' does not imply a change in lifestyle, but only represents a greater power for purchasing industrialised goods. See Almeida, H.B. 2015. '"Classe media" para a indústria cultural.' *Psicologia USP* 26(1): 27–36.

15 This stratum is composed of the population with the average household income in Brazil (located between the affluent A and B and the poor D and E), which expanded in size during the 2000s generally in association with a growth in formal employment among the most vulnerable socioeconomic groups. See Neri, M. C. 2011. 29–31, 143–4.

16 See Miller, D. et al, 2016. 1–9.

17 Lemos, R. and Martini, P. 2010. 'LAN Houses: A new wave of digital inclusion in Brazil.' *Information Technologies & International Development* 6(SE): 31–5.

18 'Classe C' represented 54 per cent of all Brazilians connected to the internet; almost half of internet users go online using smartphones. In Google/Instituto Data Popular, 2015. *Os novos donos da internet: Classe C, de conectados. Think with Google*. Available at: https://www.thinkwithgoogle.com/intl/pt-br/research-studies/novos-donos-internet-classe-c-conectados-brasil.html (accessed 23 January 2017).

19 Neri, M.C. 2008. 'A nova classe média.' *Rio de Janeiro: FGV/Ibre, CPS*:16.

20 Such as in this talk by Pochmann (see minutes 26 to 27), stating that it was the state that was mainly responsible for the changes taking place in recent decades. See Pochmann, M. 2013. Nova classe média? *YouTube*. Available at: https://www.youtube.com/watch?v=UswLAb-Oshc (accessed January 23, 2017).

21 Fonseca refers to a decline in the interest ethnologists have shown for the urban poor, referring to how researchers refuse to attend Pentecostal services. Fonseca, C. 2000. 111.

22 Lima's ethnography on Pentecostalism in Brazil challenges the stereotyped vision of these low-income evangelical Christians as being naïvely influenced by a dishonest religious institution. Her informants refer to their individual decision as making personal changes, with positive consequences for their professional status. See Lima, D. N. D. O. 2007. '"Trabalho", "mudança de vida" e "prosperidade" entre fiéis da Igreja Universal do Reino de Deus.' *Religião & Sociedade* 27(1): 132–55.

23 I am referring here to broad categories of north and south, which correspond respectively to the predominantly poor area inhabited mainly by descendants of Africans and Amerindians and the predominantly affluent area inhabited mainly by European descendants. The cross-comparison of data about race and location from the 2010 census exposes this visually explicit divide. See Nexo Jornal, 2015. Mapa revela segregação racial no Brasil. Available at: https://www.nexojornal.com.br/especial/2015/12/O-que-o-mapa-racial-do-Brasil-revela-sobre-a-segregação-no-pa%C3%ADs (accessed 23 January 2017).

24 This ambiguity appears also in Scalco's ethnography of a low-income neighborhood in the Southern region of Brazi. See Scalco, L. M. 2012. 'Máquinas, conexões e saberes: as práticas de "inclusão digital" em famílias de grupos populares.' Doctoral thesis, Universidade Federal do Rio Grande do Sul, Rio Grande do Sul.

25 Neri refers to the expressed desire of this low-income population to improve their socioeconomic condition. He refers to them as a group that made the dream of prosperity happen as,

for this population, (my translation) 'Where you will end up is more important than the position where you came from and where you are.' Neri, M. C. 2011. 25.

26 See more about this in Scalco, L. M. and Pinheiro-Machado, R. 2010. 'Os sentidos do real e do falso: o consumo popular em perspectiva etnográfica.' *Revista de Antropologia* 53(1): 321–59.

27 It is important to note that displaying financial prosperity and displaying belief are often treated as distinct social phenomena, or are debates associated with different research groups within the social sciences. Displaying faith is at the core of the Protestant movement, as believers have direct access to God through reading the Bible; they also evangelise and promote the idea of salvation. On the subject of consumption see Veblen, Bourdieu and Campbell. Veblen, T. 2005. *The theory of the leisure class; an economic study of institutions*. Delhi: Aakar Books. Bourdieu, P. 1984. *Distinction: A social critique of the judgement of taste*. Cambridge, Massachusetts: Harvard University Press. Campbell, C. 2005. *The romantic ethic and the spirit of modern consumerism*. Great Britain: WritersPrintShop. In contemporary Brazil, Lima uses the term 'emergent ethos' to describe a social type that associates positively hard work and conspicuous consumption. Lima, D. N. D. O. 2007. 'Ethos emergente: notas etnográficas sobre o "sucesso".' *Revista Brasileira de Ciências Sociais* 22(65): 73–83.

28 boyd and Ellison list three features that together define social network sites, one of which is allowing users to 'articulate a list of other users with whom they share a connection'. boyd, d. and Ellison, N. 2007. 'Social network sites: Definition, history, and scholarship.' *Journal of Computer-Mediated Communication* 13(1): 210–30.

29 Yaccoub noted the emergence of a local elite at a low-income locality in Rio de Janeiro as a differentiation based on economic prosperity. Haynes's research at a low-income mining town in Chile reports the opposite scenario: a local elite hiding their economic distinction in favour of preserving a collective identity as workers. See Yaccoub, H. 2011. 'A chamada "nova classe média": cultura material, inclusão e distinção social.' *Horizontes antropológicos* 17(36): 197–231. Haynes, N. 2016. *Social Media in Northern Chile*. London: UCL Press.

30 In 2015 Facebook and Messenger had over 63 million users in Brazil. LinkedIn came second with close to 10 million. *Statista, Brazil: most popular social networks 2015 | Statistic*. Available at: https://www.statista.com/statistics/254734/most-popular-social-networking-sites-in-brazil/ (accessed 23 January 2017).

31 boyd, d. 2013. 'White flight in networked publics? How race and class shaped American teen engagement with MySpace and Facebook.' *Race after the Internet*. Nakamura, L. and Chow-White, P. A., eds. New York and London: Routledge. 203–22.

32 See Scalco, L. M. 2012. 36.

33 A simple search on the internet for the term 'orkutização' returns countless links to pages. This is an example of this phenomenon being debated in the media. Revista Exame. 2012. 'Usuários discutem orkutização do Instagram.' Available at http://exame.abril.com.br/tecnologia/usuarios-discutem-orkutizacao-do-instagram/ (accessed 23 January 2017).

34 There are many social scientists among Brazilians and Brazilianists who are studying different aspects of working-class Brazilians (in relation to topics such as politics, religion, gender, violence and health, among others): it would be unfair to name only a few.

35 *Index Mundi*, Countries ranked by GINI index (World Bank estimate). Available at: http://www.indexmundi.com/facts/indicators/SI.POV.GINI/rankings (accessed 23 January 2017).

36 *The Economist*, 2016. 'Slavery's legacies.' Available at http://www.economist.com/news/international/21706510-american-thinking-about-race-starting-influence-brazil-country-whose-population (accessed 23 January 2017).

37 In 2012 the Northeast scored 0.54 in the Gini coefficient. The other regions of Brazil are North (0.53), Centre-West (0.51), Southeast (0.50) and South (0.47). Source: Plano CDE / IPEADATA.

38 Source: Plano CDE / IBGE PNAD 2012.

39 Source: Plano CDE / DATASUS / IDB 2012.

40 Source: Plano CDE / IBGE PNAD 2012.

41 Source: Plano CDE / IBGE PNAD 2012.

42 Source: Plano CDE / Todos pela Educação. This is directly related to social welfare programmes requesting proof of school attendance as a condition to receive government aid.

43 Source: Plano CDE / IBGE PNAD 2012. According to the 'Inaf' (Indicador de Alfabetismo Funcional), functional illiteracy has been progressively reduced in Brazil. The number dropped by 10 per cent since the early 2000s to about 30 per cent of Brazilians in 2015. However, less

than 10 per cent of the remaining population that is considered functionally literate are fully capable of reading and interpreting written content. *Nexo Jornal*, 2016. A evolução do analfabetismo funcional no Brasil. Available at: https://www.nexojornal.com.br/grafico/2016/11/21/A-evolu%C3%A7%C3%A3o-do-analfabetismo-funcional-no-Brasil (accessed 23 January 2017).

44 I use the fictional name of Balduíno for the settlement in which I lived from April 2013 to July 2014. At the end of this chapter further information is supplied about the ethical aspects of my research, applied to protect informants' privacy.

45 Kottak's ethnography of Arembepe, a settlement similar to Balduíno and also located in the northern coast of Bahia, developed through several visits to the site from 1962. It focuses on the transformation resulting from factors such as the incorporation of motor boats among the professional fishermen, industrial pollution and suburbanisation brought to the region. See Kottak, C. P. 1991. *Assault on paradise: the globalization of a little community in Brazil*. New York and London: McGraw-Hill.

46 Fausto's work is a respected scholarly introduction to the historical formation of Brazil. Fausto, B. 2014. *A concise history of Brazil*. New York: Cambridge University Press.

47 Reis stresses the importance of considering the formation of Bahian society beyond the dichotomy of slaves and masters. Its social structure allowed degrees of mobility and yet it is clearly divided according to skin colour. See Reis, J. J.1995. *Slave rebellion in Brazil: the Muslim uprising of 1835 in Bahia*. Baltimore and London: Taylor & Francis.

48 Nearly 40% of all Africans who crossed the Atlantic as slaves were brought to Brazil. See Appiah, A. and Gates Jr, H. L., eds. 2005. *Africana: The encyclopedia of the African and African American experience*. New York: Oxford University Press.

49 Ferreira, J. P., Filho, V. C. and Faissol, S. 1958. *Enciclopédia dos municípios brasileiros*. Rio de Janeiro: Instituto Brasileiro de Geografia e Estatística - IBGE. 117–99.

50 Risério notes that, in the passage from the nineteenth to the twentieth centuries, the state of Bahia fell behind the southern states economically; it remained tied to an outmoded model of agricultural production during a period of national industrialisation. See Risério, A. 2016. *Uma história da cidade da Bahia*. Rio de Janeiro: Versal Editores.

51 Nazaré, H. F. S. 1999. *Camaçari, Minha Cidade, Nossa História – Memória de Idosos*. Prefeitura de Camaçari, Secretaria de Ação Social/Secretaria de Esporte, Lazer e Cultura.

52 Nazaré, H. F. S. 1999. 52.

53 In the 1960s and early 1970s Kottak mentions taking three hours to drive 60 km on unpaved roads from Salvador to Arembepe. Kottak, C. P. 1991. 6.

54 McCallum's class analysis in a similar context in Bahia reports that the local thinking refers to 'a relatively disempowered "us" (variously *o povo* (the people); *classe média*, median class; or *classe humilde*, humble class) and a relatively powerful "them" (*os barões*, the barons; *os ricos*, the rich; *os brancos*, the whites).' McCallum, C. 1999. 'Restraining Women: Gender, Sexuality and Modernity in Salvador da Bahia.' *Bulletin of Latin American Research* 18(3): 275–93.

55 I have seen and heard locals talking about this tradition. It is also mentioned in Rosa Cruz, C. 2014. *Linha Verde: Salvador – Aracaju Pelo Litoral*. Aracaju: Vaza-Barris.

56 Nazaré, H. F. S. 1999. 56.

57 McCallum, C. 2005. 'Racialized bodies, naturalized classes: moving through the city of Salvador da Bahia.' *American Ethnologist* 32(1): 100–17.

58 Kottak refers to a similar process of urbanisation as the middle and upper classes build country houses and transform a virtually isolated location into a neighbourhood of Salvador. See Kottak, C. P. 1999. 27–8.

59 See also Robben, A. C., Phillips, M. and Aspelin, P. 1982. 'Tourism and change in a Brazilian fishing village; Tourism in the Amazon; "What you don't know, won't hurt you".' *Cultural Survival Quarterly* 6(3): 18–21.

60 McCallum, C. 1999. 275–93.

61 Velho, G. 2007. 'Metrópole, cultura e conflito', in Velho, G. ed. *Rio de Janeiro: cultura, política e conflito*. Rio de Janeiro: Jorge Zahar. 9–30.

62 Interview with Joilson Souza, head of IBGE library in Bahia. He explains that 'isolated urban areas are those that are clearly urban, although without a connection with the main urban agglomeration (city).'

63 Reflecting the shared perception of young visitors in the 1960s, Kottak writes that: 'Arembepe belonged to a movie. (Some French photographers did use the chapel as a backdrop for fashion ads that appeared in Vogue in 1966.) This conjunction of natural beauty with middle-class

appeal of a "quaint" village subsisting on a wind-powered, hook-and-line fishing industry had already drawn a handful of tourists and summer residents to Arembepe in 1962.' Kottak, C. P. 1991. 8.

64 Vilas do Atlântico, a gated affluent community built in the outskirts of Salvador in the 1980s, represents what Caldeira has called 'fortified enclaves'. See Caldeira, T. P. D. R. 2000. *City of walls: crime, segregation, and citizenship in São Paulo*. Berkeley, Los Angeles and London: University of California Press.

65 I am borrowing the concept of 'gated communities' and expanding its meaning to describe the appeal that these types of large and closed tourist resorts offer. Such places relate not just to the 'all inclusive holidays' associated with places like Las Vegas, but also to the exclusivity and the walled protection that provides security to visitors. In relation to the discourse of fear, see Low, S. M. 2001. 'The edge and the center: Gated communities and the discourse of urban fear.' *American Anthropologist* 103(1): 45–58.

66 A more detailed description of the region can be found at Rosa Cruz, C. 2014.

67 Kottak describes the arrival of affluent urbanites and the divisions in Arembepe: 'Previously, variations in house placement and building materials had provided evidence for slight differences in wealth, although all arembepeiros had been members of the national lower class. Beach houses with tile roofs had been concentrated in the main square and just to the north, in an area that had begun as a secondary square but was lengthening into an open rectangle. Moving north, on either side of the two parallel rows, brick houses had gradually given way to wattle and daub, and tiles to palm-frond roofs. The same change had taken place south of the central square, which opened into the narrow Street Down There, whose seaside houses were much nearer the surf than those in the north. Crude huts with palm-front roofs had reappeared at the southern end of this street, inhabited by the poorest arembepeiros.' Kottak, C. P. 1991. 30.

68 While some of the original settlements became tourist destinations – such as Arembepe and Praia do Forte – others such as Balduíno were pushed away from the coast and have not benefited from being part of an ethnic community as described by Grünewald. Those like Vanessa are in the opposite condition, providing a faceless, inexpensive manual workforce. See Grünewald, R. D. A. 2003. 'Turismo e etnicidade.' *Horizontes antropológicos* 9(20): 141–59.

69 For more on domestic servants see Rizzini, I. and Fonseca, C. 2002. *As meninas e o universo do trabalho doméstico no Brasil: aspectos históricos, culturais e tendências atuais*. Brasília: Sistema de Informação Regional sobre Trabalho Infantil, SIRTI – Organização Internacional do Trabalho.

70 Brites, J. 2007. 'Afeto e desigualdade: gênero, geração e classe entre empregadas domésticas e seus empregadores.' *Cadernos Pagu* (29): 91–109.

71 According to the 2012 National Census (Plano CDE / IBGE PNAD 2012), 56% of the low-income population in the Northeast works informally or is self-employed. Formal employment is an important topic in Balduíno, especially since the late 1990s, when the opening of large-scale resorts quickly increased the number of work opportunities in the formal sector. However, informality in work is still very important in the region. Tourist resources depend on temporary labour during the summer months to cope with the increase of visitors, and many locals either prefer being self-employed – for example as motorcycle taxi drivers, builders or waiters and cooks at beach tents – or have periodic incursions into formal employment positions which then enable them to work informally while benefiting from job seekers' allowances.

72 This is an established practice in Pentecostal organisations in Brazil and is supported by scripture passages such as in the New Testament (2 Corinthians 9:7): 'Each of you must give as you have made up your mind, not reluctantly or under compulsion, for God loves a cheerful giver.'

73 The recent scholarly work about religion in Brazil, both from sociological and anthropological perspectives, is vast, especially in regard the shift from Catholicism to Protestantism among the low-income population. Below is only a sample of this body of literature. Pierucci analysed the decline of Catholicism, Lutheranism and Umbanda in contemporary Brazil. Pierucci, A. F. 2004. '"Bye bye, Brasil": o declínio das religiões tradicionais no Censo 2000.' *Estudos avançados* 18(52): 17–28. Mariano studied the growth of Brazil's Pentecostal movement. Mariano, R. 2004. 'Expansão pentecostal no Brasil: o caso da Igreja Universal.' *Estudos avançados* 18(52): 121–38. Mariz contrasts the sociological perspectives about whether Pentecostalism promotes or limits socio-political change. Mariz, C. L. 1995. 'Perspectivas sociológicas sobre o pentecostalismo e o neopentecostalismo.' *Revista de Cultura Teológica. ISSN (impresso) 0104-0529 (eletrônico) 2317-4307* (13): 37–52. For the growing influence of Pentecostalism in state politics see Oro, A. P. 2003. 'A política

da Igreja Universal e seus reflexos nos campos religioso e político brasileiros.' *Revista brasileira de ciências sociais* 18(53): 53–69. Machado, M. D. D. C. 2015. 'Religion and politics in contemporary Brazil: an analysis of Pentecostal and Catholic Charismatics.' *Religião & Sociedade* 35(2): 45–72. Machado, M. D. D. C. and Burity, J. 2014. 'A ascensão política dos pentecostais no Brasil na avaliação de líderes religiosos.' *Dados – Revista de Ciências Sociais* 57(3): 601–31. Pierucci, A. F. 2011. 'Eleição 2010: desmoralização eleitoral do moralismo religioso.' *Novos Estudos-CEBRAP* (89): 6–15. Mariano, R. and Pierucci, A. F. 1992. 'O envolvimento dos pentecostais na eleição de Collor.' *Novos Estudos Cebrap* 34: 92–106. For Pentecostalism and gender see Machado, M. D. D. C. 2005. 'Representações e relações de gênero nos grupos pentecostais.' *Estudos feministas* 13(2): 387–96. Machado, M. D. D. C. and de Barros, M. L. 2009. 'Gênero, geração e classe: uma discussão sobre as mulheres das camadas médias e populares do Rio de Janeiro.' *Estudos Feministas* 7(2): 369–93. Machado, M. D. D. C. 2013. 'Conversão religiosa e a opção pela heterossexualidade em tempos de aids: notas de uma pesquisa.' *Cadernos Pagu* (11): 275–301. On Pentecostalism and divinity see Birman, P. 2012. 'O poder da fé, o milagre do poder: mediadores evangélicos e deslocamento de fronteiras sociais.' *Horizontes Antropológicos* 18(37): 133–53.

74 A detailed analysis of this shift away from Catholicism can be found in Birman, P. and Leite, M. P. 2000. 'Whatever happened to what used to be the largest Catholic country in the world?' *Daedalus* 129(2): 271–90.

75 Mafra raised questions about the interpretations of the 2010 census data from Brazil concerning religion, especially in relation to the use of these numbers to negotiate political alliances. See Mafra, C. 2013. 'Números e narrativas.' *Debates do NER* 2(24): 13–25.

76 This number includes everything between families associated with the same church for two or more generations and individuals who sympathise with Protestantism but have not yet committed to becoming part of a denomination.

77 Similar to the context of Balduíno, Swatowiski examined Pentecostalism as an enabler for the low-income population to embrace modernity and prosperity through entrepreneurship. See Swatowiski, C. 2009. 'Dinâmicas espaciais em Macaé: lugares públicos e amientes religiosos.' *Religiões e cidades: Rio de Janeiro e São Paulo.* Mafra, C. and Almeida, R., eds. São Paulo: Terceiro Nome. 51–68.

78 The Universal Church of the Kingdom of God (UCKG) is among the Brazilian Christian organisations most successful in capturing the interest of social scientists, in part because of the controversies related to what is now called the 'theology of prosperity'. Mafra, Swatowiski and Sampaio argue that (my translation) 'In peripheral countries and in post-colonial contexts, [the UCKG] operates successfully exactly where the population learned to submit to a high level of social control as a strategy to access "social goods"'. Mafra, C., Swatowiski, C. and Sampaio, C. 2012. 'O projeto pastoral de Edir Macedo. Uma igreja benevolente para indivíduos ambiciosos?' *Revista Brasileira de Ciências Sociais* 27(78): 81–96.

79 Mafra, C. 2001. *Os evangélicos.* Rio de Janeiro: Zahar.

80 Mariano, R. 2004. 'Expansão pentecostal no Brasil: o caso da Igreja Universal.' *Estudos avançados* 18(52): 121–38.

81 On Pentecostalism and poverty in Brazil see also Mariz, C. 1992. 'Religion and poverty in Brazil: a comparison of Catholic and Pentecostal communities.' *Sociology of Religion* 53 (Special Issue): S63–S70. Souza, B. M. 1969. *A experiência da salvação: pentecostais em São Paulo*, vol. 1. São Paulo: Duas Cidades.

82 Pierucci refers to a religious form that works as an (my translation) *'in fieri* community [that] disconnects the people from their mother-culture, of a context that earlier seemed natural to them [..] making the stranger the true neighbour'[.] Pierucci, A. F. 2006. 'Religião como solvente: uma aula.' *Novos Estudos-CEBRAP* (75): 111–27.

83 On gospel music in Brazil see also Dolghie, J. Z. 2004. 'A Igreja Renascer em Cristo e a consolidação do mercado de música gospel no Brasil: uma análise das estratégias de marketing.' *Ciencias Sociales y Religión/Ciências Sociais e Religião* 6(6): 201–20.

84 The person who wants to be saved through baptism and be accepted as part of an evangelical church needs to give up the consumption of alcoholic beverages and of any other type of drug (including cigarettes). But non-evangelical Christians do not consider that they are committing to the practices of evangelical churches simply because they listen to gospel music.

85 On the dispute between Pentecostals and practicioners of Afro-Brazilian religions see Mariz, C. L. 1997. 'Reflexões sobre a reação afro-brasileira à guerra santa.' *Debates do NER* 1(1): 96–103. Oro, A. P. 1997. 'Neopentecostais e afro-brasileiros: quem vencerá esta guerra?.' *Debates do NER* 1(1): 10–36.

86   See Mariano, R. 2010. 'Mudanças no campo religioso brasileiro no censo 2010.' *Debates do NER* 2(24): 119–37.
87   In Weber's study of Protestant ethics, economic progress among historical Protestants is a result of an austere lifestyle that does not reject but actually engages with the world through work and generation of wealth. However, Schama's history of Dutch culture during their 'golden age' of economic prosperity cautions the reader regarding Weber's fetishisation of Protestant asceticism and the actual influence its ethics had on the development of capitalism. Campbell advances this critique, pointing out the tense complement – absent in Weber's explanatory model – of utilitarian Puritanism and Romanticism as dual phenomena of the Modern Age, fundamental to the development of capitalism. Pentecostal churches are a late nineteenth-century phenomenon; their participants place a significant importance on a personal experience with God which is manifested through the use of 'spiritual gifts', such as healing, incorporating the Holy Spirit or speaking in tongues. Originating in the mid-twentieth century in the United States, neo-Pentecostal churches directly associate religious conversion with a path to achieve material wealth and upward mobility, and are thus commonly described as preaching a 'theology of prosperity'. Lima argues that the success enjoyed by neo-Pentecostal churches in Brazil among the low-income population since the 1990s reflects a context of national promotion of neoliberal capitalist values concerning individual aspiration and achievement. See Weber, M. 2002. *The Protestant ethic and the "spirit" of capitalism and other writings*. London: Penguin. Schama, S. 1988. *The embarrassment of riches: An interpretation of Dutch culture in the Golden Age*. Berkeley, Los Angeles and London: University of California Press. Campbell, C. 2005. Lima, D. N. D. O. 2007. 132– 55.
88   Mariano, R. 1996. 'Os neopentecostais e a teologia da prosperidade.' *Novos Estudos* 44(44): 24–44.
89   Machado has analysed the reduction of the differences between Pentecostals and neo-Pentecostals in Brazil. Machado, M. D. D. C. 2001. 'Além da religião.' *Cadernos CERU* 12: 139–50.
90   This recent move at the local Assembly of God from displaying modesty and acting as well-behaved people (*gente direita*) to displaying aspiration and economic prosperity has not been fully embraced among the church's members. Dissidents complain more or less openly, saying, among other things, that there are people now not coming to services because they are ashamed of the clothes they have in relation to the very fine and expensive clothes that other participants are now wearing. The head minister is also criticised for placing a high value on ostentation and offering positions of status to individuals and families able to contribute more money to the church. In fact, prestige and financial success are so important for the Assembly of God in Balduíno that the church's leadership incorporated aristocratic practices. For example, during the head minister's birthday party, guests were announced and offered their gifts publicly, as part of the service. These were all from prestigious brands. During the dinner that followed the ceremony, prestigious guests sat separately at a high table, served with special food. See also Mesquita, W. A. B. 2007. 'Um pé no reino e outro no mundo: consumo e lazer entre pentecostais.' *Horizontes Antropológicos* 13(28): 117–44.
91   I use the term 'non-church goers' because people in Balduino very rarely identified themselves as atheists. The part of the population who do not go to church and are not associated with Afro-Brazilian religions identify themselves as 'faithful' and say that they have their own particular ways of communicating with God. See also Novaes, R., 2004. 'Os jovens "sem religião": ventos secularizantes, "espírito de época" e novos sincretismos. Notas preliminares.' *Estudos avançados* 18(52): 321–30.
92   Harding argues Christians are a type of 'other' often rejected by anthropologists as anti-modern (instead of non-modern) and a group that rejects the passive position of other vulnerable 'others'. Harding, S. 1991. 'Representing fundamentalism: The problem of the repugnant cultural other.' *Social research* 58(2): 373–93. In Brazil progressive affluent circles tend to frame Pentecostals as being homogenous and intrinsically backward. See Alexandre, R. 2014. *Afinal, quem são os evangélicos?* *Carta Capital*. Available at: http://www.cartacapital.com.br/sociedade/afinal-quem-sao-201cos-evangelicos201d-2053.html (accessed 23 January 2017). Mariz points to the need to 'criticize the criticism' social scientists make of religious movements, pointing to Pentecostals being criticised either because of their political alienation or because they participate in politics, either because they are too dogmatic and place greater importance on salvation or for being too flexible and too materialistic. Mariz, C. L. 1995. 37–52.

93 Birman and Lehmann discuss the unease that Pentecostalism brought to Brazil's affluent society and how this strain has echoed in public debates. Birman, P. and Lehmann, D. 1999. 'Religion and the Media in a Battle for Ideological Hegemony: the Universal Church of the Kingdom of God and TV Globo in Brazil.' *Bulletin of Latin American Research* 18(2): 145–64.

94 For Pentecostalism's influence to 'recycle' the lives of criminals see Birman, P. and Machado, C. 2012. 'A violência dos justos: evangélicos, mídia e periferias da metrópole.' *Revista Brasileira de Ciências Sociais* 27: 55–69. See also Machado, C. B. 2014. 'Pentecostalismo e o sofrimento do (ex-) bandido: testemunhos, mediações, modos de subjetivação e projetos de cidadania nas periferias.' *Horizontes antropológicos* 20(42): 153–80.

95 See also Robben, A. C. 1994. 'Conflicting discourses of economy and society in coastal Brazil.' *Man* 29(4): 875–900.

96 Bernard, H. R. 2011. *Research methods in anthropology: Qualitative and quantitative approaches.* Lanham, MD: Rowman Altamira.

97 Malinowski, B. 2015. *Argonauts of the Western Pacific.* np: Routledge.

98 Boellstorff, T. 2015. *Coming of age in Second Life: An anthropologist explores the virtually human.* Princeton, NJ: Princeton University Press. Boellstorff, T. 2012. *Ethnography and virtual worlds: A handbook of method.* Princeton, NJ: Princeton University Press.

99 Wesch, M. 2008. *An anthropological introduction to YouTube. YouTube.* Available at: https://www.youtube.com/watch?v=TPAO-lZ4_hU (accessed 23 January 2017).

100 Spyer, J. 2011. *Making up art, videos and fame.* MSc dissertation, University College London, London.

Chapter 2

1 I acknowledge, as Weintraub and Kumar posited, that public and private are often used imprecisely as organising categories. Sheller and Urry argue that there are multiple 'privates' and 'publics' to consider. However, the results coming from this ethnography suggest that socioeconomic background reflects on different understandings regarding the use of content filters. See Weintraub, J. and Kumar, K. 1997. 'Preface.' Weintraub, J. and Kumar, K., eds. *Public and private in thought and practice: Perspectives on a grand dichotomy.* Chicago and London: University of Chicago Press. xi–xii. Sheller, M. and Urry, J. 2003. 'Mobile transformations of public and private life.' *Theory, Culture & Society* 20(3): 107–25.

2 I am following Weintraub's choice of considering the public/private dichotomy by viewing the public both in terms of what is exposed and what concerns the collective audience. Anonymous collective conversations in Balduíno frequently relate to both aspects, so a case of robbery, for example, will generally include sharing the personal information of those affected. See Weintraub, J. 1997. 'The theory and politics of the public/private distinction.' Weintraub J. and Kumar K., eds. *Public and Private in Thought and Practice.* Chicago and London: University of Chicago Press. 1–42.

3 Fernandes writes about Afro-Brazilians becoming the 'main victim, that results from the persistency of the past'. See Fernandes, F. 2015. *O negro no mundo dos brancos.* São Paulo: Global Editora. 139. Scheper-Hughes writes that the people of her field site in the Northeast of Brazil 'are invisible and discounted in many other ways. [...] Their deaths, like their lives, are quite invisible, and we may as well speak of their bodies, too, as having been disappeared.' Scheper-Hughes, N. 1993. *Death without weeping: The violence of everyday life in Brazil.* Berkeley, Los Angeles and London: University of California Press. Velho, G. 2000. 'O desafio da violência.' *Estudos Avançados* 14(39): 56–60. On the topic of imposed subordination see Rowlands, M. 2005. 'A materialist approach to materiality', in Miller, D., ed. *Materiality.* Durham, NC: Duke University Press. 72–87.

4 Speaking specifically about intimacy, Shapiro writes about low-income Brazilians from Maranhão rendering 'invisible actions that challenge conventional moral injunctions'. Shapiro, M. 2016. 'Paradoxes of Intimacy: Play and the Ethics of Invisibility in North-east Brazil.' *Journal of Latin American Studies*: 1–25.

5 Schwarcz, L. M. 2013. 'Raça e Silêncio.' *Nem Preto Nem Branco, Muito Pelo Contrário: Cor E Raça Na Sociabilidade Brasileira.* São Paulo: Claro Enigma. 69.

6 Schwarcz, L. M. 2013. 'Cultura Jurídica: Raça Como Silêncio E Como Afirmação.' *Nem Preto Nem Branco, Muito Pelo Contrário: Cor E Raça Na Sociabilidade Brasileira.* São Paulo: Claro Enigma. 69–77.

7 Schwarcz, L. M. 2013. 23.

8 Fernandes, F. 1969. *The Negro in Brazilian Society.* New York: Columbia UP.

9 Schwarcz points to how lifts became instruments of social and racial discrimination as buildings in Brazil have the 'social' lift for residents and their guests and the 'service' lift for those providing manual labour. Schwarcz, L. M. 2013. 'Nas Falácias Do Mito: Falando Da Desigualdade Racial.' *Nem Preto Nem Branco, Muito Pelo Contrário: Cor E Raça Na Sociabilidade Brasileira.* São Paulo: Claro Enigma. 58–68.

10 Schwarcz, L. M. 2013. 58–68.

11 As Schwarcz explains (my translation): 'the slave labor and the African presence in Brazil cannot be understood only as passive responses to an adverse environment. In fact, they invented their conditions of life and survival in the slave regime in two main ways: by negotiation and conflict. Through negotiation, bluff, bargaining and daily arrangements, enslaved forced the limits of slavery in endless negotiations, sometimes successful, sometimes unsuccessfully. Forms of negotiation included both demands for land and better working conditions as the defence of a playful and autonomous spiritual life – the right to play music, sing and play without the overseer's consent, or to honour their gods by practicing *Candomblé* without police intrusion. Sometimes a bit of deterrence was necessary: when the state banned the worship of black deities, they appealed to Christians saints, a correspondence relationship in force today in the country. But when the negotiations failed, either by intransigence of the lord or impatience of the enslaved, this opened ways to conflict: individual and collective escapes, the formation of quilombos and, of course, uprisings and slave revolts.' Schwarcz, L. M. 2013. 'Pela História: Um País De Futuro Branco Ou Branqueado.' *Nem Preto Nem Branco, Muito Pelo Contrário: Cor E Raça Na Sociabilidade Brasileira.* São Paulo: Claro Enigma. 29–35.

12 Spivak, G. C. 1988. 'Can the subaltern speak?', in Morris, R. C., ed., *Can the subaltern speak? Reflections on the history of an idea.* New York and Chichester: Columbia University Press. 21–78. According to Fernandes, racism in Brazil often erases conflicts and differences by exchanging the reference of a subordinate strata for terms such as 'black' and 'negro'. Fernandes, F. 1969.

13 Drawing on Bourdieu's studies about taste and distinction, Souza theorises about invisible networks that (my translation) 'disqualify individuals and precarious social groups as by-products and sub-citizens'. Souza, J. 2013. 'Em defesa da Sociologia: O economicismo e a invisibilidade das classes sociais.' *Revista Brasileira de Sociologia* 1(01): 129–58.

14 Bayat's original and 'emic' assessment of political activism in Middle East countries provides useful frameworks for analysing situations in which contestation and subversion take place through non-explicit actions and apparent submission. See Bayat, A. 2013. *Life as politics: How ordinary people change the Middle East.* Stanford, CA: Stanford University Press.

15 *Sacis* offer us particular insights in regard to the idea of visibility and invisibility; they have the power of invisibility until their red caps are taken from them, whereupon they assume a subordinate role.

16 Carroll, M. P. 1984. 'The Trickster as Selfish-Buffoon and Culture Hero.' *Ethos* 12(2): 105–31. Dube, M. W. 2016. 'The Subaltern Can Speak: Reading the Mmutle (Hare) Way.' *Journal of Africana Religions* 4(1): 54–75.

17 Amado, J. 1977. *Dona Flor and her two husbands.* New York: Avon.

18 Schwarcz notes that the 'malandro' represents a popular character who rejects regular work and takes advantages of temporary means to live a good life, including comfort and personal enjoyment. This popular figure has subsequently been introduced to the world through Walt Disney's character 'José (Zé) Carioca' in the 1942 movie *Saludos Amigos.* Schwarcz, L. M. 2013. 'Nos Anos 1930 a Estetização Da Democracia Racial: Somos Todos Mulatos.' *Nem Preto Nem Branco, Muito Pelo Contrário: Cor E Raça Na Sociabilidade Brasileira.* São Paulo: Claro Enigma. 36–57.

19 Direct exchanges are a constant cause of distress in Balduíno as Chapter 4 considers in detail. Mobile phones and social media profiles are constantly being spied upon by others, particularly partners. McQuire refers to the technological inscriptions that expose content which is meant to remain hidden. McQuire, S. 2008. *The Media City. Media, Architecture and Urban Space.* London: Sage.

20 It is useful analytically to frame the process of growing up and the learning associated with growing up through the concepts of communities of practice and of legitimate peripheral participation (LPP). See Lave, J. and Wenger, E. 1991. *Situated learning: Legitimate peripheral participation.* Cambridge and New York: Cambridge University Press. See also Lave,

J. 2011. *Apprenticeship in critical ethnographic practice*. Chicago and London: University of Chicago Press; Lave, J. 1996. 'Teaching, as learning, in practice.' *Mind, culture, and activity* 3(3): 149–64.

21 And, as Shaw argues, in other areas historically affected and marked by the Atlantic slave trade, both in the Americas and Africa. Shaw, R. 2002. *Memories of the Slave Trade: ritual and the historical imagination in Sierra Leone*. Chicago and London: University of Chicago Press.

22 In Jorge Amado's novel *Jubiabá*, the protagonist Antônio Balduíno, a poor orphan of African descent, learns 'with the beatings […] to be disingenuous (*dissimulado*). Now he smoked when no one was looking, he swore quietly, [and] lied shamelessly.' Amado, J. 1989. *Jubiabá*. New York: Avon.

23 Fonseca finds similarities between her research among low-income populations in urban Southern Brazil and other ethnographies about ghettos of Afro-descendants in the United States and France. She argues that these urban poor give up employment through being subjected to harassment by the affluent. I was surprised to see affluent employers in Balduíno openly offending their workers by making comments about their behaviour or morals. These employers made this comments in the presence of employees, as if they were not paying attention or were not intelligent enough to understand – or if such comments were an established truth. Fonseca, C. 2000. *Família, fofoca e honra: etnografia de relações de gênero e violência em grupos populares*. Porto Alegre, RS: Editora da Universidade Federal do Rio Grande do Sul. 7–12. Stack, C. B. 1975. *All our kin: Strategies for survival in a black community*. New York: Basic Books.

24 Birman's study of Pentecostalism in a Brazilian fishing settlement points to a similar moral geography, one in which the young people who challenge church norms and values in the outskirts of the settlement – named 'Hell's Corner' (*Canto do Inferno*) – behave differently when they walk the central areas. Birman, P. 2006. 'O Espírito Santo, a mídia e o território dos crentes.' *Ciencias Sociales y Religión/Ciências Sociais e Religião* 8(8): 41–62.

25 Blum-Kulka, S. 1987. 'Indirectness and politeness in requests: Same or different?' *Journal of pragmatics* 11(2): 131–46.

26 Brenneis, D. 1986. 'Shared territory: audience, indirection and meaning.' *Text - Interdisciplinary Journal for the Study of Discourse* 6(3): 339–47.

27 Searle, J. R. 1975. 'Indirect speech acts.' Cole, P. and Morgan, J. L., eds, *Syntax and Semantics*, vol. 3: *Speech Acts*. New York: Academic Press. 59–82.

28 Lempert explains that different fields study indirectness, from linguistics to anthropology to rhetoric to communication studies, but that there has not so far been an attempt to consolidate and synthesise the existing research. He adds that there is not a common definition of it that all parties accept. Lempert, M. 2012. 'Indirectness.' *The handbook of intercultural discourse and communication*. Paulston, C. B. et al., eds. West Sussex: Blackwell Publishing. 180–204.

29 Brenneis refers to these language acts as 'the product not of literary creativity but of ongoing cultural and individual practice'. See Brenneis, D. 1987. 'Talk and transformation.' *Man* 22(3): 499–510.

30 Brenneis, D. 1987. 499–510.

31 Brenneis, D. 1987. 499–510.

32 Indirection as it has been conceptualised and discussed in edited volumes, such as Brenneis and Myers (1984) and Watson-Gegeo and White (1990), are under-studied in Brazil, particularly considering the potential it has to engage with ethnographies of race and gender relations and low-income populations. Among the few mentions I found in the literature are those of Caldeira (1988), in a paper about political discussion in an interclass context, and Pereira's study of the linguistic strategies adopted by women occupying leadership positions in the corporate domain. However, Caldeira's publication was released in an English-speaking journal and Pereira's work, having been released as an edited volume, is difficult to access considering the budget limitations university libraries in Brazil often have. The conceptual framing of indirection is used in Portuguese and has been translated as '*indiretividade*', but is more commonly applied in Brazil by linguists. Brenneis, D. and Myers, F. 1984. *Dangerous words. Language and Politics in the Pacific*. New York and London: New York University Press. White, G. M. and Watson-Gegeo, K. A. 1990. 'Disentangling discourse', in Watson-Gegeo, K. A. and White, G. M., eds., *Disentangling: Conflict discourse in Pacific societies*. Stanford, CA: Stanford University Press. 3–49. Caldeira, T. P. D. R. 1988. 'The Art of Being Indirect: Talking about Politics in Brazil.' *Cultural Anthropology* 3(4): 444–54. Pereira, M. G. D. 2006. 'Estratégias De Manutenção Do Poder De Uma Ex-Chefe

Em Uma Reunião Empresarial: Indiretividade E Diretividade Em Atos De Comando.' *Linguagem E Gênero: No Trabalho, Na Mídia E Em Outros Contextos.* Heberle, V. M. et al., eds. Florianópolis: Editora Da UFSC.

33 Fonseca refers to 'networks of mutual help'. In Fonseca, C. 2000. 35.

34 Fonseca, C. 2000. 13.

35 Out of the various cases of indirect communication Thin refers to, a recurrent motivation is to establish privacy. Thin, N. 2001. 'Indirect speech.' *An Anthropology of Indirect Communication* (37): 201. Josephides analyses strategies and the context for hidden talks. See Josephides, L. 2001. 'Straight talk, hidden talk, and modernity: shifts in discourse strategy in Highland New Guinea', in Hendry, J. and Watson, C. W., eds, *An anthropology of indirect communication.* London: Routledge. 218–31.

36 Argenti-Pillen's study of colonial violence in Sri Lanka includes a chapter on discursive strate- gies in relation to conversations about potentially dangerous subjects. She explores several examples of these strategies used by women, whose informal discourse is 'evasive' to avoid being exposed to danger. However, as Brenneis cautions, the use of oblique and allusive speech is not only related to a situation of domination, but also aims to help maintain long-term social relations in egalitarian forms of social organisation, where direct leadership is dangerous to all involved. Argenti-Pillen, A. 2003. '"Those and These Things Happened': Ambigous Forms of Speech.' *Masking Terror: How Women Contain Violence in Southern Sri Lanka.* Philadelphia, PA: University of Pennsylvania Press.102–33. Brenneis, D. 1984. 'Straight talk and sweet talk: political discourse in an occasionally egalitarian community', in Brenneis, D. and Myers, F., eds. *Dangerous words: Language and politics in the Pacific.* New York and London: New York University Press. 69–84.

37 Brenneis and Myers describe language 'as a sensitive index of social relations as well as an important sort of action with material consequences'. They posit that some 'speech events […] do not exercise power so much as they reproduce already existing relations of dominance. In Balduíno, women are the masters of oblique speech, and not coincidently they use it as means to alienate men from participating on some more sensitive topics of conversation.' See Brenneis, D. and Myers, F., eds. 1984. 1–29.

38 For example, Besnier refers to the use of nouns such as 'those' and 'they' that refer to people that were not introduced previously in the narrative, so the listener has to try to deduce who 'those' and 'they' are. In her study of violence in southern Sri Lanka, Argenti-Pillen explains that the interpretation of the narrative depends on the knowledge and the position of the interlocutor, so 'A well-practiced deployment [of this technique] forces the audience to be an important coauthor of the discourse'. The narratives are carefully constructed to include various levels of understanding to be relevant to listeners with different degrees of close- ness. In Balduíno locals can discuss sensitive information in the streets using such linguistic strategies without worrying much about being overheard, because a significant part of the interpretation of the information depends on the previous knowledge of the part of those listening. Besnier, N., 1985. 'The local organization of zero-anaphora in Tuvaluan conversa- tion.' *Te Reo* 28: 119–47. Argenti-Pillen, A. 2003. 115–116. See also Brenneis, D. and Myers, F., eds. 1984. 69–84.

39 This short video made in the field features informants talking about their experiences of encrypted conversation: Why We Post, 2016. Northeast Brazil: Context - Speaking in code. *YouTube.* Available at http://goo.gl/HpJ6VD (accessed 23 January 2017).

40 Morgan, M. 2002. *Language, discourse and power in African American culture,* vol. 20. Cambridge: Cambridge University Press.

41 Scott analyses indirectness in contexts of domination. Caldeira notes that the 'context of class reversal [that] would probably be significant in any society, […] acquires special meaning in the case of a strongly stratified society like Brazil. The relationship among members of different classes in Brazil is based on various factors of recognition of social position that involves submission, use of honorific address forms, assumption of a weaker position and so forth on the part of the working-class members. Moreover, poor people have to negotiate carefully their right to talk as the social structure usually puts them in the position of listeners when interacting with members of the upper classes.' The ethnography in Balduíno presents, then, cases in which those in more vulnerable positions also use indi- rection as a strategy to ridicule the powerful. Scott, J. C. 1990. *Domination and the arts of resistance: Hidden transcripts.* New Haven, CN: Yale University Press. Caldeira, T. P. D. R. 1988. 444–54.

42 Silva, S. R. 2012. 'On Emotion and Memories: the Consumption of Mobile Phones as "Affective Technology"'. *International Review of Social Research* 2(1): 157–72.

43 Silva, S. R. 2007. '"Eu Não Vivo Sem Celular": sociabilidade, consumo, corporalidade e novas práticas nas culturas urbanas.' *Intexto* 2(17): 1–17.

44 Calls to clients of the same providers cost less in top-up 'pay as you go' plans.

45 Madianou, M. and Miller, D. 2011. 'Mobile phone parenting: Reconfiguring relationships between Filipina migrant mothers and their left-behind children.' *New media & society* 13(3): 457–70.

46 Castells, M. 2008. 'Afterword.' *Handbook of Mobile Communication Studies.* Katz, J. E., ed. Cambridge, MA: The MIT Press, 447–51.

47 Similarly, Horst and Miller argue against interpretations that consider the economic value of mobiles to low-income populations, indicating that social relationships are at the core of the motivation to access these new possibilities of communication. See Horst, H. and Miller, D. 2006. *The cell phone: An anthropology of communication.* Oxford and New York: Berg.

48 Lange, P. G. 2007. 'Publicly private and privately public: Social networking on YouTube.' *Journal of computer-mediated communication* 13(1): 361–80.

49 There are promising comparisons to be made between this anonymous public sphere, Lange's notion of 'privately public' and boyd's concept of 'social steganography'. See Lange. 2007. 361–80. boyd, d. 2010. *Social steganography: Learning to hide in plain sight* (web blog message). Available at http://www.zephoria.org/thoughts/archives/2010/08/23/social-steganography-learning-to-hide-in-plain-sight.html (accessed 29 April 2017).

50 Generational tensions are commonly related to the use of new communication technologies, as discussed in Chapter 4. See also the chapter 'Comunicando, traindo e atraindo: o telefone celular entre gêneros e gerações', in Silva, S. R. 2010. *'Estar no tempo, estar no mundo: a vida social dos telefones celulares em um grupo popular.'* Ph.D dissertation, Universidade Federal De Santa Catarina, Santa Catarina.

51 Miller, D. et al. 2016. 155.

52 Lange, P. G. 2007. 361–80.

53 A study conducted in the Northeastern state of Maranhão indicated that almost 30 per cent of pregnant mothers were teenagers; it also found that this group featured women from a lower socioeconomic background and 34.5 per cent did not have a partner. Simões, V. M. F., Silva, A. A. M. D., Bettiol, H., Lamy-Filho, F., Tonial, S. R. and Mochel, E. G. 2003. 'Characteristics of adolescent pregnancy, Brazil.' *Revista de Saúde Pública* 37(5): 559–65.

54 'Indiretas' here refers to a local modality of indirection and as such is similar to 'indirectas', as Morris describes this practice of Puerto Rican women. Morris, M. 1981. *Saying and Meaning in Puerto Rico: Some Problems in the Ethnography of Discourse.* Oxford: Pergamon Press.

55 Irvine, J. T. 1993. 'Insult and responsibility: Verbal abuse in a Wolof village.' Hill, J. and Irvine, J., eds. *Responsibility and evidence in oral discourse.* Cambridge: Cambridge University Press.105–34.

56 Kardozo describes 'indiretas' as (my translation) 'vague or decontextualized or encrypted messages whose author expects only intimate partners understand its meaning precisely'. Kardozo, F. C. M. 2013. 'Confissões no Facebook: educação e subjetivação nas redes sociais.' PhD dissertation, Universidade Federal do Ceará, Ceará. The ethnography about England that is part of the Why We Post project identified the same practice taking place among teenagers. See Miller, D. 2016. 'The Social Media Landscape.' *Social Media in an English Village.* London: UCL Press. In Turkey, Tufekci reported about people from different sides of an argument talking 'at' each other without mentioning each other. Tufekci, Z. 2013. 'Turkish Twitterverse is a sea of "subtweets"—folks from diff "sides" are talking "at" each other in lengthy conversations, but no mentions!' *Twitter.* Available at https://twitter.com/zeynep/status/412907669708898304 (accessed 23 January 2017).

57 Fisher documented similar occurrences, which he calls 'dropping remarks', in the Caribbean island of Barbados. Like *indiretas*, they are pejorative and typically delivered during a conflict. Fisher, L. E. 1976. '"Dropping Remarks" and the Barbadian Audience.' *American Ethnologist* 3(2): 227–42.

58 See Foster, G. M. 1965. 'Peasant society and the image of limited good.' *American Anthropologist* 67(2): 293–315. Foster, G. M. 1972. 'A second look at limited good.' *Anthropological Quarterly* 45(2): 57–64. See also Rubel, A. J. 1977. '"Limited Good" and "Social Comparison": Two Theories, One Problem.' *Ethos* 5(2): 224–38.

59   See more about narrative techniques applied to avoid responsibility in McKellin, W. H. 1984. 'Putting down roots: information in the language of Managalase exchange.' Brenneis, D. and Myers, F., eds. *Dangerous Words: Language and Politics in the Pacific.* New York and London: New York University Press.108–28. Watson-Gegeo, K. A. and White, G. M., eds. 1990. 3–49.

60   As the cases presented in this chapter should help make clear, a common outcome of using Facebook to attack someone's reputation indirectly is to create confusion, and also to raise curiosity about a situation of conflict inside a given social circle. Given the 'strategic ambiguity' used to diffuse responsibility, it is common for part of the audience to wonder whether the message was directed at them. They may check this possibility, either contacting the sender privately or discussing the matter with people in shared relationships who may be informed about the situation that caused the indirect. Similarly, people not involved in the matter often will respond to the indirect, contacting the sender privately to talk about the matter, to learn more about the situation and to try to find out the name of the intended recipient of the attack. The success of this strategy consists in creating a situation to hurt the reputation of the foe in such a way that she or he has to take the punishment in silence; responding directly to such an attack tends to increase the circulation of rumours. Typically, then, the retaliation against an indirect comes in the form of another indirect and as this 'dialogue' through Facebook posts escalate, it becomes more and more clear who is fighting with whom.

61   On the practice of 'giving' offspring among low-income groups in Brazil, see Fonseca, C. 2000. 15. See also Fonseca, C. 1998. 'A modernidade diante de suas próprias ficções: o caso da adoção internacional', in Dora, D. D. et al., eds, *Direitos humanos, ética e direitos reprodutivos.* Porto Alegre: Themis-Assessoria Jurídica e Estudos de Gênero. 43–60.

62   Legendre, F., Lenders, V., May, M. and Karlsson, G. 2008. 'Narrowcasting: an empirical performance evaluation study.' *Proceedings of the third ACM workshop on Challenged networks.* San Francisco: ACM Press. 11–8.

63   Lange, P. G. 2007. 361–80.

64   Spyer, J. 2011. 'Making up art, videos and fame'. MSc dissertation, University College London, London. 32–4.

65   Fonseca conducted field work at a similar context to Balduíno. Fonseca, C. 2000. 20.

66   Although many of these exchanges happen on the streets, the exchanges are controlled depending on the sensitivity of the event. It is relevant to note this because it is generally easy to associate streets with external (hence public) domains, while in this case the participants control what they say in relation to who might be listening. This communication may take place outside of homes, in places like streets or during bus trips, but the information exchanged is not available to all.

67   I have applied Munn's study of value creation in Kula exchanges to frame the 'fame' of YouTube videos. Similarly to Kula objects that are ceremonially exchanged, these videos 'travel' through direct referral from groups of amateur video producers. The travelling object creates the fame of the travellers who exchange them. See Spyer, J. 2011. Munn, N. D. 1992. *The fame of Gawa: A symbolic study of value transformation in a Massim (Papua New Guinea) society.* Durham, NC and London: Duke University Press.

68   Foster, G. M. 1965. 293–315.

69   An interesting contrast comes from the ethnography carried out in England, where a patient with cancer uses social media to inform others of his condition and hence receive a level of comfort. See Miller, D. 2016. 220.

70   My description follows how informants explained the meaning of the term, but their perspective is not dissimilar to that present in other academic work. See Cerqueira Lana, L. C., Corrêa, L. G. and Rosa, M. G. 2012. 'A cartilha da mulher adequada: ser piriguete e ser feminina no Esquadrão da Moda.' *Revista Contracampo* 1(24): 120–39. Nascimento, C. 2009. 'Entrelaçando corpos e letras: representações de gênero nos pagodes baianos.' Masters dissertation, Universidade Federal da Bahia, Salvador, BA.

71   According to this source, 50 quick tester kits were offered only to women who voluntarily sought to be tested for sexually transmitted diseases. The result showed that three out of ten tested positive, and that one in ten was infected with HIV.

72   This is an example of market research commissioned by Google: *Google / Instituto Data Popular, 2015. Os novos donos da internet: Classe C, de conectados. Think with Google.* Available at https://www.thinkwithgoogle.com/intl/pt-br/research-studies/novos-donos-internet-classe-c-conectados-brasil.html [accessed 23 January 2017].

73　Brazil is often depicted on news reports as being a place of high online activity. For an example see Holmes, R. 2013. 'The Future Of Social Media? Forget About The U.S., Look To Brazil.' Available at http://www.forbes.com/forbes/welcome/?toURL=http%3A%2F%2Fwww.forbes.com%2Fsites%2Fciocentral%2F2013%2F09%2F12%2Fthe-future-of-social-media-forget-about-the-u-s-look-to-brazil%2F [accessed 23 January 2017].

74　*Statista, Facebook users by country*. Available at https://www.statista.com/statistics/268136/top-15-countries-based-on-number-of-facebook-users/ (Accessed 23 January 2017).

75　These works argue about social media promoting cosmopolitanism. See Cross, M. 2011. *Bloggerati, Twitterati: How Blogs and Twitter are Transforming Popular Culture*. Santa Barbara, Denver and Oxford: Praeger.

76　Scalco, L. M. and Pinheiro-Machado, R. 2010. 321–59.

77　Content filters are technical solutions that services such as Facebook use to limit access to online content. They enable the user to select the audience that views each post.

78　Lange applies the notion of 'privately public' to indicate how internet users publish content publicly and yet are knowledgeable and use social and technical mechanisms to limit access. See Lange, P. G. 2007. 361–80.

79　Madianou, M. and Miller, D. 2013. *Migration and new media: Transnational families and polymedia*. London and New York: Routledge.

80　Spyer, J. 2016. 'They flirt, they share porn and they gossip.' Available at http://blogs.ucl.ac.uk/global-social-media/2016/02/05/they-flirt-they-share-porn-and-they-gossip/ (accessed 23 January 2017).

Chapter 3

1　Edwards has discussed the understanding of photography, especially in how it is used by some anthropologists, as simply a form of evidence. Edwards, E. 2015. 'Anthropology and photography: A long history of knowledge and affect.' *Photographies* 8(3): 235–52. For other current anthropological debates on photography see Pinney, C. 2011. *Photography and anthropology*. London: Reaktion.

2　Miller, D. 2016. *Social Media in an English Village*. London: UCL Press. 45–92.

3　Edwards, E. 2015. 235–52.

4　Barthes, R. 1981. *Camera lucida: Reflections on photography*. New York: Hill and Wang.

5　Sontag, S. 1977. *On photography*. New York: Farrar, Straus, and Giroux.

6　Benjamin, W. 2008. *The work of art in the age of mechanical reproduction*. London: Penguin.

7　For example see Gómez Cruz, E. and Lehmuskallio, A., eds. 2016. *Digital Photography and Everyday Life: Empirical Studies on Material Visual Practices*. London: Routledge.

8　In fact the two essential claims regarding visual images in our comparative volume are that 'the vast majority of photography today is social media photography [and] that our relationship to visual images has reached a level of ubiquity that is historically unprecedented.' Miller, D. et al. 2016. *How the world changed social media*. London: UCL Press.

9　See Gibbs, M. et al. 2015. '# Funeral and Instagram: Death, social media, and platform vernacular.' *Information, Communication & Society* 18(3): 255–68, and Gómez Cruz, E. and Meyer, E. T. 2012. 'Creation and control in the photographic process: iPhones and the emerging fifth moment of photography.' *Photographies* 5(2): 203–21. For more regarding the social uses of photography see David, G. 2010. 'Camera phone images, videos and live streaming: a contemporary visual trend.' *Visual Studies* 25(1): 89–98. Okabe, D. 2006. 'Everyday contexts of camera phone use: Steps toward techno-social ethnographic frameworks', in Höflich, J. and Harmann, M., eds. *Mobile communications in everyday life: Ethnographic views, observations, and reflections*. Berlin: Frank and Timme. 79–102.

10　Fonseca's research on low-income Brazilians includes a theoretical discussion about orality and oral culture. She notes that most of her informants – similarly to mine in Balduíno – were either illiterate or functionally illiterate, and oral communication was key to the circulation of local information. However, her field work took place in the 1980s, a period in which mobile telephone networks did not exist in Brazil and landlines were expensive even for middle-class families and individuals. Thirty years later mobile phones are necessary and common communication equipment for contemporary working-class Brazilians. Fonseca refers to Ong's and other studies of orality, and it would be interesting to go back to this bibliography to consider the use of social media among functionally illiterate users. The ability to read is broadly dispensable as informants now both have the support of younger family members to help them with the technological aspects of using social media and are using social media based on audio-visual information. See Fonseca, C. 2000. *Familia, Fofoca E Honra: etnografia de relações de gênero e violência em grupos populares*. Porto Alegre, RS: Editora da Universidade Federal do Rio Grande do Sul. 113–33; Ong, W. J. 2012. *Interfaces of the Word: Studies in the Evolution of Consciousness and Culture*. Ithaca and London: Cornell University Press.

11 Scalco also notes how the home that has a computer gains prestige; neighbours will show up in different circumstances asking to access the internet. Scalco, L. M. 2012. *Máquinas, conexões e sabers*: as práticas de 'inclusão digital' em famílias de grupos populares.' Doctoral thesis, Universidade Federal do Rio Grande do Sul, Rio Grande do Sul. 238.

12 In her ethnography of Yemen, Meneley provides a rich comparison to the situation in Balduíno by describing how the home is the public space for women while the street is anonymous. Miller and Sinanan compared visual postings on Facebook between England and Trinidad, arguing that the contrast helps to visualise the practices related to photography in each place. See Meneley, A. 2016. *Tournaments of value: Sociability and hierarchy in a Yemeni town*. Buffalo and London: University of Toronto Press. Miller, D. and Sinanan, J. 2017. *Visualising Facebook*. London: UCL Press.

13 I am using the term 'neighbour' as a particular category of social relation. Neighbours are people they know from the settlement, but with whom they are not sufficiently close to invite them to the home. In occasional encounters, interactions happen outside the home.

14 As analytical categories, 'lights on' and 'lights off' resemble Goffman's notions of front and backstage. As Turkle argues, social life has always depended on roles and frames. I am not implying that one is less socially constructed than the other or that locals are more spontaneous when in a 'lights off' condition. The differences refer to conventions and types of relationships that exist in Balduíno. My categories derive from Bourdieu's notion of habitus (as seen in Chapter 2), referring to what uneducated peasants in the settlement learn about what they should avoid doing openly. 'Lights on' and 'lights off' represent ethnographically grounded alternatives to the often vague and imprecise use of 'public' and 'private'. See Goffman, E. 1959. *The presentation of self in everyday life*. Garden City, AT: Doubleday. Turkle, S. 2006. *Life on the screen: Identity in the age of the internet*. New York: Simon & Schuster. Bourdieu, P. 1977. *Outline of a Theory of Practice,* vol. 16. Cambridge: Cambridge University Press. Weintraub, J. and Kumar, K. 1997. 'Preface', in Weintraub, J. and Kumar, K., eds. *Public and private in thought and practice*. Chicago and London: University of Chicago Press. 1–42.

15 Scalco, L. M. and Pinheiro-Machado, R. 2010. '*Os sentidos do real e do falso: o consumo popular em perspectiva etnográfica.*' *Revista de Antropologia* 53(1): 321–59.

16 These could refer to the type of files (photo, video), to a technical aspect (use of filter) or to the type of content (humour, religion, politics), among many other possibilities.

17 Torresan, A. 2011. 'RoundTrip: Filming a Return Home.' *Visual Anthropology Review* 27(2): 119–30. MacDougal, D. 1998. 'Visual anthropology and the ways of knowing.' *Transcultural cinema* 61: 92.

18 Novaes, S. C. 2008. 'Imagem, magia e imaginação: desafios ao texto antropológico.' *Mana* 14(2): 455–75.

19 Chapter 6 presents further cases in which social media is used to mediate conflicts of interest between strangers.

20 The general perception is that though the attacks happened in the place they lived, they resulted from problems and disputes between police or criminal outsiders. Goldstein reports on an everyday humour among poor Brazilians that 'makes fun of dead, sexualized, and grotesque bodies and of the death of poor bodies.' Goldstein, D. 2013. *Laughter out of place: Race, class, violence, and sexuality in a Rio shantytown*. Berkeley, Los Angeles and London: University of California Press. 34.

21 The 'Why We Post' channel on YouTube includes some of these clips, which can be watched here: Why We Post, 2016. Northeast Brazil: The plague of WhatsApp for Brazilian parents. *YouTube*. Available at https://youtu.be/C2TG15TT1nQ (accessed 23 January 2017). Why We Post, 2016. Northeast Brazil: Technology and generational differences – INSTAGRAM. *YouTube*. Available at https://youtu.be/9oYBreWYwag (accessed 23 January 2017). Why We Post, 2016. Northeast Brazil: Technology and generational differences – THE VIRUS. YouTube. Available at https://youtu.be/LBTi0zx4HCo (accessed 23 January 2017).

22 Munn's (1992) study of value creation in relation to the circulation of ceremonial goods taking place in the Kula Ring offers a useful theoretical framework to discuss the circles of exchange of videos online. See Munn, N. D. 1992. *The fame of Gawa: A symbolic study of value transformation in a Massim (Papua New Guinea) society*. Durham, NC and London: Duke University Press. See also in Spyer, J. 2011. *Making up art, videos and fame. MSc dissertation*, University College London: London. 30–5.

23 These circuses still exist. The one that came to Balduíno had clearly three types of attractions: humour (primarily sex and cursing), danger (risk of death) and sex (exotic dancers). Both the exotic dancers and most of the audience were younger than 18 years old, so technically minors. The circus then seemed in line with the types of 'attractions' popular on 'lights off' exchanges. This type of content also resonates with the notions of carnival and grotesque realism discussed by Bakhtin. Other studies of Brazilian low-income groups also make reference to this genre of communication. See Bakhtin, M. 1984. *Rabelais and His World*, Bloomington, IN: Indiana University Press. Goldstein, D. 2013. 11. Fonseca, C. 2000. 80.

24 Bourdieu, P. and Bourdieu, M. C. 2004. 'The peasant and photography.' *Ethnography* 5(4): 601–16.

25 Bahia notes how these types of photos are not displaying individuals but the social roles that they represent. Bahia, J. 2005. 'O uso da fotografia na pesquisa de campo.' *Revista Vivência* (29): 349–60.

26 See Agier, M. 2007. 'Espaço urbano, familia e status social: O novo operariado baiano nos seus bairros.' *Caderno CRH* 3(13). Azevedo, T. D.1966. 'Família, casamento e divórcio.' *Cultura e situação racial no Brasil*. Rio de Janeiro: Civilizacao Brasileira. Woortmann, K. 1987. *A família das mulheres*. Rio de Janeiro: Biblioteca Tempo Universitário, Tempo Brasileiro. Bourdieu, P. and Whiteside, S. 1996. *Photography: A middle-brow art*. Stanford, CA: Stanford University Press.

27 As Chapter 2 explains, locals expose controlled content showing intimacy. This argument follows also the idea that privacy does not need to be conceptualised as a territory with clear boundaries, but as the capacity to control the information about ourselves. See Müller, C. 2004. 'It's not about privacy, it's about control! Critical remarks on CCTV and the public/private dichotomy from a sociological perspective.' *Presentation at the Conference 'CCTV and Social Control:The politics and practice of video surveillance – European and Global perspectives'*. Sheffield, UK.

28 Recent studies suggest that private and personal are no longer synonymous, and that sharing intimate content may 'facilitate [contact or encounter with strangers], because of the multiple positive aspects of these encounters…'. Lasén, A. and Gómez-Cruz, E. 2009. 'Digital photography and picture sharing: Redefining the public/private divide.' *Knowledge, Technology & Policy* 22(3): 205–15.

29 Bartlett's historic research echoes a mode of thinking held by older adults in Balduíno, namely that education corresponds to learning how to value family bonds and acquiring working skills from relatives. Bartlett, L. 2007. 'Literacy, speech and shame: The cultural politics of literacy and language in Brazil.' *International Journal of Qualitative Studies in Education* 20(5): 547–63.

30 Services such as Facebook notify the user of particular occurrences related to his or her online presence. These can include cases of comments or 'liking' of the user's posts.

31 Baran, M. D. 2007. '"Girl, You Are Not Morena. We Are Negras!": Questioning the Concept of "Race" in Southern Bahia, Brazil.' *Ethos* 35(3): 383–409.

32 "Caldwell, K. L. 2003. '"Look at Her Hair": The Body Politics of Black Womanhood in Brazil.' *Transforming Anthropology* 11(2): 18–29.

33 In research conducted at a low-income neighbourhood in Brazil, Pinheiro-Machado and Scalco address the phenomenon of the consumption of expensive branded items, noting the importance these acts have in displaying self-esteem and claiming a broader condition of citizenship. Pinheiro-Machado, R. and Scalco, L. M. 2012. 'Brand Clans: Consumption and Rituals Among Low-income Young People in the City of Porto Alegre.' *International Review of Social Research* 2(1): 107–26.

34 The visions of aspiration appear differently in the field sites of the 'Why We Post' Project. Latin America, Trinidad and North Chile represent opposing examples of how, respectively, consumption is made visible to differentiate individuals or how values of collectivity predominate. In rural and industrial China, migrant industrial workers reflect their purpose of obtaining wealth by staging fantasies of consumption, while in rural China economic aspirations are shaped through tradition. Haynes, N. 2016. *Social Media in Northern Chile*. London: UCL

Press. McDonald, T. 2016. *Social Media in Rural China*. London: UCL Press. Wang, X. 2016. *Social Media in Industrial China*. London: UCL Press. Sinanan, J. Forthcoming. *Social Media in Trinidad*. London: UCL Press.

35 *Pagodão* and *Pagofunk* are both genres native to Bahia. They fuse gangsta-rap ostentatious style with musical influences ranging from samba and Brazilian funk to Caribbean Reggaeton.

36 Mothers, as well as partners, are often the most critical of women's embrace of formal employment, as this short video shows: Why We Post, 2016. Northeast Brazil: Context – An act of rebellion. *YouTube*. Available at https://youtu.be/VESJuboJZoM (accessed 23 January 2017).

37 This ideological tension is discussed in detail in Chapter 1.

38 See pieces in popular media outlets such as Holmes, R. 2013. 'The Future Of Social Media? Forget About The U.S., Look To Brazil.' Available at http://www.forbes.com/forbes/welcome/?toURL=http%3A%2F%2Fwww.forbes.com%2Fsites%2Fciocentral%2F2013%2F09%2F12%2Fthe-future-of-social-media-forget-about-the-u-s-look-to-brazil%2F (accessed 23 January 2017). Chao, L. 2013. 'Brazil: The Social Media Capital of the Universe.' *The Wall Street Journal*. Available at http://www.wsj.com/articles/SB10001424127887323301104578257950857891898 (accessed 23 January 2017).

39 See Margarete's case in Chapter 2.

40 A possible contrast to these cases of people avoiding situations that would cause conflict is Gilsenan's (1982) discussion of situations in which people 'agree' not to see each other in public spaces (such as the market) since to acknowledge that they have seen each other creates a moral obligation to fight. Gilsenan, M.1982. *Recognising Islam: an anthropologist's introduction*. London: Croom Helm.

41 Miller, D. 2016. 170–4.

42 Bourdieu analyses peasant photography in terms of how it represents unity. Empson's ethnography on Mongolian herding families examines how photographs placed in the house represent or manifest kinship diagrams; a similar claim can be made in relation to the photos internet users choose to publish on their public-facing social media outlets. Bourdieu, P. and Bourdieu, M. C. 2004. 601–16. Empson, R. 2011. *Harnessing fortune*. Oxford: Oxford University Press.

43 Many locals today, including adults, still carry hundreds of photos on their phones. These are often shown as people encounter one another in their daily lives.

Chapter 4

1 This is the argument in Turkle, S. *Alone together: Why we expect more from technology and less from each other*. New York: Basic Books.

2 To consider how the low-income people of Balduíno perceive what is intimate, it is useful to apply a sociological definition of what intimacy means. Argentinean sociologist Viviana Zelizer conceptualised intimate associations as 'longer-term, wider-ranging, more intense relationships in which at least one party gains access to intimate' knowledge of physical, informational and emotional information. In other words Zelizer describes personal closeness in terms of the knowledge about a person that only very few others access. This definition needs to be considered in relation to the particularities of local social life, which will be presented in each section. Another advantage of using this definition is because it describes intimacy independently of it being neutral or positive. The knowledge intimately connected locals have of people in Balduíno is often used for attacking and shaming. The importance of indirectness in such situations, as Chapter 2 suggests, derives from the efforts to create instances of privacy. Zelizer, V. A. 2000. 'The purchase of intimacy.' *Law & Social Inquiry* 25(3): 817–48.

3 The sources available to examine intimate relations in the past are very limited. The history of illiterate poor Brazilians represents a challenge to scholars of the humanities, particularly when it comes to discussing the intimate domain, as this passage from Falci reveals (my translation): 'The free poor, the washerwomen, the vendors, the seamstresses and lacemakers – so well known in the songs of the Northeast –, the water pickers in the streams, the coconut breakers and midwives, all of these we have more difficulty to know: they did not leave properties after death, and their children did not open inventories, they did not write or speak of their yearnings, fears, anguish, because they were illiterate and had, in their day to day work, to fight for survival. If they dreamed, in order to survive, we cannot know.' Falci, M. K. 2004.

'Mulheres do sertão nordestino', in Del Priore, M., ed., *História das mulheres no Brasil*. São Paulo: Contexto. 241–77.

4 Depending on the case, underage criminals are taken to juvenile facilities and incarceration time is reduced in comparison with adult criminals.

5 A classic sociological study on this topic is Elias, N. and Scotson, J. L. 1994. *The established and the outsiders*, vol. 32. London, Thousand Oaks and New Delhi: Sage.

6 Koury has mapped the growing body of literature produced in Brazil on the anthropology of emotions, and based on this work the topic of non-kin attachment beyond urban middle-class settings in Brazil is currently under-studied. See Koury, M. G. P. 2005. 'A antropologia das emoções no Brasil.' *Revista Brasileira de Sociologia da Emoção* 4(12): 239–52.

7 For a bibliography review of anthropological research on greeting, see Duranti, A. 1997. 'Universal and Culture-Specific Properties of Greetings.' *Journal of Linguistic Anthropology* 7(1): 63–97. Greeting is examined in the context of low-income urban settings in the following papers: Lyons, B. J. 2005. 'Discipline and the arts of domination: rituals of respect in Chimborazo, Ecuador.' *Cultural Anthropology* 20(1): 97–127. Kivland, C. 2014. 'Becoming a force in the zone: Hedonopolitics, masculinity, and the quest for respect on Haiti's streets.' *Cultural Anthropology* 29(4): 672–98.

8 Pina-Cabral and Aparecida Silva refer (my translation) to '*consideração*' (mutual respect) as the glue that connects the kinship ties, from the most basic to the more distant. '[*Consideração*], then, can create kinship where it did not exist before. (my translation)' Pina-Cabral, J. 2013. *Gente livre: consideração e pessoa no Baixo Sul da Bahia*. São Paulo: Terceiro Nome. 29.

9 Locals are sensitive to these displays of distinction and a case of avoiding greeting a person is normally interpreted as being very offensive. Consequently an initial sign of distancing from another person tends to escalate and become a more serious estrangement. And yet, depending on the necessity or the circumstance, these differences can also be renegotiated.

10 See boyd, d. 2006. 'Friends, Friendsters, and MySpace Top 8: Writing Community Into Being on Social Network Sites.' [Electronic Version]. *First Monday*. 11.

11 The topic of gift giving and reciprocation is at the core of anthropological study of social relations. The foundation study on this topic is Mauss, M. 2002. *The gift: forms and functions of exchange in archiac societies*. London: Routledge.

12 For a review of the current bibliography on the theme of house sociality, including collective building practices, see Pina-Cabral, J. 2013. Pina-Cabral and Silva confirm Fonseca's observation about the important relation between the place of residence and sociality in the form of networks of mutual support. Fonseca, C. 2000. *Família, Fofoca e Honra: etnografia de relações de gênero e violência em grupos populares*. Porto Alegre, RS: Editora da Universidade Federal do Rio Grande do Sul. 13–52. See also Marcelin, L. H. 1999. 'A linguagem da casa entre os negros no recôncavo baiano.' *Mana* 5(2): 31–60.

13 In contrast to women and children, men tend to be welcoming and helpful to newcomers. Kottak's ethnography on a neighbouring settlement in Bahia presents similar evidences. See Kottak, C. P. 1991. *Assault on paradise: the globalization of a little community in Brazil*. New York and London: McGraw Hill. 64–5.

14 The most important recent work on gossiping (*fofoca*) and low-income Brazilians is by Fonseca. As she explains, in such communities gossiping is (my translation) 'instrumental to the definition of the limits of the group – there is no gossiping about strangers because the same norms do not apply to them; to be the object, subject of gossiping, represents the integration in the group. [...] Through gossiping, even the poorest from the group can bring something to the network of exchanges.' This specific chapter also includes a review of anthropological debates on gossiping and especially in the context of low-income Brazilians. Fonseca, C. 2000. 13–52.

15 Foster has analysed similar levelling mechanisms in relation to a peasant village in Mexico. See Foster, G. M. 1967. *Tzintzuntzan; Mexican peasants in a changing world*. Boston, MA: Little, Brown and Co. Similarly Kottak found a tendency to use levelling systems in a settlement also in the Coconut Coast. He found that the individual desire to progress is curbed by the proportional increase in responsibility that comes with economic advancement. See Kottak, C. P. 1991. 58. See also Kottak, C. P. 1967. 'Kinship and class in Brazil.' *Ethnology* 6(4): 427–43. A local driver working in Balduíno explained that it was only fair that hotel owners gave money to the police (he did not use the negative word 'bribing') in exchange for the police not giving tickets for recurrent illicit parking by hotel vehicles. As he understands it, 'where a person eats, everyone eats' – meaning that if the hotel is making money, others in the locality should have also a share.

16 Fonseca, C. 2000. 89–112.

17 Fonseca, C. 2000. 89–112.

18 Fonseca, C. 2000. 89–112. Also for modes of social regulation see Comerford, J. C. 2003. *Como uma família*. Rio de Janeiro: Relume Dumará. 25; 30–4; 60–3; 81–5; 130–2. Gluckman, M. 1963. 'Gossip and scandal.' *Current anthropology* 4(3): 307–16. Paine, R. 1967. 'What is gossip about? An alternative hypothesis.' *Man* 2(2): 278–85. Haviland, J. B. 1977. 'A plea for gossip' and 'The ethnographic context.' *Gossip, Reputation and Knowledge in Zinacantan*. Chicago: The University of Chicago Press.1–27. Elias, N. and Scotson, J. L. 1994. 121–33. Simmel, G. 1950. 'Secrecy.' Wolff, K. H., ed. *The Sociology of Georg Simmel*. New York: The Free Press. 330–44.

19 Fonseca, C. 2000. 89–112.

20 Fonseca, C. 2000. 89–112.

21 For this section, though both male and female homosexuality has been common and publicly visible in the settlement since at least the recent past, given space constraints the cases discussed here relate only to heterosexual relations.

22 Among the anthropological research published in recent years that focus on low-income families, see Pina-Cabral, J. 2013. Duarte, L. F. D. and de Campos Gomes, E. 2008. *Três famílias: identidades e trajetórias transgeracionais nas classes populares*. Rio de Janeiro: FGV Editora; Fonseca, C. 2000; Agier, M. 2007. 'Espaço urbano, familia e status social: O novo operariado baiano nos seus bairros.' *Caderno CRH* 3(13).

23 Fonseca, C. 2000. 133–64.

24 See McCallum, C. 2005. *Racialized bodies, naturalized classes: moving through the city of Salvador da Bahia.' American Ethnologist* 32(1): 100–17. Agier, M. 1995. 'Racism, culture and black identity in Brazil.' *Bulletin of Latin American Research* 14(3): 245–64. Butler, K. D. 1998. 'Ginga Bahiana-The politics of race, class, culture and power in Salvador, Brazil', in Kraay, H., ed. *Afro-Brazilian culture and politics: Bahia, 1790s to 1990s*. Armonk, NY: M. E. Sharpe.158–75. Moutinho, L. 2004. *Razão, "cor" e desejo: uma análise comparativa sobre relacionamentos afetivo-sexuais "inter-raciais" no Brasil e na África do Sul*. São Paulo: Unesp. Goldstein, D. 1999. '"Interracial" sex and racial democracy in Brazil: twin concepts?' *American Anthropologist* 101(3): 563–78. Goldstein, D. 2013. *Laughter out of place: Race, class, violence, and sexuality in a Rio shantytown*. Berkeley, Los Angeles and London: University of California Press.

25 Fonseca alerts to controversies of the notion of 'popular culture', which she finds useful to refer to the specificities of a 'symbolic universe' without implying homogeneity. Fonseca, C. 2000. 89–112.

26 Falci refers to the tradition of more affluent men in the hinterlands of the Northeast changing older partners for new, younger ones, and of men also heading two or more families. In these situations the official wife and children are supplemented by parallel stable but unofficial partnerships with younger women without social status or possessions. Such young women could, through this arrangement, gain an unprecedented socioeconomic lift that would be otherwise impossible for them to achieve. Complementary to this argument, Lindisfarne suggests that women associated with men who are poorer and more vulnerable have greater autonomy. Falci, M. K. 2004. 241–77. Lindisfarne, N. 1994. 'Variant masculinities, variant virginities: Rethinking "honour and shame".' Cornwall, A. and Lindisfarne, N., eds. *Dislocating masculinity: Comparative ethnographies*. London and New York: Routledge. 82–96.

27 See also Durham, E. R. 1973. *A caminho da cidade: a vida rural e a migração para São Paulo*, vol. 77. São Paulo: Editora Perspectiva. Agier, M. 1990. 'O sexo da pobreza. Homens, e famílias numa "avenida" em Salvador da Bahia.' *Tempo Social* 2(2): 35–60. Viveiros de Castro, E. 2007. 'Filiação intensiva e aliança demoníaca.' *Novos estudos-CEBRAP* (77): 91–126.

28 Brazilian sexuality is at the beginning of Brazilian social sciences, being a core topic in Freyre's classic work. See Freyre, G. 1970. *The Masters and the Slaves: A Study in the Development of Brazilian Civlization*. New York: Alfred A. Knopf. Goldstein analyses the topic based on an ethnography of low wage populations in Rio de Janeiro, indicating how the 'sex-positiveness' of Brazilians needs to be pondered through a feminist critique of gendered power relations and normative heterosexual relations. See Goldstein, D. 2013.

29 See Fonseca, C. 2000. 133–64.

30 Chapter 1 has an introduction on the theme of Protestant Christianity in Brazil and also indicates key references on the subject.

31 Writing about indigenous family relations in the Brazilian coast, Raminelli explains that (in my translation) 'After obtaining the permission of the relatives, the bride and groom considered themselves married. There were no ceremonies, no reciprocal promise of indissolubility or

perpetuity of the relationship. The husband could expel the woman and vice versa. If they got tired of living together, the union would be undone. Both could then look for other partners, without any major constraints.' Using census information, criminal proceedings and also references from nineteenth-century literary work, Seihon claims that formal marriages were not predominant among working-class Brazilians. Fonseca's ethnography during the 1980s at a low-income conclave in urban Brazil also declares that 'official marriages are extremely rare'. Raminelli, R. 2004. 'Eva Tupinambá', in Del Priore, M., ed. *História das mulheres no Brasil.* São Paulo: Contexto.11–44. Soihet, R. 2004. 'Mulheres pobres e violência no Brasil urbano', in Del Priore, M., ed. *História das mulheres no Brasil.* São Paulo: Contexto.362–400. Fonseca, C. 2000. 13–52.

32   For teenage pregnancy in low-income communities in Brazil see Heilborn, M. L. et al. 2002. 'Aproximações socioantropológicas sobre a gravidez na adolescência.' *Horizontes antropológicos* 8(17): 13–45. Aquino, E. M. et al. 2003. 'Adolescência e reprodução no Brasil: a heterogeneidade dos perfis sociais Adolescence and reproduction in Brazil: the heterogeneity of social profiles.' *Cad. Saúde Pública* 19(Sup 2): S377–S88. Cabral, C. S. 2003. 'Contracepção e gravidez na adolescência na perspectiva de jovens pais de uma comunidade favelada do Rio de Janeiro: Teenage contraception and pregnancy from the perspective of young, low-income fathers in a slum area in Rio de Janeiro.' *Cad. saúde pública* 19(Sup 2): S283–S92. Dias, A. C. G. and Teixeira, M. A. P. 2010. 'Gravidez na adolescência: um olhar sobre um fenômeno complexo.' *Paidéia* 20(45): 123–31. McCallum, C. and Reis, A. P. D. 2005. 'Childbirth as Ritual in Brazil: young mothers' experiences.' *Ethnos* 70(3): 335–60. McCallum, C. and Reis, A. P. D. 2006. 'Re-significando a dor e superando a solidão: experiências do parto entre adolescentes de classes populares atendidas em uma maternidade pública de Salvador, Bahia, Brasil.' *Cad. Saúde Pública* 22(7): 1483–91.

33   Matrifocality is a theme I discuss in the following section about parenthood.

34   For masculinity in Bahia see Souza, R. 2010. 'Rapazes negros e socialização de gênero: sentidos e significados de "ser homem".' *Cadernos Pagu* (34): 107–42. Pinho, O. 2014. '"Brincar, Jogar Bola, Mulher" – A Desigualdade Racial no Brasil e a Etnografia das Masculinidades no Recôncavo da Bahia.' *Antropolítica: Revista Contemporânea de Antropologia* (34). Pinho, O. 2005. 'Etnografias do brau: corpo, masculinidade e raça na reafricanização em Salvador.' *Revista Estudos Feministas* 13(1): 127–45.

35   Beyond this more simplistic framing of gender and moral disputes, Shapiro proposes the notion of 'the intimate event' to theorise the dynamic of affective alliances in a low-wage neighbourhood in Northeast Brazil. Shapiro, M. 2016. 'Paradoxes of Intimacy: Play and the Ethics of Invisibility in North-east Brazil.' *Journal of Latin American Studies.* 1–25.

36   The Brazilian popular expression *novinha* is so popular and powerful that it is the only non-English term that appears among the most used search words on pornographic websites. *The Economist*, 2015. Naked capitalism. Available at http://www.economist.com/news/international/21666114-internet-blew-porn-industrys-business-model-apart-its-response-holds-lessons (accessed 23 January 2017).

37   For more recent categories related to gender relations see Cerqueira Lana, L. C., Corrêa, L.G. and Rosa, M. G. 2012. 'A cartilha da mulher adequada: ser piriguete e ser feminina no Esquadrão da Moda.' *Revista Contracampo* 1(24): 120–39.

38   Historically among low-income women in urban Brazil, male infidelity appears as a passive circumstance. Men were not particularly responsible as they are expected to have 'weaknesses' that justified them falling for seduction. Soihet, R. 2004. 362–400.

39   The economic understanding of these relationships is also present in Sarti's ethnography about low-income families in São Paulo. She points to the reciprocity among partners, one in which the woman's body is the 'reward' for the man who in return provides material means to the household. Sarti, C. A. 1994. *A família como espelho: um estudo sobre a moral dos pobres na periferia de São Paulo.* Doctoral dissertation, University of São Paulo, São Paulo.

40   This passage from Raminelli is not a suggestion that female adultery in contemporary Brazil is directly linked to the very particular cultural background of a specific Amerindian population, but refers rather to the fact that this perception is not exclusively associated with European *patriarcalismo.* Among the Tupinambá people, (my translation) 'Female adultery caused great horror. The deceived man could repudiate the guilty woman, expel her or even, in extreme cases, kill her... [However], In addition to the rigidity of punishment against the deficient woman, the reports show perplexity in the face of the sexual freedom permitted before marriage. The girls could have relations with young men and European adventurers without this

resulting in their dishonor. […] But sexual instincts were curtailed by marriage, when husbands watched them closely, motivated by jealousy.' Writing about working-class women in early twentieth-century urban settings, Soihet argues that masculine infidelity was considered to be a private issue while female infidelity constituted a crime. Raminelli, R. 2004. 11–44. Soihet, R. 2004. 362–400.

41 Drawing from Peristiany's studies about masculinity in the Iberian peninsula, Fonseca writes that (my translation) 'there, the honour of a man depends to a great extent on his control over female sexuality. It may be a tragedy to lose a woman, but it is an almost unbearable humiliation to have lost her to another man.' Fonseca, C. 2004. 'Ser mulher, mãe e pobre', in Del Priore, M., ed. *História das mulheres no Brasil*. São Paulo: Contexto. 510–53. Peristiany, J. G. 1965. *Honour and shame: The values of Mediterranean society*. London: Weidenfeld and Nicolson.

42 boyd and Ellison's definition of social network sites includes three necessary attributes allowing individuals to '(1) construct a public or semi-public profile within a bounded system, (2) articulate a list of other users with whom they share a connection, and (3) view and traverse their list of connections and those made by others within the system'. The research team of the 'Why We Post' project presented a critique of this definition. boyd, d. m. and Ellison, N. B. 2007. 'Social network sites: Definition, history and scholarship.' *Journal of Computer-Mediated Communication* 13(1): 210–30. Miller, D. et al. 2016. *How The World Changed Social Media*. London: UCL Press. 1–9.

43 Fonseca noted also in regard to literacy among low-income Brazilians that romance is also the only instance that motivated her informants to practice writing. Fonseca, C. 2000. 113–32.

44 Porta dos Fundos, 2014. SENHA. *YouTube*. Available at: https://www.youtube.com/watch?v=-bDS63bEpyc (accessed 23 January 2017).

45 Fonseca recommends caution against forms of 'internal colonialism' in which (my translation) 'any difference of values is seen negatively, making even progressive agents to deny the notion of cultural alterity', indicating that Brazilian working-class women 'have considerable power, in spite of ideas about the relationships between spouses being different from those of the middle classes'. Fonseca, C. 2000. 133–64.

46 Soihet's historical study depicts women in urban Brazil as having very different attributes from how the more affluent women were expected to behave. She writes that (my translation) 'Since their participation in the "world of work" was substantial, although kept in subaltern positions, popular women largely did not adapt to the characteristics given to women as universal: submission, modesty, delicacy, fragility. They were hard-working women, most of whom were not formally married, fought in the street, pronounced profanity, and [thus] escaped, on a large scale, the stereotypes attributed to the fragile sex.' Soihet, R. 2004. 362–400.

47 This refers to explicit images or videos of a person posted on the internet, typically by a former partner. See also Sinanan, J. 2016. 'The Internet: Deviation — Cultural Anthropology.' *Cultural Anthropology*. Available at https://culanth.org/fieldsights/857-the-internet-deviation (accessed 23 January 2017). On this same topic we are also reminded of boyd's description of the affordances that emerge in what she called 'networked publics': persistence, replicability, scalability and searchability. boyd, d. 2010. 'Social Network Sites as Networked Publics: Affordances, Dynamics, and Implications.' *Networked Self: Identity, Community, and Culture on Social Network Sites*. 39–58.

48 See, for instance Kitzinger, S. et al.1996. *Mães: um estudo antropológico da maternidade*. Lisboa: Editorial Presença. Scavone, L. 2001. 'Maternidade: transformações na família e nas relações de gênero.' *Interface-Comunicação, Saúde, Educação* 5(8): 47–59. Scavone, L. 2001. 'A maternidade e o feminismo: diálogo com as ciências sociais.' *Cadernos Pagu* 16: 137–50. Scavone, L. 2013. 'As múltiplas faces da maternidade.' *Cadernos de Pesquisa* 54: 37–49. Fonseca, C. 2003. 'De afinidades a coalizões: uma reflexão sobre a "transpolinização" entre gênero e parentesco em décadas recentes da antropologia.' *Ilha Revista de Antropologia* 5(2): 5–31. Del Priore, M. 1993. *Ao sul do corpo: condição feminina, maternidades e mentalidades no Brasil Colônia*. Rio de Janeiro: José Olympio.

49 See Fonseca, C. 2006. 'Da circulação de crianças à adoção internacional: questões de pertencimento e posse.' *Cadernos Pagu* 26: 11–43. Fonseca, C. 2002. 'Mãe é uma só?: Reflexões em torno de alguns casos brasileiros.' *Psicologia USP* 13(2): 49–68. Fonseca, C. 2009. 'Abandono, adoção e anonimato: Questões de moralidade materna suscitadas pelas propostas legais de "parto anônimo".' *Sexualidad, Salud y Sociedad-Revista Latinoamericana* 1: 30–62.

50 Writing about social relations during the nineteenth century in Brazil, Falci refers to cases of emancipation of slaves in the hinterlands of the states of Ceará and Piauí, in which the freed

slave stayed in a state of servitude working for the formal owner in exchange for housing and subsistence. In Bahia the temporary giving of children represented a similar arrangement. Fonseca refers to the complex and often painful outcome of such practices when the popular tradition of giving the offspring temporarily leads mothers to leave their offspring at official adoption centres, only to find out later that they cannot retrieve their offspring. Citing French historian Phillipe Ariès, Fonseca explains that during pre-modern Europe the sending of children aged six and upwards to be domestic servants in more affluent homes was common practice in England and France. Falci, M. K. 2004. 241–77. Fonseca, C. 2000. 209–28. Ariès, P. 1981. *História social da criança e da família*. São Paulo: Zahar. Fonseca, C. 2004. 'Ser mulher, mãe e pobre', in Del Priore, M., ed. *História das mulheres no Brasil*. São Paulo: Contexto. 510–53.

51 The existence of a blood tie, however, does not constitute family relations. See Duarte, L. F. D. and de Campos Gomes, E. 2008.

52 See Fonseca, C. 2004. 510–53.

53 Venkatraman, S. 2017. *Social Media in South India*. London: UCL Press.

54 On the topic of matrifocal families in general and the notion in relation to families in Bahia see Smith, R. T. 1973. 'The matrifocal family.' *The character of kinship*. Goody, J., ed. London: Cambridge University Press. 121–44. Blackwood, E. 2005. 'Wedding bell blues: Marriage, missing men, and matrifocal follies.' *American Ethnologist* 32(1): 3–19. Scott, R. P. 2013. 'O homem na matrifocalidade: gênero, percepção e experiências do domínio doméstico.' *Cadernos de pesquisa* (73): 38–47. Woortmann, 2004. *A família das mulheres*. Woortmann, K. and Woortmann, E. F., eds. *Monoparentalidade e chefia feminina: conceitos, contextos e circunstâncias*. Série Antropológica, no. 357. Brasília: Departamento De Antropologia, UNB. Agier, N. 2007. McCallum, C. and Bustamante, V. 2012. 'Parentesco, gênero e individuação no cotidiano da casa em um bairro popular de Salvador da Bahia.' *Etnográfica. Revista do Centro em Rede de Investigação em Antropologia* 16(2): 221–46. For a broader discussion about this theme among Brazilian low-income families, see Fonseca, C. 2000. 53–88.

55 Legal guarantees regarding holidays, payment and job security, access to bank service and credit, plus various benefits that companies offer to retain employees, for instance private health insurance for the worker's family.

56 Spyer, J. 2013. 'An Ethnographic Account of the Riots in Brazil Seen From the Periphery — Cultural Anthropology'. *Cultural Anthropology*. Available at https://culanth.org/fieldsights/440-an-ethnographic-account-of-the-riots-in-brazil-seen-from-the-periphery (accessed 23 January 2017).

57 Feltran, G. S. 2011. *Fronteiras de tensão: política e violência nas periferias de São Paulo*. São Paulo: UNESP/CEM-Centro de Estudos da metropole. 171.

58 For a detailed criticism of this topic see section A, 'Definição intranquila de alteridades familiares', in Fonseca, C. 2000. 53–88.

Chapter 5

1 The paddles were applied by the teacher in instances of bad behaviour or by the students themselves during regular, one-to-one challenges about topics being taught. The latter were effectively competitions in which two students challenged each other with questions about a particular subject; answering incorrectly meant being struck in the hand by the opponent. Though these were obviously painful, the adults I spoke to about these experiences recalled them with excitement, as a type of game.

2 Fonseca provides a detailed analysis of the literature on topics related to non-literate societies, particularly illiteracy in relation to low-income Brazilians. Fonseca, C. 2000. *Família, Fofoca e Honra: etnografia de relações de gênero e violência em grupos populares*. Porto Alegre, RS: Editora da Universidade Federal do Rio Grande do Sul. 113–32. According to the 'Inaf' (Indicador de Alfabetismo Funcional), about 30 per cent of Brazilians were functionally illiterate in 2015. See Nexo Jornal, 2016. *A evolução do analfabetismo funcional no Brasil*. Available at https://www.nexojornal.com.br/grafico/2016/11/21/A-evolu%C3%A7%C3%A3o-do-analfabetismo-funcional-no-Brasil (Accessed 23 January 2017).

3 Kuznesof's recent study argues that low-income families in Brazil historically preferred their offspring to learn (in the practical and in the moral sense) through beginning to work at an

early age. See Kuznesof, E. A. 1998. 'The puzzling contradictions of child labor, unemployment, and education in Brazil.' *Journal of Family History* 23(3): 225–39.

4 Balduíno also has a private school that until recently provided 12 years of compulsory schooling, but now caters only for students in years 1 to 8.

5 Attuned with the various professional opportunities open to working-class individuals in this region, these programmes provide short and relatively less expensive instruction in subjects such as Excel, general office management and Autocad, software used to design the structure of houses and buildings. They also offer a basic introduction to computers.

6 During the ethnography I heard informally of one serious case of a secondary school teacher who had allegedly seduced students. Apparently the teacher was quietly dismissed but the case was never taken to the police.

7 The books and computers that these institutions receive are often locked away, or piled up in various locations within the school.

8 See Soares, S. and Sátyro, N. 2009. *O Programa Bolsa Família: desenho institucional, impactos e possibilidades futuras*. Texto para Discussão (N° 1424). Brasília: Instituto de Pesquisa Econômica Aplicada (IPEA).

9 Venkatraman's study in Tamil Nadu, southern India, also found that while more affluent families tended to see social media as a problem that damaged educational results, those from lower income groups saw social media more positively, its use indicating that their children might have the chance of a better paid job in that sector. Venkatraman, S. 2017. *Social Media in South India*. London: UCL Press.

10 These conceptual tools have been proposed in the context of this research about learning and technology. Ito, M. et al. 2009. *Hanging out, messing around, and geeking out: Kids living and learning with new media*. Cambridge, Mass and London: The MIT Press.

11 Fonseca refers to schools as part of normalising forces, acting in conjunction with more employment stability and access to bank credit. See Fonseca, C. 2000. 89–112.

12 Collins argues that it remains a problem in the social sciences to understand how social inequality results from the relationships between schools, classrooms and society. Collins, J. 2009. 'Social reproduction in classrooms and schools.' *Annual Review of Anthropology* 38: 33–48.

13 According to Fonseca, (my translation) 'the contempt [for employment] can be interpreted as self-defence, since many […] have at some point been brutally dismissed by a potential boss.' Fonseca, C. 2000. 12–52.

14 An informant explained that in this region a person of African ancestry will not succeed in a job interview for an office position if they have an Afro hairstyle.

15 See Fonseca, C. 2008. 'Preparando-se para a vida: reflexões sobre escola e adolescência em grupos populares.' *Em Aberto* 14(61).

16 For the ways in which the education system contributes to the maintenance of inequality see: Swartz, D. 1977. 'Pierre Bourdieu: The cultural transmission of social inequality.' *Harvard Educational Review* 47(4): 545–55. For a classic study of issues of work and education see Willis, P. E. 1977. *Learning to labor: How working class kids get working class jobs*. New York: Columbia University Press.

17 Teachers in Balduíno have been given incentives to buy computers, but in general they are not comfortable with the challenges that digital communication brings to their work. For more on this topic see Santos Abreu, R. D. A. and Nicolaci-da-Costa, A. M. 2003. 'Internet: um novo desafio para os educadores.' *Paidéia* 13(25): 27–40. Medeiros, Z. and Ventura, P. C. S. 2008. 'Cultura tecnológica e redes sociotécnicas: um estudo.' *Educação e Pesquisa* 34(1): 63–75. Santos, G. L. 2011. 'Ensinar e aprender no meio virtual: rompendo paradigmas.' *Educação e pesquisa* 37(2): 307–20. Santos, G. L. 2011. 'Uma pesquisa longitudinal sobre professores e computadores.' *Educação & Realidade* 36(3).

18 Another example of how conversations are carried on from social media to face-to-face situations appears in this quote from a teenager: 'When night comes, everybody goes to the square where the conversations roll loose… we chit-chat til break of dawn. But the conversations there already begin in the middle, you know? The whole conversation starts on Face (Facebook), and continues at the square.' Nemer, D. 2013. *Favela Digital: The other side of technology*. Vitoria, Brazil: Editora GSA. 50.

19 Costa, E. 2016. *Social Media in Southeast Turkey*. London: UCL Press. McDonald, T. 2016. *Social Media in Rural China*. London: UCL Press. Venkatraman, S. 2017. Miller, D. 2016. *Social media in an English village*. London: UCL Press. 220.

20 See chapters on education, work and inequality in Miller, D. et al. 2016. *How the world changed social media*. London: UCL Press.

21 For more about using social media in the context of learning in Brazil, see Belloni, M. L. and Gomes, N. G. 2008. 'Infância, mídias e aprendizagem: autodidaxia e colaboração.' *Educação & Sociedade* 29(104): 717–46.

22 For more on YouTube and learning see Snickars, P. and Vonderau, P. 2009. *The YouTube Reader*. Stockholm: National Library of Sweden. Wesch, M. 2008. *An anthropological introduction to YouTube. YouTube*. Available at: https://www.youtube.com/watch?v=TPAO-lZ4_hU (accessed 23 January 2017). Spyer, J. 2011. *Making up art, videos and fame*. MSc dissertation, University College London, London.

23 For more about mental health in low-income Brazil see, for example, Duarte, L. F. D. 1988. *Da vida nervosa nas classes trabalhadoras urbanas*. Rio de Janeiro: Zahar. Fonseca, C. 1999. 'Quando cada caso não é um caso.' *Revista Brasileira de Educação* 10: 58–78. Duarte, L. F. D. 2003. 'Indivíduo e pessoa na experiência da saúde e da doença.' *Ciência & Saúde Coletiva* 8(1): 173–83. Silveira, M. L. D. 2000. *O nervo cala, o nervo fala: a linguagem da doença. Coleção Antropologia & Saúde*. Rio de Janeiro: Fiocruz.

24 On reading as a social practice and how it relates to the use of electronic media see Griswold, W., McDonnell, T. and Wright, N. 2005. 'Reading and the reading class in the twenty-first century.' *Annual Review of Sociology* 31: 127–41.

25 This phenomenon was then captured by young people using their phones and circulated nationally among low-income online networks as in the following videos: Why We Post, 2016. Northeast Brazil: The plague of WhatsApp for Brazilian parents. *YouTube*. Available at: https://youtu.be/C2TG15TT1nQ (accessed 23 January 2017). Why We Post, 2016. Northeast Brazil: Technology and generational differences – THE VIRUS. *YouTube*. Available at https://youtu.be/LBTi0zx4HCo (accessed 23 January 2017). Why We Post, 2016. Northeast Brazil: Technology and generational differences – INSTAGRAM. *YouTube*. Available at https://youtu.be/9oYBreWYwag (accessed 23 January 2017).

26 For literacy and issues of shame among poor Brazilians see Bartlett, L. 2007. 'Literacy, speech and shame: The cultural politics of literacy and language in Brazil.' *International Journal of Qualitative Studies in Education* 20(5): 547–63.

27 This solution is an appropriation of Google's Autocomplete service, which suggests to its search engine users common words or phrases associated with the content being typed. Young people in Balduíno are not interested in searching, but they consider that the most common results showing on Autocomplete will probably be the formal version. For example, searching for '*nos va*' brings out as the first alternative showing the correct verbal tense '*nós vamos*' ('we go').

28 For popular culture and oral culture in Brazilian low-income groups see Fonseca, C. 2000. 113–32.

29 In the Brazilian public school system students have classes during only half of the day. This enables schools to serve more people by operating in three shifts: morning, afternoon and evening.

30 Such as Friv.com, The Best Free Online Games! [Jogos | Juegos]. Available at http://www.friv.com/ (accessed 23 January 2017).

31 For more on apprenticeship and communities of practice see Lave, J. 2011. *Apprenticeship in critical ethnographic practice*. Chicago and London: Chicago University Press. Lave, J. and Wenger, E. *Situated learning: Legitimate peripheral participation*. Cambridge and New York: Cambridge University Press. Lave, J. 1988. *Cognition in practice: Mind, mathematics and culture in everyday life*. Cambridge and New York: Cambridge University Press.

32 Brazilian public universities are often among the best in the country, while elementary and middle-level public schools often provide precarious education. This means that most students that have high scores in the exams enabling them to enter public universities are of middle or upper class background and their families could afford higher quality private schools. More recently, the increasing number of low-income Brazilians interested in having a university diploma created an opportunity for new private universities that charge fees within reach of their earnings and have entrance exams more compatible with the reality of public schools.

33 This type of usage, of affluent teenagers using a variety of social media platforms to accomplish different purposes, is described in Miller, D. 2016. 220.

34 Rainie, L. and Wellman, B. 2012. *Networked: The new social operating system*. Cambridge, MA and London: The MIT Press. 6–7.

35 Rainie, L. and Wellman, B. 2012. 6.

36 Rainie, L. and Wellman, B. 2012. 7.

Chapter 6

1   Instead of focusing on 'formal politics', the chapter will examine the informal aspects related to how one person or group negotiates and influences the actions and decisions of others. See Painter, J. and Jeffrey, A. 2009. *Political geography*. London: Sage.

2   The inadequate help that public services provide is compensated for by collaboration inside the family domain. Citing Durham, Sarti (1994: 60) writes (my translation) that the relationships among the urban poor in Brazil are established 'in a code of loyalties and reciprocities and mutual obligations, typical of family relations, that make feasible and shape its way of life also in the city, making the family and the code of reciprocity implicit in it a value to the poor'. Sarti, C.A. 1994. 'A família como espelho: um estudo sobre a moral dos pobres na periferia de São Paulo.' Doctoral dissertation, University of São Paulo, São Paulo. Durham, E. R. 1973. *A caminho da cidade: a vida rural e a migração para São Paulo*, vol. 77. São Paulo: Editora Perspectiva.

3   Although the topic of gated communities is not new in the social sciences, not many studies have related this phenomenon to tourism. See Donaldson, R. 2009. 'The making of a tourism-gentrified town: Greyton, South Africa.' *Geography* 94(2): 88–99. On gated communities, see Low, S. M. 2001. 'The edge and the center: Gated communities and the discourse of urban fear.' *American anthropologist* 103(1): 45–58. Caldeira, T. P. 1996. 'Fortified Enclaves: The New Urban Segregation.' *Public culture* 8(2): 303–28.

4   Chapter 5 of this book analyses local schools in relation to the presence of organised crime.

5   Fonseca has described physical strength in low-income Brazil as an important element to organise social relations. Fonseca, C. 2000. *Família, Fofoca e Honra: etnografia de relações de gênero e violência em grupos populares*. Porto Alegre, RS: Editora da Universidade Federal do Rio Grande do Sul. 13–52.

6   Fonseca notes how working-class morality imposes a limit to harming women and children outside of the domestic space. One reason this became such a talked-about event is probably because the victim was a child. Fonseca, C. 2000. 41.

7   In The Book of Job, Satan challenges God to test Job's integrity. Job is a virtuous and prosperous family man who, through God's actions, faces horrendous disasters that take away his health, his property and his children.

8   O'Donnell's colour classification system describe 'brown areas' corresponding to locations in Brazil where the state is unable to enforce its legality, so local politics depend on clientelism and similarly personal forms of relationships. Paradoxically police services do not attend the population, but the lack of legality justifies the use of oppressive force against residents of these areas. O'Donnell, G. 1993. 'On the state, democratization and some conceptual problems: A Latin American view with glances at some postcommunist countries.' *World Development* 21(8): 1355–69.

9   For a recent ethnographic study of urban violence in urban Brazil see, among others, Feltran, G. S. 2011. *Fronteiras de tensão: política e violência nas periferias de São Paulo*. São Paulo: UNESP/CEM-Centro de Estudos da metropole.171. Zaluar, A. 1985. *A Máquina e a Revolta: As Organizações Populares e o Significado da Pobreza*. São Paulo: Brasiliense. Zaluar, A. 2012. 'Juventude violenta: processos, retrocessos e novos percursos.' *Revista Dados* 55(2): 327–65. Goldstein, D. 2013. *Laughter out of place: Race, class, violence, and sexuality in a Rio shantytown*. Berkeley, Los Angeles and London: University of California Press. Scheper-Hughes, N. 1993. *Death without weeping: The violence of everyday life in Brazil*. Berkeley, Los Angeles and London: University of California Press.

10   See this online publication for a great number of cases and analysis concerning these protests: Dent, A. and Pinheiro-Machado, R., eds. 2013. 'Protesting Democracy in Brazil – Cultural Anthropology.' *Cultural Anthropology*. Available at https://culanth.org/fieldsights/426-protesting-democracy-in-brazil (accessed 23 January 2017).

11   Costa discusses online activism in the context of ethnic tensions in Turkey. Costa, E. 2016. *Social Media in Southeast Turkey*. London: UCL Press. Haynes provides an interesting parallel about social media being used in a mining town to declare loyalties to the region, which locals see as marginalised by the national government. Haynes, N. 2016. *Social Media in Northern Chile*. London: UCL Press.

12   For political clientelism see, for example, Wilkis, A. 2016. 'Money, morality, and politics in the slums of Buenos Aires.' *Horizontes Antropológicos* 22(45): 49–76. Colabella, L. 2010. 'Patrões e clientes ou redistribuição entre iguais? Uma reflexão sobre clientelismo e suas transposições

contextuais.' *Revista Mana. Estudos de Antropologia Social* 16(2): 287–310. Graham, R. 1997. *Clientelismo e política no Brasil do século XIX*. Rio de Janeiro: Editora UFRJ.

13 Feltran's study of low-income areas of São Paulo describes how crime organisations become progressively closer to the population as providers of protection. Feltran, G. S. 2011.

14 Brazilian judges have on several occasions ordered the suspension of access to WhatsApp in relation to its use by criminals. *The Economist*, 2008. 'Faulty powers.' Available at http://www. economist.com/node/10566838 (accessed 23 January 2017).

15 Feltran shares a conversation with a teenager explaining that he prefers to die young than to have the life his father had. Feltran, G. S. 2011. 171.

16 On the topic of the conversion of criminals through evangelical organisations see Machado, C.B. 2014. 'Pentecostalismo e o sofrimento do (ex-) bandido: testemunhos, mediações, modos de subjetivação e projetos de cidadania nas periferias.' *Horizontes antropológicos* 20(42): 153–80. For more about the interactions of evangelicals and crime see Birman, P. 2009. 'Feitiçarias, territórios e resistências marginais.' *Mana* 15(2): 321–48.

17 A reference to scriptures from the Bible such as 'Ah, Lord God! It is you who made the heavens and the earth by your great power and by your outstretched arm! Nothing is too hard for you' (Jer. 32:17) and 'See, I am the Lord, the God of all flesh; is anything too hard for me?' (Jer. 32:27). Coogan, M. D. et al. 2010. 'Jeremiah 32.' *The new Oxford annotated Bible: with the Apocrypha*. New York: Oxford University Press.1112–13.

18 See Mafra, C. 2013. 'Números e narrativas.' *Debates do NER* 2(24): 13–25.

19 It is not only evangelical Christian parents who do this, of course. However, they are in general more concerned with the whereabouts of their children.

20 Non-evangelicals, especially those with lower earnings, have a similar perspective. They say that it is better for their children to be busy using social media and playing games at internet cafés rather than getting into trouble elsewhere. For a similar argument see Nemer, D. 2013. *Favela Digital: The other side of technology*. Vitoria, Brazil: Editora GSA. 16.

21 As Chapter 1 has presented, there are significant differences within this community – for example between historic Protestant denominations such as the Baptists, which arrived in Brazil in the mid-1800s, Pentecostal organisations such as the Assembly of God, established in the early 1900s, and neo-Pentecostal churches such as the Universal Church of the Reign of God, formed in the 1970s and famous for promoting the 'theology of prosperity'.

22 Sandra's case is further detailed in Miller, D. et al. 2016. 128–41.

23 See Fonseca, C. 2002. 'Inequality near and far: adoption as seen from the Brazilian favelas.' *Law and Society Review* 36(2): 397–432. Fonseca, C. 2002. 'The politics of adoption: child rights in the Brazilian setting.' *Law & Policy* 24(3): 199–227. Fonseca, C. 2003. 'Patterns of shared parenthood among the Brazilian poor.' *Social text* 21(1):111–27. Fonseca, C. 2004. 'The circulation of children in a Brazilian working-class neighborhood.' *Cross-cultural approaches to adoption*. Bowie, F., ed. Abingdon, Oxfordshire: Routledge. 165.

24 Duarte also argues that the culture of the Brazilian urban working classes is (my translation) '"hierarchical" or "holistic" in contrast to the "individualism" considered as the ideal, educated values of the middle and upper sectors of society'. Duarte, L. F. D. 1988. *Da vida nervosa nas classes trabalhadoras urbanas*. Rio de Janeiro: Zahar.

25 On gossip and low-income populations in Brazil see Fonseca, C. 2000. 13–52.

26 For indirectness in everyday communication in Balduíno, and particularly for postings called 'indireta', see Chapter 2.

27 Sarti explains that the importance of faith among the poor is that they can be morally rich to compensate for lacking economic and political wealth. Sarti, C. A. 1994. 189.

Chapter 7

1 Lemos, R. and Martini, P. 2010. 'LAN Houses: A new wave of digital inclusion in Brazil.' *Information Technologies & International Development* 6(SE): 31–5.

2 Cruz, R. D. C. 2012. 'Social prejudice on the Internet: propagation of prejudice and social segregation from an analysis of sites and social networks.' *Perspectivas em Ciência da Informação* 17(3): 121–36.

3 Neri, M. C. 2008. *A nova classe média: o lado brilhante da base da pirâmide*. São Paulo: Editora Saraiva.

4   See Souza, J. 2012. *Os batalhadores brasileiros: nova classe média ou nova classe trabalhadora?* Belo Horizonte: Editora UFMG. See also Pochmann, M. 2012. *Nova classe média?: o trabalho na base de pirâmide socail brasileira*. São Paulo: Boitempo Editorial.

5   Fonseca advises against a romantic, 'missionary' type of study of low-income populations; she argues that this idealism limits the perception of contradictions and conflicts inside a given social group. In this book I have extended the same advice to idealising and romanticising the transformative power of the internet. Fonseca, C. 2006. 'Classe e a recusa etnográfica.' Brites, J. and Fonseca, C., eds. *Etnografias da participação*. Santa Cruz: EDUNISC.

6   Madianou, M. and Miller, D. 2013. *Migration and new media: Transnational families and polymedia*. London and New York: Routledge.

7   Brenneis, D. 1984. 'Straight talk and sweet talk: political discourse in an occasionally egalitarian community.' Brenneis, D. and Myers, F., eds. *Dangerous words: Language and politics in the Pacific*. New York and London: University Press. 69–84. Watson-Gegeo, K. A. and White, G. M. 1990. *Disentangling: Conflict discourse in Pacific societies*. Stanford, CA: Stanford University Press. Caldeira, T. P. D. R. 1988. 'The Art of Being Indirect: Talking about Politics in Brazil.' *Cultural Anthropology* 3(4): 444–54.

8   See Fonseca, C. 2000. *Família, fofoca e honra: etnografia de relações de gênero e violência em grupos populares*. Porto Alegre, RS: Editora da Universidade Federal do Rio Grande do Sul.

9   Fonseca, C. 2000. 108.

10 Schwarcz, L. M. 2013. 'Nas Falácias Do Mito: Falando Da Desigualdade Racial.' *Nem Preto Nem Branco, Muito Pelo Contrário: Cor E Raça Na Sociabilidade Brasileira*. São Paulo: Claro Enigma.58-68.

11 As Fonseca writes (my translation): 'Even today, the idea that there can exist, among popular groups, forms of otherness that are worth of analysis meets resistance in and outside the academic world. [They cite] proofs that, deep down, all that a poor person wants is to be a bourgeois. Examples of class conversion are mentioned – that is, when this or that person move up socially, and soon adopts behaviours fitting with (his or her) new social class – to then produce biased interpretations, arguing that the person wanted since always to live this way. In a projection of their own class values, the researcher wants to convince us that these are deep cravings that only now, with a relative prosperity, the individual finally can achieve.' Fonseca, C. 2000. 125.

12 Kugel, S. 2006. A Web Site Born in U.S. Finds Fans in Brazil. Available at http://www.nytimes.com/2006/04/10/technology/a-web-site-born-in-us-finds-fans-in-brazil.html (accessed 23 January 2017).

13 See Kuznesof, E. A. 1998. 'The puzzling contradictions of child labor, unemployment, and education in Brazil.' *Journal of Family History* 23(3): 225–39.

14 Fonseca, C. 2000. 89–112.

15 Velho, G. 2007. 'Metrópole, cultura e conflito.' *Rio de Janeiro: cultura, política e conflito*. Rio de Janeiro: Jorge Zahar. 9–30.

16 I refer particularly here to Bloch's analysis of feudalism being economically based on payment for the use of land through moveable objects. In Balduíno peasants also paid for land use in products. Local fishermen still work using the same system: they pay to be part of a crew by giving the boat's owner half of their catches and selling the other half for a determined price. Locals still complain today about working according to the clock (instead of the season of the year). They also resent the fact that they work with strangers rather than with extended families and friends, and that they have to leave their families behind and be subordinate to bosses who often show prejudice. See Bloch, M. 2014. *Feudal society*. New York and London: Routledge.

17 See Castells, M. 2011. *The rise of the network society: The information age: Economy, society, and culture*, vol. 1. Chichester: John Wiley & Sons. Rainie, L. and Wellman, B. *Networked: The new social operating system*. Cambridge, MA and London: The MIT Press.

18 Costa, E. 2016. *Social Media in Southeast Turkey*. London: UCL Press.

19 Miller, D. et al. 2016. *How the world changed social media*. London: UCL Press. Chapter 2.

References

Agier, M. 1990. 'O sexo da pobreza. Homens, e famílias numa "avenida" em Salvador da Bahia.' *Tempo Social* 2(2): 35–60.

Agier, M. 1995. 'Racism, culture and black identity in Brazil.' *Bulletin of Latin American Research* 14(3): 245–64.

Agier, M. 2007. 'Espaço urbano, familia e status social: O novo operariado baiano nos seus bairros.' *Caderno CRH* 3(13).

Almeida, H. B. 2015. '"Classe média" para a indústria cultural".' *Psicologia USP* 26(1): 27–36.

Amado, J. 1977. *Dona Flor and her two husbands*. New York: Avon.

Amado, J. 1989. *Jubiabá*. New York: Avon.

Appiah, A. and Gates Jr, H. L., eds. 2005. *Africana: The encyclopedia of the African and African American experience*. New York: Oxford University Press.

Aquino, E. M. et al. 2003. 'Adolescência e reprodução no Brasil: a heterogeneidade dos perfis sociais' *Cadernos de Saúde Pública* 19(Sup 2): S377–S388.

Argenti-Pillen, A. 2013. *Masking terror: How women contain violence in Southern Sri Lanka*. Philadelphia: University of Pennsylvania Press.

Ariès, P. 1981. *História social da criança e da família*. São Paulo: Zahar.

Azevedo, T. D. 1966. 'Família, casamento e divórcio.' *Cultura e situação racial no Brasil*. Rio de Janeiro: Civilizacao Brasileira.

Bahia, J. 2005. 'O uso da fotografia na pesquisa de campo.' *Revista Vivência* (29): 349–60.

Bakhtin, M. 1984. *Rabelais and His World*, trans. Hélène Iswolsky. Bloomington: Indiana University Press.

Baran, M. D. 2007. '"Girl, You Are Not Morena. We Are Negras!": Questioning the Concept of "Race" in Southern Bahia, Brazil.' *Ethos* 35(3): 383–409.

Barros, R. P. D., Henriques, R. and Mendonça, R. 2001. 'A estabilidade inaceitável: desigualdade e pobreza no Brasil.' *Desigualdade e Pobreza no Brasil*. Henriques, R., ed. Rio de Janeiro: IPEA. 1–24.

Barthes, R. 1981. *Camera lucida: Reflections on photography*. New York: Hill and Wang.

Bartlett, L. 2007. 'Literacy, speech and shame: The cultural politics of literacy and language in Brazil.' *International Journal of Qualitative Studies in Education* 20(5): 547–63.Bayat, A. 2013. *Life as politics: How ordinary people change the Middle East*. Stanford, CA: Stanford University Press.

Belloni, M. L. and Gomes, N. G. 2008. 'Infância, mídias e aprendizagem: autodidaxia e colaboração.' *Educação & Sociedade* 29(104): 717–46.

Benjamin, W. 2008. *The work of art in the age of mechanical reproduction*. London: Penguin.

Bernard, H. R. 2011. *Research methods in anthropology: Qualitative and quantitative approaches*. Lanham, MD: Rowman Altamira.

Besnier, N. 1985. 'The local organization of zero-anaphora in Tuvaluan conversation.' *Te Reo* 28: 119–47.

Birman, P. and Lehmann, D. 1999. 'Religion and the Media in a Battle for Ideological Hegemony: the Universal Church of the Kingdom of God and TV Globo in Brazil.' *Bulletin of Latin American Research* 18(2): 145–64.

Birman, P. and Leite, M. P. 2000. 'Whatever happened to what used to be the largest Catholic country in the world?' *Daedalus* 129(2): 271–90.

Birman, P. and Machado, C. 2012. 'A violência dos justos: evangélicos, mídia e periferias da metrópole.' *Revista Brasileira de Ciências Sociais* 27: 55–69.

Birman, P. 2006. 'O Espírito Santo, a mídia e o território dos crentes.' *Ciencias Sociales y Religión/ Ciências Sociais e Religião* 8(8): 41–62.

Birman, P. 2009. 'Feitiçarias, territórios e resistências marginais.' *Mana* 15(2): 321–48.

Birman, P. 2012. 'O poder da fé, o milagre do poder: mediadores evangélicos e deslocamento de fronteiras sociais.' *Horizontes Antropológicos* 18(37): 133–53.

Blackwood, E. 2005. 'Wedding bell blues: Marriage, missing men, and matrifocal follies.' *American Ethnologist* 32(1): 3–19.

Bloch, M. 2014. *Feudal society*. London and New York: Routledge.

Blum-Kulka, S. 1987. 'Indirectness and politeness in requests: Same or different?' *Journal of pragmatics* 11(2): 131–46.

Boellstorff, T. 2012. *Ethnography and virtual worlds: A handbook of method*. Princeton, NJ: Princeton University Press.

Boellstorff, T. 2015. *Coming of Age in Second Life: An anthropologist explores the virtually human*. Princeton, NJ: Princeton University Press.

Bourdieu, P. 1977. *Outline of a Theory of Practice*, vol. 16. Cambridge: Cambridge University Press.

Bourdieu, P. 1984. *Distinction: A social critique of the judgement of taste*. Cambridge, Massachusetts: Harvard University Press.

Bourdieu, P. and Whiteside, S. 1996. *Photography: A middle-brow art*. Stanford, CA: Stanford University Press.

Bourdieu, P. and Bourdieu, M.C. 2004. 'The peasant and photography.' *Ethnography* 5(4): 601–16.

boyd, d. 2006. 'Friends, Friendsters, and MySpace Top 8: Writing Community Into Being on Social Network Sites.' (electronic version). *First Monday*, 11.

boyd, d. 2010. 'Social Network Sites as Networked Publics: Affordances, Dynamics, and Implications.' *Networked Self: Identity, Community, and Culture on Social Network Sites*. 39–58.

boyd, d. 2013. 'White flight in networked publics? How Race and Class Shaped American Teen Engagement with Myspace and Facebook.' *Race after the Internet*. Nakamura, L. and Chow-White, P. A., eds. New York and London: Routledge. 203–22.

Brenneis, D. 1984. 'Straight talk and sweet talk: political discourse in an occasionally egalitarian community.' *Dangerous words: Language and politics in the Pacific*. Brenneis, D. and Myers, F., eds. New York and London: New York University Press. 69–84.

Brenneis, D. 1986. 'Shared territory: audience, indirection and meaning.' *Text - Interdisciplinary Journal for the Study of Discourse* 6(3): 339–47.

Brenneis, D. 1987. 'Talk and transformation.' *Man* 22(3): 499–510.

Brenneis, D. and Myers, F. 1984. *Dangerous words. Language and Politics in the Pacific*. New York and London: New York University Press.

Brites, J. 2007. 'Afeto e desigualdade: gênero, geração e classe entre empregadas domésticas e seus empregadores.' *Cadernos Pagu* (29): 91–109.

Butler, K. D. 1998. 'Ginga Bahiana – The politics of race, class, culture and power in Salvador, Brazil.' *Afro-Brazilian culture and politics: Bahia, 1790s to 1990s*. Kraay, H., ed. Armonk, NY: M. E. Sharpe. 158–75.

Cabral, C. S. 2003. 'Contracepção e gravidez na adolescência na perspectiva de jovenspais de uma comunidade favelada do Rio de Janeiro Teenage contraception and pregnancy from the perspective of young low-income fathers in a slum area in Rio de Janeiro.' *Cad. saúde pública* 19(Sup 2): S283–S92.

Caldeira, T.P.D.R. 1988. 'The Art of Being Indirect: Talking about Politics in Brazil.' *Cultural Anthropology* 3(4): 444–54.

Caldeira, T.P. 1996. 'Fortified Enclaves: The New Urban Segregation.' *Public culture* 8(2): 303–28.

Caldeira, T. P. D. R. 2000. *City of walls: crime, segregation, and citizenship in São Paulo*. Berkeley, Los Angeles and London: University of California Press.

Caldwell, K. L. 2003. '"Look at Her Hair": The Body Politics of Black Womanhood in Brazil.' *Transforming Anthropology* 11(2): 18–29.

Campbell, C. 2005. *The romantic ethic and the spirit of modern consumerism*. Great Britain: Alcuin Academicals.

Carroll, M. P. 1984. 'The Trickster as Selfish-Buffoon and Culture Hero.' *Ethos* 12(2): 105–31.

Castells, M. 2008. 'Afterword.' *Handbook of Mobile Communication Studies*. Katz, J. E., ed. Cambridge, MA: The MIT Press, 447–51.

Castells, M. 2011. *The rise of the network society: The information age: Economy, society, and culture*, vol. 1. Chichester: John Wiley & Sons.

Cerqueira Lana, L. C., Corrêa, L. G. and Rosa, M. G. 2012. 'A cartilha da mulher adequada: ser piriguete e ser feminina no Esquadrão da Moda.' *Revista Contracampo* 1(24): 120–39.

Colabella, L. 2010. 'Patrões e clientes ou redistribuição entre iguais? Uma reflexâo sobre clientelismo e suas transposições contextuais.' *Revista Mana. Estudos de Antropologia Social* 16(2): 287–310.

Collins, J. 2009. 'Social reproduction in classrooms and schools.' *Annual Review of Anthropology* 38: 33–48.

Comerford, J. C. 2003. *Como uma família.* Rio de Janeiro: Relume Dumará.

Coogan, M. D. et al. 2010. 'Jeremiah 32.' *The new Oxford annotated Bible: with the Apocrypha.* New York: Oxford University Press.112–13.

Costa, E. 2016. *Social Media in Southeast Turkey: Love, Kinship and Politics.* London: UCL Press.

Cross, M. 2011. *Bloggerati, Twitterati: How Blogs and Twitter are Transforming Popular Culture.* Santa Barbara, Denver and Oxford: Praeger.

Cruz, R. D. C. 2012. 'Social prejudice on the Internet: propagation of prejudice and social segregation from an analysis of sites and social networks.' *Perspectivas em Ciência da Informação* 17(3): 121–36.

David, G. 2010. 'Camera phone images, videos and live streaming: a contemporary visual trend.' *Visual Studies* 25(1): 89–98.

Del Priore, M. 1993. *Ao sul do corpo: condição feminina, maternidades e mentalidades no Brasil Colônia.* Rio de Janeiro: José Olympio.

Dias, A. C. G. and Teixeira, M.A.P. 2010. 'Gravidez na adolescência: um olhar sobre um fenômeno complexo.' *Paidéia* 20(45): 123–31.

Donaldson, R. 2009. 'The making of a tourism-gentrified town: Greyton, South Africa.' *Geography* 94(2): 88–99.

Dolghie, J. Z. 2004. 'A Igreja Renascer em Cristo e a consolidação do mercado de música gospel no Brasil: uma análise das estratégias de marketing.' *Ciencias Sociales y Religión/Ciências Sociais e Religião* 6(6): 201–20.

Duarte, L. F. D. 1988. *Da vida nervosa nas classes trabalhadoras urbanas.* Rio de Janeiro: Zahar.

Duarte, L. F. D. 1995. 'Horizontes do indivíduo e da ética no crepúsculo da família.' *Famílias em processos contemporâneos: inovações culturais na sociedade brasileira,* vol 10. Ribeiro, I. and Ribeiro, A. C., eds. São Paulo: Edições Loyola. 27–41

Duarte, L. F. D. 2003. 'Indivíduo e pessoa na experiência da saúde e da doença.' *Ciência & Saúde Coletiva* 8(1): 173–83.

Duarte, L. F. D. and de Campos Gomes, E. 2008. *Três famílias: identidades e trajetórias transgeracionais nas classes populares.* Rio de Janeiro: FGV Editora.

Dube, M. W. 2016. 'The Subaltern Can Speak: Reading the Mmutle (Hare) Way.' *Journal of Africana Religions* 4(1): 54–75.

Duranti, A. 1997. 'Universal and Culture-Specific Properties of Greetings.' *Journal of Linguistic Anthropology* 7(1): 63–97.

Durham, E. R. 1973. *A caminho da cidade: a vida rural e a migração para São Paulo,* vol. 77. São Paulo: Editora Perspectiva.

The Economist, 2008. 'Faulty powers.' Available at http://www.economist.com/node/10566838 (accessed 23 January 2017).

The Economist, 2015. 'Naked capitalism.' Available at http://www.economist.com/news/international/21666114-internet-blew-porn-industrys-business-model-apart-its-response-holds-lessons (accessed 23 January 2017).

The Economist, 2016. 'Slavery's legacies.' Available at http://www.economist.com/news/international/21706510-american-thinking-about-race-starting-influence-brazil-country-whose-population (accessed 23 January 2017).

Edwards, E. 2015. 'Anthropology and photography: A long history of knowledge and affect.' *Photographies* 8(3): 235–52.

Elias, N. and Scotson, J. L. 1994. *The established and the outsiders,* vol. 32. London, Thousand Oaks and New Delhi: Sage.

Ellison, N. B. 2007. 'Social network sites: Definition, history, and scholarship.' *Journal of Computer-Mediated Communication* 13(1): 210–30.

Empson, R., 2011. *Harnessing fortune.* Oxford: Oxford University Press.

Falci, M. K. 2004. 'Mulheres do sertão nordestino.' *História das mulheres no Brasil.* Del Priore, M., ed. São Paulo: Contexto. 241–77.

Fausto, B. 2014. *A concise history of Brazil.* New York: Cambridge University Press.

Feltran, G, S. 2011. *Fronteiras de tensão: política e violência nas periferias de São Paulo*. São Paulo: UNESP/CEM-Centro de Estudos da metropole. 171.

Fernandes, F. 1969. *The Negro in Brazilian Society*. New York: Columbia Univeristy Press.

Fernandes, F. 2015. *O negro no mundo dos brancos*. São Paulo: Global Editora.

Ferreira, J. P., Filho, V. C. and Faissol, S. 1958. *Enciclopédia dos municípios brasileiros*. Rio de Janeiro: Instituto Brasileiro de Geografia e Estatística - IBGE.117-99.

Fisher, L. E. 1976. '"Dropping Remarks" and the Barbadian Audience.' *American Ethnologist* 3(2): 227–42.

Fonseca, C. 2004. 'Ser mulher, mãe e pobre.' *História das mulheres no Brasil*. Del Priore, M., ed. São Paulo: Contexto. 510–53.

Fonseca, C. 1998. 'A modernidade diante de suas próprias ficções: o caso da adoção internacional.' *Direitos humanos, ética e direitos reprodutivos*. Dora, D. D. et al., eds. Porto Alegre: Themis-Assessoria Jurídica e Estudos de Gênero. 43–60.

Fonseca, C. 1999. 'Quando cada caso não é um caso.' *Revista Brasileira de Educação* 10: 58–78.

Fonseca, C. 2000. *Família, fofoca e honra: etnografia de relações de gênero e violência em grupos populares*. Porto Alegre, RS: Editora da Universidade Federal do Rio Grande do Sul.

Fonseca, C. 2002. 'Mãe é uma só?: Reflexões em torno de alguns casos brasileiros.' *Psicologia USP* 13(2): 49–68.

Fonseca, C. 2002. 'Inequality near and far: adoption as seen from the Brazilian favelas.' *Law and Society Review* 36(2): 397–432.

Fonseca, C. 2002. 'The politics of adoption: child rights in the Brazilian setting.' *Law & Policy* 24(3): 199–227.

Fonseca, C. 2003. 'De afinidades a coalizões: uma reflexão sobre a "transpolinização" entre gênero e parentesco em décadas recentes da antropologia.' *Ilha Revista de Antropologia* 5(2): 005–031.

Fonseca, C. 2003. 'Patterns of shared parenthood among the Brazilian poor.' *Social text* 21(1): 111–27.

Fonseca, C. 2004. 'The circulation of children in a Brazilian working-class neighborhood.' *Cross-cultural approaches to adoption*. Bowie, F., ed. Abingdon, Oxfordshire: Routledge. 165.

Fonseca, C. 2005. 'Concepções de família e práticas de intervenção: uma contribuição antropológica.' *Saúde e sociedade* 14(2): 50–9.

Fonseca, C. 2006. 'Da circulação de crianças à adoção internacional: questões de pertencimento e posse.' *Cadernos Pagu* 26: 11–43.

Fonseca, C. 2006. 'Classe e recusa etnográfica.' *Etnografias da participação*. Brites, J. and Fonseca, C., eds. Santa Cruz: EDUNISC.

Fonseca, C. 2008. 'Preparando-se para a vida: reflexões sobre escola e adolescência em grupos populares.' *Em Aberto* 14(61).

Fonseca, C. 2009. 'Abandono, adoção e anonimato: Questões de moralidade materna suscitadas pelas propostas legais de "parto anônimo".' *Sexualidad, Salud y Sociedad-Revista Latinoamericana* 1: 30–62.

Foster, G. M. 1965. 'Peasant society and the image of limited good.' *American Anthropologist* 67(2): 293–315.

Foster, G. M. 1967. *Tzintzuntzan: Mexican peasants in a changing world*. Boston, MA: Little, Brown and Company.

Foster, G. M. 1972. 'A second look at limited good.' *Anthropological Quarterly* 45(2): 57–64.

Freyre, G. 1970. *The Masters and the Slaves: A Study in the Development of Brazilian Civlization*. New York: Alfred A. Knopf.

Gibbs, M. et al. 2015. '# Funeral and Instagram: Death, social media, and platform vernacular.' *Information, Communication & Society* 18(3): 255–68.

Gilsenan, M. 1982. *Recognising Islam: an anthropologist's introduction*. London: Croom Helm.

Gluckman, M. 1963. 'Gossip and scandal.' *Current anthropology* 4(3): 307–16.

Goldstein, D. 1999. '"Interracial" sex and racial democracy in Brazil: twin concepts?' *American Anthropologist* 101(3): 563–78.

Goldstein, D. 2013. *Laughter out of place: Race, class, violence, and sexuality in a Rio shantytown*. Berkeley, Los Angeles and London: University of California Press.

Goffman, E. 1959. *The presentation of self in everyday life*. Garden City, NY: Doubleday.

Gómez Cruz, E. and Meyer, E. T. 2012. 'Creation and control in the photographic process: iPhones and the emerging fifth moment of photography.' *Photographies* 5(2): 203–21.

Gómez Cruz, E. and Lehmuskallio A., eds. 2016. *Digital Photography and Everyday Life: Empirical Studies on Material Visual Practices*. London: Routledge.

Graham, R. 1997. *Clientelismo e política no Brasil do século XIX*. Rio de Janeiro: Editora UFRJ.

Griswold, W., McDonnell, T. and Wright, N. 2005. 'Reading and the reading class in the twenty-first century.' *Annual Review of Sociology* 31: 127–41.

Grünewald, R. D. A. 2003. 'Turismo e etnicidade.' *Horizontes antropológicos* 9(20): 141–59.

Harding, S. 1991. 'Representing fundamentalism: The problem of the repugnant cultural other.' *Social research* 58(2): 373–93.

Haviland, J. B. 1977. *Gossip, Reputation and Knowledge in Zinacantan*. Chicago: University of Chicago Press.

Haynes, N. 2016. *Social Media in Northern Chile*. London: UCL Press.

Heilborn, M. L. et al. 2002. 'Aproximações socioantropológicas sobre a gravidez na adolescência'. *Horizontes antropológicos* 8(17): 13–45.

Horst, H. and Miller, D. 2006. *The cell phone: An anthropology of communication*. Oxford and New York: Berg.

Irvine, J. T. 1993. 'Insult and responsibility: Verbal abuse in a Wolof village.' *Responsibility and evidence in oral discourse*. Hill, J. and Irvine, J., eds. Cambridge: Cambridge University Press. 105–34.

Ito, M. et al. 2009. *Hanging out, messing around, and geeking out: Kids living and learning with new media*. Cambridge, MA and London: The MIT Press.

Josephides, L. 2001. 'Straight talk, hidden talk, and modernity: shifts in discourse strategy in Highland New Guinea.' *An anthropology of indirect communication*. Hendry, J. and Watson, C. W., eds. London: Routledge. 218–31.

Kardozo, F. C. M. 2013. 'Confissões no Facebook: educação e subjetivação nas redes sociais.' Doctoral dissertation, Universidade Federal do Ceará, Ceará.

Kitzinger, S. et al. 1996. *Mães: um estudo antropológico da maternidade*. Lisboa: Editorial Presença.

Kivland, C. 2014. 'Becoming a force in the zone: Hedonopolitics, masculinity, and the quest for respect on Haiti's streets.' *Cultural Anthropology* 29(4): 672–98.

Kottak, C. P. 1967. 'Kinship and class in Brazil.' *Ethnology* 6(4): 427–43.

Kottak, C.P. 1991. *Assault on paradise: the globalization of a little community in Brazil*. New York and London: McGraw-Hill.

Koury, M. G. P. 2005. 'A antropologia das emoções no Brasil.' *Revista Brasileira de Sociologia da Emoção* 4(12): 239–52.

Kuznesof, E. A. 1998. 'The puzzling contradictions of child labor, unemployment, and education in Brazil.' *Journal of Family History* 23(3): 225–39.

Lange, P. G. 2007. 'Publicly private and privately public: Social networking on YouTube.' *Journal of computer-mediated communication* 13(1): 361–80.

Lasén, A. and Gómez-Cruz, E. 2009. 'Digital photography and picture sharing: Redefining the public/private divide.' *Knowledge, Technology & Policy* 22(3): 205–15.

Lave, J. 1988. *Cognition in practice: Mind, mathematics and culture in everyday life*. Cambridge and New York: Cambridge University Press.

Lave, J. 1996. 'Teaching, as learning, in practice.' *Mind, culture, and activity* 3(3): 149–64.

Lave, J. 2011. *Apprenticeship in critical ethnographic practice*. Chicago and London: University of Chicago Press.

Lave, J. and Wenger, E. 1991. *Situated learning: Legitimate peripheral participation*. Cambridge and New York: Cambridge University Press.

Legendre, F., Lenders, V., May, M. and Karlsson, G. 2008. 'Narrowcasting: an empirical performance evaluation study.' *Proceedings of the third ACM workshop on Challenged networks*. ACM Press. 11–18.

Lemos, R. and Martini, P. 2010. 'LAN Houses: A new wave of digital inclusion in Brazil.' *Information Technologies & International Development* 6(SE): 31–5.

Lempert, M. 2012. 'Indirectness.' *The handbook of intercultural discourse and communication*. Paulston, C. B. et al, eds. Chichester: Blackwell Publishing.180–204.

Lima, D. N. D. O. 2007. '"Trabalho", "mudança de vida" e "prosperidade" entre fiéis da Igreja Universal do Reino de Deus.' *Religião & Sociedade* 27(1): 132–55.

Lima, D. N. D. O. 2007. 'Ethos emergente: notas etnográficas sobre o "sucesso".' *Revista Brasileira de Ciências Sociais* 22(65).

Lindisfarne, N. 1994. 'Variant masculinities, variant virginities: Rethinking " honour and shame".' *Dislocating masculinity: Comparative ethnographies*. Cornwall, A. And Lindisfarne, N. eds. London and New York: Routledge. 82–96.

Low, S. M. 2001. 'The edge and the center: Gated communities and the discourse of urban fear.' *American anthropologist* 103(1): 45–58.

Lyons, B. J. 2005. 'Discipline and the arts of domination: rituals of respect in Chimborazo, Ecuador.' *Cultural Anthropology* 20(1): 97–127.

MacDougal, D. 1998. 'Visual anthropology and the ways of knowing.' *Transcultural cinema* 61: 92.

Machado, C. B. 2014. 'Pentecostalismo e o sofrimento do (ex-) bandido: testemunhos, mediações, modos de subjetivação e projetos de cidadania nas periferias.' *Horizontes antropológicos* 20(42): 153–80.

Machado, M. D. D. C. and Burity, J. 2014. 'A ascensão política dos pentecostais no Brasil na avaliação de líderes religiosos.' *Dados – Revista de Ciências Sociais* 57(3): 601–31.

Machado, M. D. D. C. and de Barros, M. L. 2009. 'Gênero, geração e classe: uma discussão sobre as mulheres das camadas médias e populares do Rio de Janeiro.' *Estudos Feministas* 17(2): 369–93.

Machado, M. D. D. C. 2001. 'Além da religião.' *Cadernos CERU* 12: 139–50.

Machado, M. D. D. C. 2005. 'Representações e relações de gênero nos grupos pentecostais.' *Estudos feministas* 13(2): 387–96.

Machado, M. D. D. C. 2013. 'Conversão religiosa e a opção pela heterossexualidade em tempos de aids: notas de uma pesquisa.' *Cadernos Pagu* (11): 275–301.

Machado, M. D. D. C. 2015. 'Religion and politics in contemporary Brazil: an analysis of Pentecostal and Catholic Charismatics.' *Religião & Sociedade* 35(2): 45–72.

Madianou, M. and Miller, D. 2011. 'Mobile phone parenting: Reconfiguring relationships between Filipina migrant mothers and their left-behind children.' *New media & society* 13(3): 457–70.

Madianou, M. and Miller, D. 2013. *Migration and new media: Transnational families and polymedia.* London and New York: Routledge.

Mafra, C. 2001. *Os evangélicos.* Rio de Janeiro: Zahar.

Mafra, C., Swatowiski, C. and Sampaio, C. 2012. 'O projeto pastoral de Edir Macedo. Uma igreja benevolente para indivíduos ambiciosos?' *Revista Brasileira de Ciências Sociais* 27(78): 81–96.

Mafra, C. 2013. 'Números e narrativas.' *Debates do NER* 2(24): 13–25.

Marcelin, L. H. 1999. 'A linguagem da casa entre os negros no recôncavo baiano.' *Mana* 5(2): 31–60.

Mariano, R. 1996. 'Os neopentecostais e a teologia da prosperidade.' *Novos Estudos* 44(44): 24–44.

Mariano, R. 2004. 'Expansão pentecostal no Brasil: o caso da Igreja Universal.' *Estudos avançados* 18(52): 121–38.

Mariano, R. 2010. 'Mudanças no campo religioso brasileiro no censo 2010.' *Debates do NER* 2(24): 119–37.

Mariano, R. and Pierucci, A. F. 1992. 'O envolvimento dos pentecostais na eleição de Collor.' *Novos Estudos Cebrap* 34: 92–106.

Mariz, C. 1992. 'Religion and poverty in Brazil: a comparison of Catholic and Pentecostal communities.' *Sociology of Religion* 53 (Special Issue): S63–S70.

Mariz, C. L. 1995. 'Perspectivas sociológicas sobre o pentecostalismo e o neopentecostalismo.' *Revista de Cultura Teológica. ISSN (impresso) 0104-0529 (eletrônico) 2317-4307* (13): 37–52.

Mariz, C. L. 1997. 'Reflexões sobre a reação afro-brasileira à guerra santa.' *Debates do NER* 1(1): 96–103.

Mauss, M. 1954. *The gift: forms and functions of exchange in archaic societies.* Abingdon, Oxon: Routledge.

McCallum, C. 1999. 'Restraining Women: Gender, Sexuality and Modernity in Salvador da Bahia.' *Bulletin of Latin American Research* 18(3): 275–93.

McCallum, C. 2005. 'Racialized bodies, naturalized classes: moving through the city of Salvador da Bahia.' *American Ethnologist* 32(1): 100–17.

McCallum, C. and Reis, A. P. D. 2005. 'Childbirth as Ritual in Brazil: young mothers' experiences.' *Ethnos* 70(3): 335–60.

McCallum, C. and Reis, A. P. D. 2006. 'Re-significando a dor e superando a solidão: experiências do parto entre adolescentes de classes populares atendidas em uma maternidade pública de Salvador, Bahia, Brasil.' *Cad Saúde Pública* 22(7): 1483–91.

McCallum, C. and Bustamante, V. 2012. 'Parentesco, gênero e individuação no cotidiano da casa em um bairro popular de Salvador da Bahia.' *Etnográfica. Revista do Centro em Rede de Investigação em Antropologia* 16(2): 221–46.

McDonald, T. 2016. *Social Media in Rural China.* London: UCL Press.

McKellin, W. H. 1984. 'Putting down roots: information in the language of Managalase exchange.' *Dangerous Words: Language and Politics in the Pacific*. Brenneis, D. L. and Myers, F. R., eds. New York and London: New York University Press.108–28.

McQuire, S. 2008. *The Media City. Media, Architecture and Urban Space*. London: Sage.

Medeiros, Z. and Ventura, P. C. S. 2008. 'Cultura tecnológica e redes sociotécnicas: um estudo.' *Educação e Pesquisa* 34(1): 063–075.

Meneley, A. 2016. *Tournaments of value: Sociability and hierarchy in a Yemeni town*. Buffalo and London: University of Toronto Press.

Mesquita, W. A. B. 2007. 'Um pé no reino e outro no mundo: consumo e lazer entre pentecostais.' *Horizontes Antropológicos* 13(28): 117–44.

Miller, D. 2016. *Social media in an English village*. London: UCL Press.

Miller, D. and Sinanan, J. 2016. *Visualising Facebook*. London: UCL Press.

Miller, D. et al. 2016. *How the world changed social media*. London: UCL Press.

Morgan, M. 2002. *Language, discourse and power in African American culture*, vol. 20. Cambridge: Cambridge University Press.

Morozov, E. 2012. *The net delusion: The dark side of Internet freedom*. New York: PublicAffairs.

Morris, M. 1981. *Saying and Meaning in Puerto Rico: Some Problems in the Ethnography of Discourse*. Oxford: Pergamon Press.

Moutinho, L. 2004. *Razão, "cor" e desejo: uma análise comparativa sobre relacionamentos afetivo-sexuais "inter-raciais" no Brasil e na África do Sul*. São Paulo: UNESP.

Müller, C. 2004. 'It's not about privacy, it's about control! Critical remarks on CCTV and the public/private dichotomy from a sociological perspective.' *Presentation at the Conference "CCTV and Social Control: The politics and practice of video surveillance – European and Global perspectives."* Sheffield, UK.

Munn, N. D. 1992. *The fame of Gawa: A symbolic study of value transformation in a Massim (Papua New Guinea) society*. Durham, NC and London: Duke University Press.

Nascimento, C. 2010. 'Entrelaçando corpos e letras: representações de gênero nos pagodes baianos.' Master dissertation, Universidade Federal da Bahia, Salvador, BA.

Nazaré, H. F. S. 1999. *Camaçari, Minha Cidade, Nossa História – Memória de Idosos*. Prefeitura de Camaçari, Secretaria de Ação Social / Secretaria de Esporte, Lazer e Cultura.

Neri, M. C. 2008. 'A nova classe média.' *Rio de Janeiro: FGV/Ibre, CPS*:16.

Neri, M. C. 2011. *A nova classe média: o lado brilhante da base da pirâmide*. São Paulo: Editora Saraiva.

Novaes, R. 2004. 'Os jovens "sem religião": ventos secularizantes, "espírito de época" e novos sincretismos. Notas preliminares.' *Estudos avançados* 18(52): 321–30.

Novaes, S. C. 2008. 'Imagem, magia e imaginação: desafios ao texto antropológico.' *Mana* 14(2): 455–75.

O'Donnell, G. 1993. 'On the state, democratization and some conceptual problems: A Latin American view with glances at some postcommunist countries.' *World Development* 21(8): 1355–69.

Okabe, D. 2006. 'Everyday contexts of camera phone use: Steps toward techno-social ethnographic frameworks.' *Mobile communications in everyday life: Ethnographic views, observations, and reflections*. Höflich, J. and Harmann, M., eds. Berlin: Frank and Timme. 79–102.

Ong, W. J. 2012. *Interfaces of the Word: Studies in the Evolution of Consciousness and Culture*. Ithaca and London: Cornell University Press.

Oro, A. P. 1997. 'Neopentecostais e afro-brasileiros: quem vencerá esta guerra?' *Debates do NER* 1(1): 10–36.

Oro, A. P. 2003. 'A política da Igreja Universal e seus reflexos nos campos religioso e político brasileiros.' *Revista brasileira de ciências sociais* 18(53): 53–69.

Paine, R. 1967. 'What is gossip about? An alternative hypothesis.' *Man* 2(2): 278–85.

Painter, J. and Jeffrey, A. 2009. *Political geography*. London: Sage.

Pereira, M. G. D. 2006. 'Estratégias De Manutenção Do Poder De Uma Ex-Chefe Em Uma Reunião Empresarial: Indiretividade E Diretividade Em Atos De Comando.' *Linguagem E Gênero: No Trabalho, Na Mídia E Em Outros Contextos*. Heberle, V. M et al., eds. Florianópolis: Editora Da UFSC.

Peristiany, J. G. 1965. *Honour and shame: The values of Mediterranean society*. London: Weidenfeld and Nicolson.

Pierucci, A. F. 2004. ' "Bye bye, Brasil": o declínio das religiões tradicionais no Censo 2000.' *Estudos avançados* 18(52): 17–28.

Pierucci, A. F. 2006. 'Religião como solvente: uma aula.' *Novos Estudos-CEBRAP* 75: 111–27.

Pierucci, A. F. 2011. 'Eleição 2010: desmoralização eleitoral do moralismo religioso.' *Novos Estudos-CEBRAP* (89): 6–15.

Pinheiro-Machado, R. and Scalco, L. M. 2012. 'Brand Clans: Consumption and Rituals Among Low-income Young People in the City of Porto Alegre.' *International Review of Social Research* 2(1): 107–26.

Pinho, O. 2005. 'Etnografias do brau: corpo, masculinidade e raça na reafricanização em Salvador.' *Revista Estudos Feministas* 13(1): 127–45.

Pinho, O. 2014. '"Brincar, Jogar Bola, Mulher" – A Desigualdade Racial no Brasil e a Etnografia das Masculinidades no Recôncavo da Bahia.' *Antropolítica: Revista Contemporânea de Antropologia* (34).

Pina-Cabral, J. 2013. *Gente livre: consideração e pessoa no Baixo Sul da Bahia*. São Paulo: Ed. Terceiro Nome.

Pinney, C. 2011. *Photography and anthropology*. London: Reaktion.

Pochmann, M. 2012. *Nova classe média?: o trabalho na base de pirâmide socail brasileira*. São Paulo: Boitempo Editorial.

Rainie, L. and Wellman, B. 2012. *Networked: The new social operating system*. Massachusetts and London: The MIT Press.

Raminelli, R. 2004. 'Eva Tupinambá.' *História das mulheres no Brasil*. Del Priore, M., ed. São Paulo: Contexto.11–44.

Reis, J. J. 1995. *Slave rebellion in Brazil: the Muslim uprising of 1835 in Bahia*. Baltimore and London: Taylor & Francis.

Risério, A. 2016. *Uma história da cidade da Bahia*. Rio de Janeiro: Versal Editores.

Rizzini, I. and Fonseca, C. 2002. *As meninas e o universo do trabalho doméstico no Brasil: aspectos históricos, culturais e tendências atuais*. Brasília: Sistema de Información Regional sobre Trabajo Infantil, SIRTI-Organization Internacional de Trabalho.

Robben, A. C. 1994. 'Conflicting discourses of economy and society in coastal Brazil.' *Man* 29(4): 875–900.

Robben, A. C., Phillips, M. and Aspelin, P. 1982. 'Tourism and change in a Brazilian fishing village; Tourism in the Amazon; "What you don't know, won't hurt you".' *Cultural Survival Quarterly* 6(3): 18–21.

Rowlands, M. 2005. 'A materialist approach to materiality.' *Materiality*. Miller, D. ed. Durham, NC: Duke University Press. 72–87.

Rosa Cruz, C. 2014. Linha Verde: Salvador – Aracaju Pelo Litoral. Aracaju: Vaza-Barris.

Rubel, A. J. 1977. '"Limited Good" and "Social Comparison": Two Theories, One Problem.' *Ethos* 5(2): 224–38.

Santos, G. L. 2011. 'Ensinar e aprender no meio virtual: rompendo paradigmas.' *Educação e pesquisa* 37(2): 307–20.

Santos, G. L. 2011. 'Uma pesquisa longitudinal sobre professores e computadores.' *Educação & Realidade* 36(3).

Santos Abreu, R. D. A. and Nicolaci-da-Costa, A. M. 2003. 'Internet: um novo desafio para os educadores' *Paidéia* 13(25): 27–40.

Sarti, C. A. 1994. 'A família como espelho: um estudo sobre a moral dos pobres na periferia de São Paulo.' Doctoral dissertation, University of São Paulo, São Paulo.

Scalco, L. M. 2012. 'Máquinas, conexões e saberes: as práticas de "inclusão digital" em famílias de grupos populares.' Doctoral thesis, Universidade Federal do Rio Grande do Sul, Rio Grande do Sul.

Scalco, L. M. and Pinheiro-Machado, R. 2010. 'Os sentidos do real e do falso: o consumo popular em perspectiva etnográfica.' *Revista de Antropologia* 53(1): 321–59.

Scavone, L. 2001. 'Maternidade: transformações na família e nas relações de gênero.' *Interface-Comunicação, Saúde, Educação* 5(8): 47–59.

Scavone, L. 2001. 'A maternidade e o feminismo: diálogo com as ciências sociais.' *Cadernos Pagu* (16): 137–50.

Scavone, L. 2013. 'As múltiplas faces da maternidade.' *Cadernos de Pesquisa* (54) 37–49.

Schama, S. 1988. *The embarrassment of riches: An interpretation of Dutch culture in the Golden Age*. Berkeley, Los Angeles and London: University of California Press.

Scheper-Hughes, N. 1993. *Death without weeping: The violence of everyday life in Brazil*. Berkeley, Los Angeles and London: University of California Press.

Schwarcz, L. M. 2013. *Nem preto nem branco, muito pelo contrário: cor e raça na sociabilidade brasileira*. São Paulo: Claro Enigma.

Scott, J. C. 1990. *Domination and the arts of resistance: Hidden transcripts*. New Haven, CT: Yale University Press.

Scott, R. P. 2013. 'O homem na matrifocalidade: gênero, percepção e experiências do domínio doméstico.' *Cadernos de pesquisa* (73): 38–47.

Searle, J. R. 1975. 'Indirect speech acts.' *Syntax and Semantics*, vol 3: Speech Acts. Cole, P. and Morgan, J. L., eds. New York: Academic Press. 59–82.

Shaw, R. 2002. *Memories of the Slave Trade: ritual and the historical imagination in Sierra Leone*. Chicago and London: University of Chicago Press.

Shapiro, M. 2016. 'Paradoxes of Intimacy: Play and the Ethics of Invisibility in North-east Brazil.' *Journal of Latin American Studies*: 1–25.

Silva, S. R. 2007. ' "Eu Não Vivo Sem Celular": sociabilidade, consumo, corporalidade e novas práticas nas culturas urbanas.' *Intexto* 2(17):1–17.

Silva, S. R. 2010. 'Estar no tempo, estar no mundo: a vida social dos telefones celulares em um grupo popular.' Doctoral dissertation, Universidade Federal De Santa Catarina, Santa Catarina.

Silva, S. R. 2012. 'On Emotion and Memories: the Consumption of Mobile Phones as " Affective Technology".' *International Review of Social Research* 2(1): 157–72.

Silveira, M. L. D. 2000. *O nervo cala, o nervo fala: a linguagem da doença. (Coleção Antropologia & Saúde)*. Rio de Janeiro: Fiocruz.

Simmel, G. 1950. 'Secrecy.' *The Sociology of Georg Simmel*. Wolff, K. H., ed. New York: The Free Press. 330–44.

Simões, V. M. F. et al., 2003. 'Characteristics of adolescent pregnancy, Brazil.' *Revista de Saúde Pública* 37(5): 559–65.

Sinanan, J. 2017. *Social Media in Trinidad*. London: UCL Press.

Sheller, M. and Urry, J. 2003. 'Mobile transformations of public and private life.' *Theory, Culture & Society* 20(3): 107–25.

Smith, R. T. 1973. 'The matrifocal family.' *The character of kinship*. Goody, J., ed. London: Cambridge University Press. 121–44.

Snickars, P. and Vonderau, P. 2009. *The YouTube Reader*. Stockholm: National Library of Sweden.

Soares, S. and Sátyro, N. 2009. *O Programa Bolsa Família: desenho institucional, impactos e possibilidades futuras*. Texto para Discussão (No.1424). Brasília: Instituto de Pesquisa Econômica Aplicada (IPEA).

Soihet, R. 2004. 'Mulheres pobres e violência no Brasil urbano.' *História das mulheres no Brasil*. Del Priore, M., ed. São Paulo: Contexto. 362–400.

Sontag, S. 1977. *On photography*. New York: Farrar, Straus, and Giroux.

Souza, B. M. 1969. *A experiência da salvação: pentecostais em São Paulo*, vol. 1. São Paulo: Duas Cidades.

Souza, J. 2012. *Os batalhadores brasileiros: nova classe média ou nova classe trabalhadora?* Belo Horizonte: Editora UFMG.

Souza, J. 2013. 'Em defesa da Sociologia: O economicismo e a invisibilidade das classes sociais.' *Revista Brasileira de Sociologia-RBS* 1(01): 129–58.

Souza, R. 2010. 'Rapazes negros e socialização de gênero: sentidos e significados de "ser homem".' *Cadernos Pagu* (34): 107–42.

Spivak, G. C. 1988. *Can the subaltern speak? Reflections on the history of an idea*. Morris, R. C., ed. New York and Chichester: Columbia University Press. 21–78.

Spyer, J. 2011. *Making up art, videos and fame*. MSc dissertation, University College London, London.

Stack, C. B. 1975. *All our kin: Strategies for survival in a black community*. New York: Basic Books.

Swartz, D. 1977. 'Pierre Bourdieu: The cultural transmission of social inequality.' *Harvard Educational Review* 47(4): 545–55.

Swatowiski, C. 2009. 'Dinâmicas espaciais em Macaé: lugares públicos e amientes religiosos.' *Religiões e cidades: Rio de Janeiro e São Paulo*. Mafra, C. and Almeida, R., eds. São Paulo: Terceiro Nome. 51–68.

Thin, N. 2001. 'Indirect speech.' *An Anthropology of Indirect Communication* (37): 201.

Torresan, A. 2011. 'RoundTrip: Filming a Return Home.' *Visual Anthropology Review* 27(2): 119–30.

Turkle, S. 2006. *Life on the screen: Identity in the age of the internet*. New York: Simon & Schuster.

Turkle, S. 2012. *Alone together: Why we expect more from technology and less from each other*. New York: Basic Books.

Veblen, T. 2005. *The theory of the leisure class; an economic study of institutions*. Delhi: Aakar Books.

Velho, G. 2000. 'O desafio da violência.' *Estudos Avançados* 14(39): 56–60.

Velho, G. 2007. 'Metrópole, cultura e conflito.' *Rio de Janeiro: cultura, política e conflito*. Velho, G., ed. Rio de Janeiro: Jorge Zahar. 9–30.

Venkatraman, S. 2017. *Social Media in South India*. London: UCL Press.

Viveiros de Castro, E. 2007. 'Filiação intensiva e aliança demoníaca.' *Novos estudos-CEBRAP* (77). 91–126.

Wang, XinYuan. 2016. *Social Media in Industrial China*. London: UCL Press.

Watson-Gegeo, K. A. and White, G. M. 1990. *Disentangling: Conflict discourse in Pacific societies*. Stanford, CA: Stanford University Press.

Weber, M. 2002. *The Protestant ethic and the "spirit" of capitalism and other writings*. London: Penguin.

Weintraub, J. and Kumar, K. 1997. 'Preface.' *Public and private in thought and practice: Perspectives on a grand dichotomy*. Weintraub, J. and Kumar, K., eds. Chicago and London: University of Chicago Press. xi–xii.

Weintraub, J. 1997. 'The theory and politics of the public/private distinction.' *Public and Private in Thought and Practice*. Weintraub J. and Kumar K., eds. Chicago and London: University of Chicago Press. 1–42.

Wellman, B. 1996. 'Are personal communities local? A Dumptarian reconsideration.' *Social networks* 18(4): 347–54.

Wilkis, A. 2016. 'Money, morality, and politics in the slums of Buenos Aires.' *Horizontes Antropológicos* 22(45): 49–76.

Willis, P. E. 1977. *Learning to labor: How working class kids get working class jobs*. New York: Columbia University Press.

White, G. M. and Watson-Gegeo, K. A. 1990. 'Disentangling discourse.' *Disentangling: Conflict discourse in Pacific societies*. Watson-Gegeo, K.A. and White, G.M eds. Stanford, CA: Stanford University Press. 3–49.

Woortmann, K. 1987. *A família das mulheres*. Rio de Janeiro: Biblioteca Tempo Universitário, Tempo Brasileiro.

Woortmann, K. and Woortmann, E. F. 2004. *Monoparentalidade e chefia feminina: conceitos, contextos e circunstâncias*. Série Antropológica, No. 357. Brasília: Departamento De Antropologia, UNB.

Yaccoub, H. 2011. 'A chamada "nova classe media": cultura material, inclusão e distinção social.' *Horizontes antropológicos* 17(36): 197–231.

Yelvington, K. A. 2001. 'The anthropology of Afro-Latin America and the Caribbean: diasporic dimensions.' *Annual Review of Anthropology* 30(1): 227–60.

Zaluar, A. 1985. *A Máquina e a Revolta: As Organizações Populares e o Significado da Pobreza*. São Paulo: Brasiliense.

Zaluar, A. 2012. 'Juventude violenta: processos, retrocessos e novos percursos.' *Revista Dados* 55(2): 327–65.

Zelizer, V. A. 2000. 'The purchase of intimacy.' *Law & Social Inquiry* 25(3): 817–48.

Internet sources

Alexandre, R. 2014. Afinal, quem são os evangélicos? *Carta Capital*. Available at http://www.carta-capital.com.br/sociedade/afinal-quem-sao-201cos-evangelicos201d-2053.html (accessed 23 January 2017).

boyd, d. 2010. Social steganography: Learning to hide in plain sight. [web blog message]. Available at http://www.zephoria.org/thoughts/archives/2010/08/23/socialsteganography-learning-to-hide-in-plain-sight.html (accessed 29 April 2017).

Chao, L. 2013. Brazil: The Social Media Capital of the Universe. *The Wall Street Journal*. Available at http://www.wsj.com/articles/SB10001424127887323301104578257950857891898 (accessed January 23, 2017).

Dent, A. and Pinheiro-Machado R., eds. 2013. Protesting Democracy in Brazil – Cultural Anthropology. *Cultural Anthropology*. Available at https://culanth.org/fieldsights/426-protesting-democracy-in-brazil (accessed 23 January 2017]).

Friv.com, The Best Free Online Games! [Jogos | Juegos]. Available at http://www.friv.com/ (accessed 23 January 2017).

Google / Instituto Data Popular, 2015. Os novos donos da internet: Classe C, de conectados. Think with Google. Available at https://www.thinkwithgoogle.com/intl/pt-br/research-studies/novos-donos-internet-classe-c-conectados-brasil.html (accessed 23 January 2017).

Holmes, R. 2013. The Future Of Social Media? Forget About The U.S., Look To Brazil. Available at http://www.forbes.com/forbes/welcome/?toURL=http%3A%2F%2Fwww.forbes.com%2Fsites%2Fciocentral%2F2013%2F09%2F12%2Fthe-future-of-social-media-forget-about-the-u-s-look-to-brazil%2F (accessed 23 January 2017).

Index Mundi, Countries ranked by GINI index (World Bank estimate). Available at http://www.indexmundi.com/facts/indicators/SI.POV.GINI/rankings (accessed 23 January 2017).

Kugel, S. 2006. A Web Site Born in U.S. Finds Fans in Brazil. Available at http://www.nytimes.com/2006/04/10/technology/a-web-site-born-in-us-finds-fans-in-brazil.html (accessed 23 January 2017).

Nexo Jornal, 2015. Mapa revela segregação racial no Brasil. Available at https://www.nexojornal.com.br/especial/2015/12/16/O-que-o-mapa-racial-do-Brasil-revela-sobre-a-segregação-no-pa%C3%ADs (accessed 23 January 2017).

Nexo Jornal, 2016. A evolução do analfabetismo funcional no Brasil. Available at https://www.nexojornal.com.br/grafico/2016/11/21/A-evolu%C3%A7%C3%A3o-do-analfabetismo-funcional-no-Brasil (accessed 23 January 2017).

Pochmann, M., 2013. Nova classe média? YouTube. Available at https://www.youtube.com/watch?v=UswLAb-Oshc (accessed 23 January 2017).

Porta dos Fundos, 2014. SENHA. YouTube. Available at https://www.youtube.com/watch?v=-bDS63bEpyc (accessed 23 January 2017).

Revista Exame. 2012. Usuários discutem orkutização do Instagram. Available at http://exame.abril.com.br/tecnologia/usuarios-discutem-orkutizacao-do-instagram/ (accessed 23 January 2017).

Statista, Brazil: most popular social networks 2015 | Statistic. Available at https://www.statista.com/statistics/254734/most-popular-social-networking-sites-in-brazil/ (accessed 23 January 2017).

Statista, Facebook users by country. Available at https://www.statista.com/statistics/268136/top-15-countries-based-on-number-of-facebook-users/ (accessed 23 January 2017).

Sinanan, J. 2016. The Internet: Deviation – Cultural Anthropology. Cultural Anthropology. Available at https://culanth.org/fieldsights/857-the-internet-deviation (accessed 23 January 2017).

Spyer, J. 2013. An Ethnographic Account of the Riots in Brazil Seen From the Periphery — Cultural Anthropology. Cultural Anthropology. Available at https://culanth.org/fieldsights/440-an-ethnographic-account-of-the-riots-in-brazil-seen-from-the-periphery (accessed 23 January 2017).

Spyer, J. 2016. 'A crise política e os evangélicos.' CartaCapital. Available at http://www.cartacapital.com.br/sociedade/a-crise-politica-e-os-evangelicos (accessed 23 January 2017).

Spyer, J. 2016. 'They flirt, they share porn and they gossip.' Available at http://blogs.ucl.ac.uk/global-social-media/2016/02/05/they-flirt-they-share-porn-and-they-gossip/ (accessed 23 January 2017).

Tufekci, Z. 2013. 'Turkish Twitterverse is a sea of "subtweets"—folks from diff "sides" are talking "at" each other in lengthy conversations, but no mentions!' Twitter. Available at https://twitter.com/zeynep/status/412907669708898304 (accessed 23 January 2017).

Wesch, M. 2008. An anthropological introduction to YouTube. YouTube. Available at https://www.youtube.com/watch?v=TPAO-lZ4_hU (accessed 23 January 2017).

'Why We Post', 2016. Northeast Brazil: Context – An act of rebellion. YouTube. Available at https://youtu.be/VESJuboJZoM (accessed 23 January 2017).

'Why We Post', 2016. Northeast Brazil: Context – Speaking in code. YouTube. Available at http://goo.gl/HpJ6VD (accessed 23 January 2017).

'Why We Post', 2016. Northeast Brazil: Technology and generational differences – INSTAGRAM. YouTube. Available at https://youtu.be/9oYBreWYwag (accessed 23 January 2017).

'Why We Post', 2016. Northeast Brazil: Technology and generational differences – THE VIRUS. YouTube. Available at https://youtu.be/LBTi0zx4HCo (accessed 23 January 2017).

'Why We Post', 2016. Northeast Brazil: The plague of WhatsApp for Brazilian parents. YouTube. Available at https://youtu.be/C2TG15TT1nQ (accessed 23 January 2017).

Index

CPSIA information can be obtained
at www.ICGtesting.com
Printed in the USA
BVHW02s1456040818
523431BV00024B/1084/P